Himouto (干物妹)

A lazy little sister who never lifts a finger around the house.
"At home, Umaru is a himouto."
Origin: a portmanteau of imouto (little sister) and himono (a woman who is elegant and polished in public, but secretly a slob at home).

From Shueisha's *Imouto Dictionary*.

Characters Inside

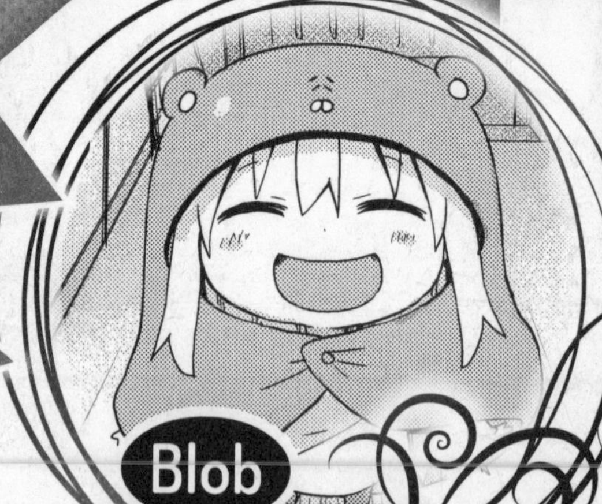

Blob

Inside Umaru

Master

Taihei's little sister. Once she steps through the front door, she turns into an irresponsible slob whose motto is, "Eat, sleep (Zzz...), play!"♪

Siblings

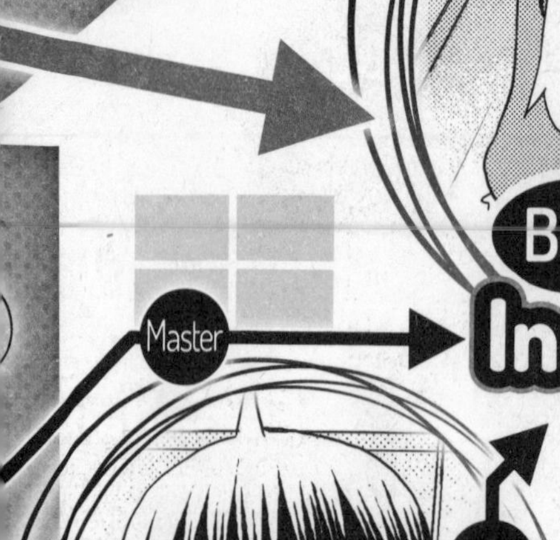

Taihei

Umaru's big brother. He has an office job, but he also works a second job doing chores and generally being a "house-husband."

Story

In the outside world, Taihei's little sis Umaru is the perfect high school girl, beloved and envied by all. ♥ But this beautiful little sister has a big secret!! Once she steps across the threshold into their home, she indulges in the himouto lifestyle of "eat, sleep, play"!!♪ And that's not all. Umaru has a third persona: UMR, gamer extraordinaire and master of the local arcade!! When Umaru (as UMR) enters a video game tournament, she's shocked to encounter none other than her classmate Sylphyn, who's also entered the competition!! The two classmates face off in the final round, but which girl will claim the ultimate title...?!

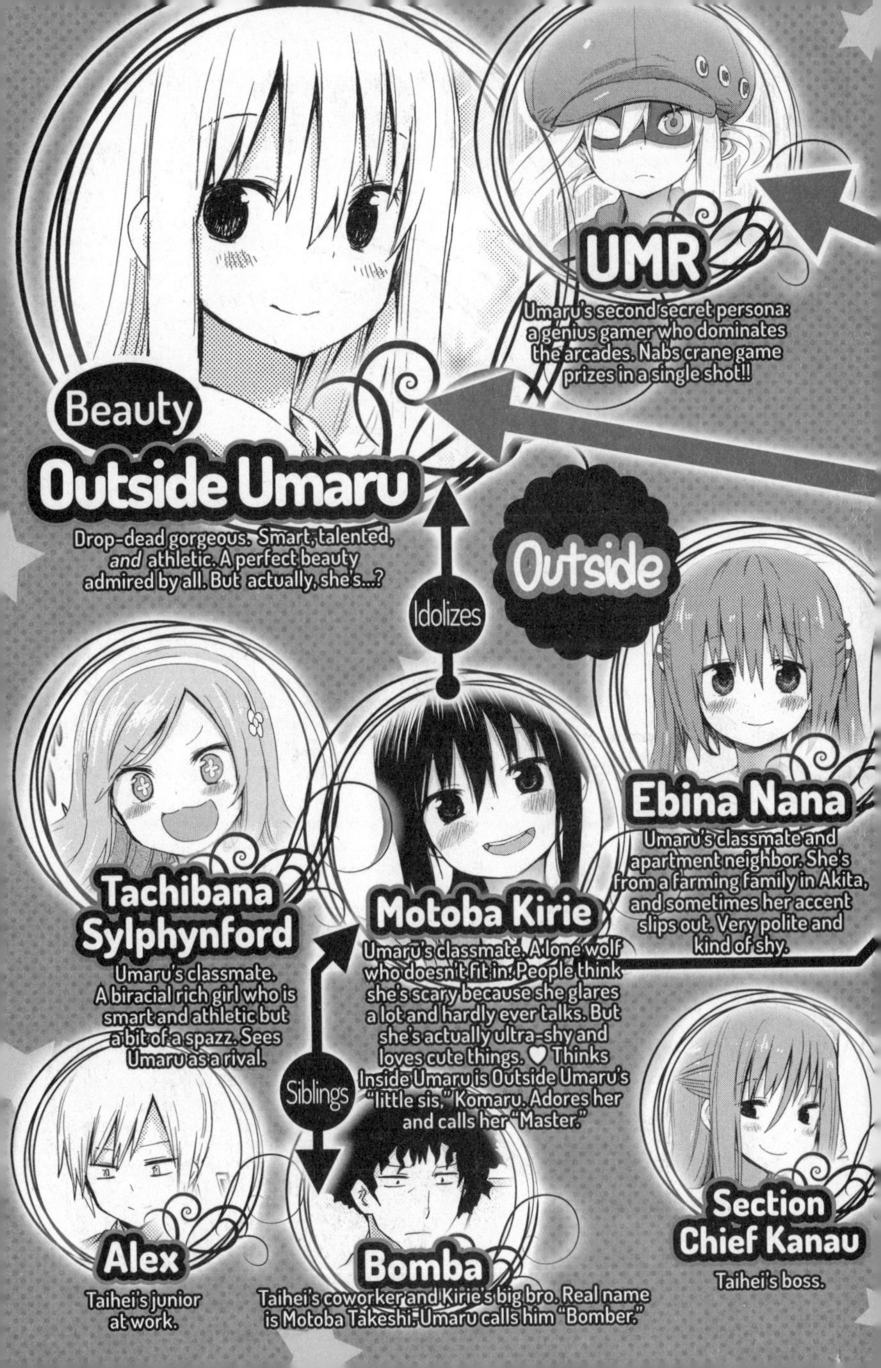

UMR
Umaru's second secret persona: a genius gamer who dominates the arcades. Nabs crane game prizes in a single shot!!
Beauty
Outside Umaru
Drop-dead gorgeous. Smart, talented, *and* athletic. A perfect beauty admired by all. But actually, she's...?
Idolizes
Outside
Ebina Nana
Umaru's classmate and apartment neighbor. She's from a farming family in Akita, and sometimes her accent slips out. Very polite and kind of shy.
Motoba Kirie
Umaru's classmate. A lone wolf who doesn't fit in. People think she's scary because she glares a lot and hardly ever talks. But she's actually ultra-shy and loves cute things. ♥ Thinks Inside Umaru is Outside Umaru's "little sis," Komaru. Adores her and calls her "Master."
Tachibana Sylphynford
Umaru's classmate. A biracial rich girl who is smart and athletic but a bit of a spazz. Sees Umaru as a rival.
Siblings
Section Chief Kanau
Taihei's boss.
Bomba
Taihei's coworker and Kirie's big bro. Real name is Motoba Takeshi. Umaru calls him "Bomber."
Alex
Taihei's junior at work.

HIMOUTO! UMARU-CHAN 4 CONTENTS

No. 53 Umaru & the Game Tournament Part 2

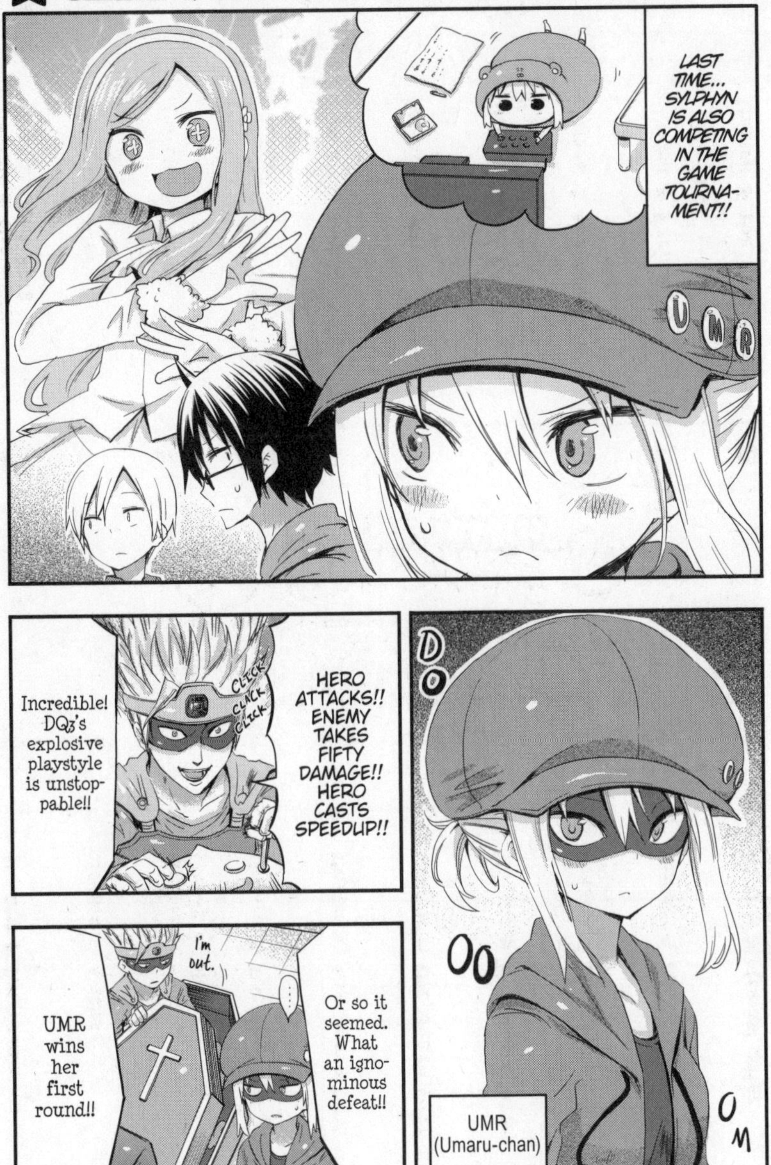
LAST TIME... SYLPHYN IS ALSO COMPETING IN THE GAME TOURNAMENT!!
UMR
DO
OO
OM
UMR (Umaru-chan)
HERO ATTACKS!! ENEMY TAKES FIFTY DAMAGE!! HERO CASTS SPEEDUP!!
CLICK CLACK CLICK
Incredible! DQ3's explosive playstyle is unstoppable!!
Or so it seemed. What an ignominious defeat!!
I'm out.
...
UMR wins her first round!!

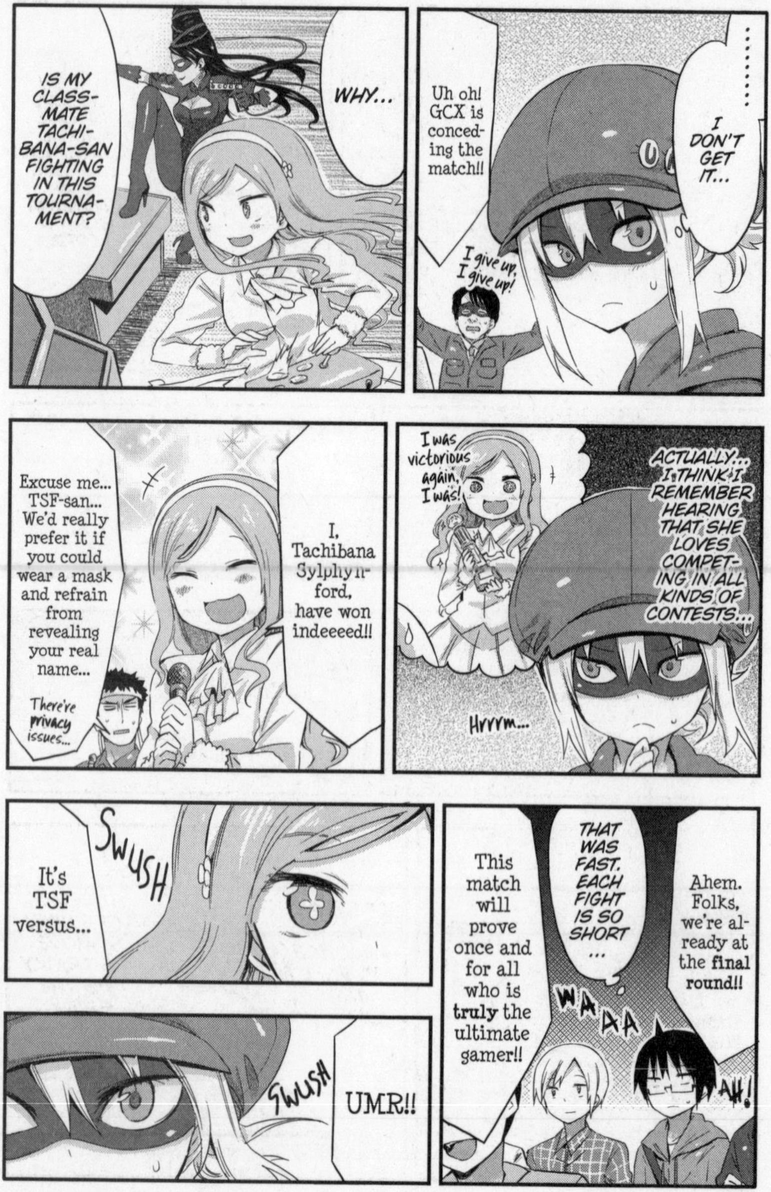
......
I DON'T GET IT...
Uh oh! GCX is conceding the match!!
I give up, I give up!
WHY...
IS MY CLASSMATE TACHIBANA-SAN FIGHTING IN THIS TOURNAMENT?
ACTUALLY... I THINK I REMEMBER HEARING THAT SHE LOVES COMPETING IN ALL KINDS OF CONTESTS...
I was victorious again, I was!
Hrrrm...
I, Tachibana Sylphynford, have won indeeeeed!!
Excuse me... TSF-san... We'd really prefer it if you could wear a mask and refrain from revealing your real name...
There're privacy issues...
Ahem. Folks, we're already at the final round!!
THAT WAS FAST. EACH FIGHT IS SO SHORT...
This match will prove once and for all who is truly the ultimate gamer!!
WAAAA
AH!
SWUSH
It's TSF versus...
UMR!!
SWUSH

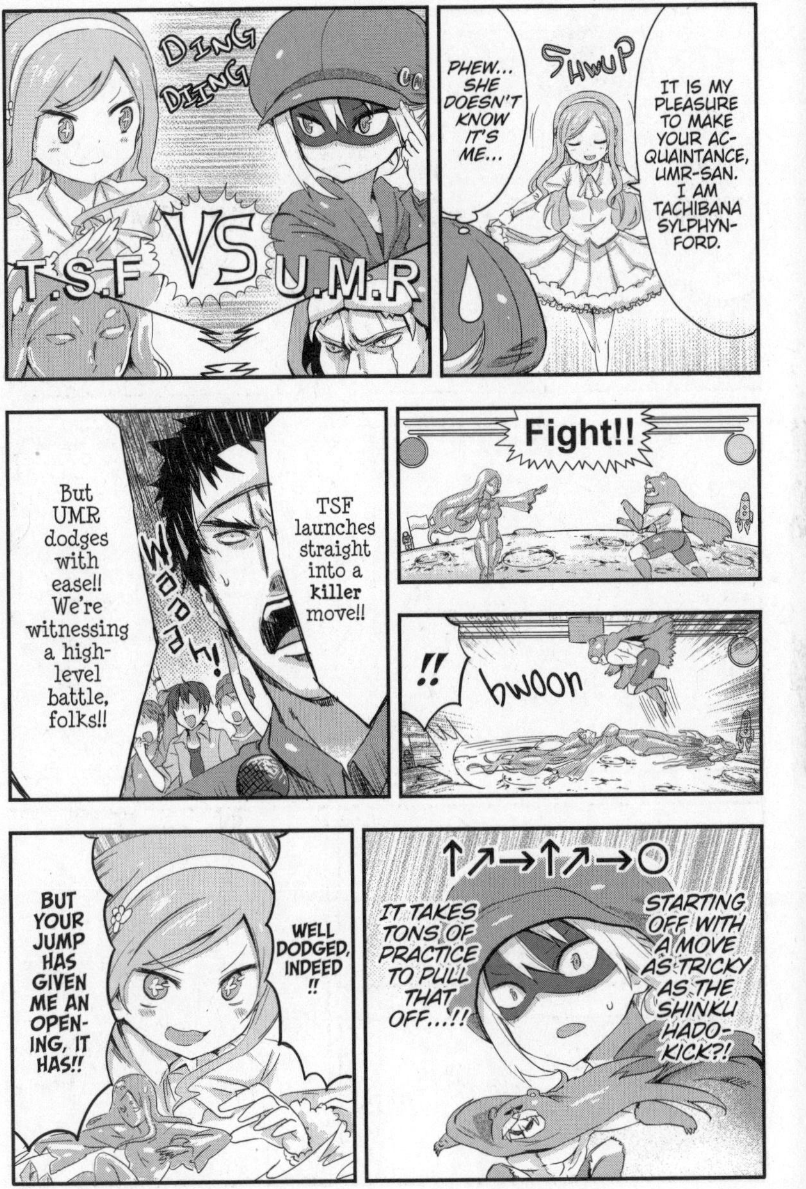
IT IS MY PLEASURE TO MAKE YOUR ACQUAINTANCE, UMR-SAN. I AM TACHIBANA SYLPHYNFORD.
SHWUP
PHEW... SHE DOESN'T KNOW IT'S ME...
DING DING
T.S.F
VS
U.M.R
Fight!!
!!
bwoon
TSF launches straight into a **killer** move!!
Waaah!
But UMR dodges with ease!! We're witnessing a high-level battle, folks!!
↑↗→↑↗→○
STARTING OFF WITH A MOVE AS TRICKY AS THE SHINKU HADO-KICK?!
IT TAKES TONS OF PRACTICE TO PULL THAT OFF...!!
WELL DODGED, INDEED!!
BUT YOUR JUMP HAS GIVEN ME AN OPENING, IT HAS!!

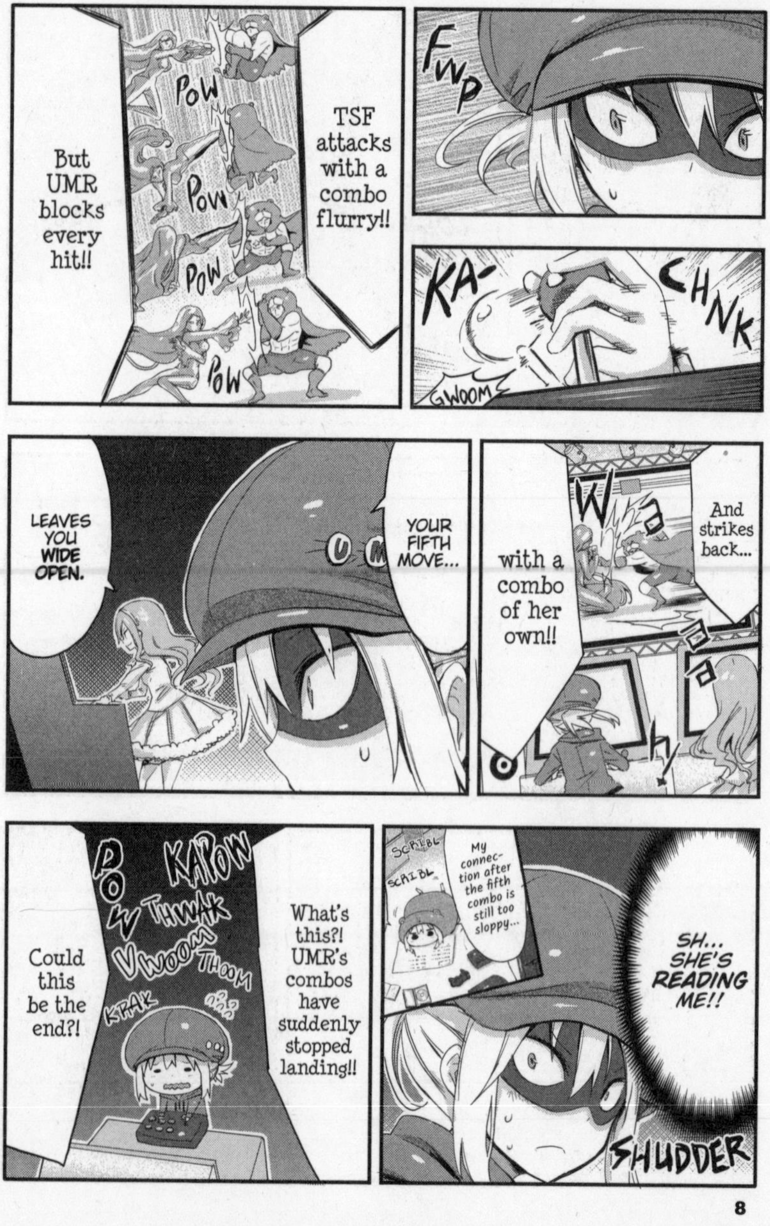
FWP
KA-
CHNK
GWOOM
TSF attacks with a combo flurry!!
POW
POW
POW
POW
But UMR blocks every hit!!
And strikes back...
with a combo of her own!!
YOUR FIFTH MOVE...
LEAVES YOU WIDE OPEN.
SCRIBL
SCRIBL
My connection after the fifth combo is still too sloppy...
SH... SHE'S READING ME!!
SHUDDER
What's this?! UMR's combos have suddenly stopped landing!!
KAPOW
POW
THWAK
VWOOM
THOOM
KRAK
Could this be the end?!

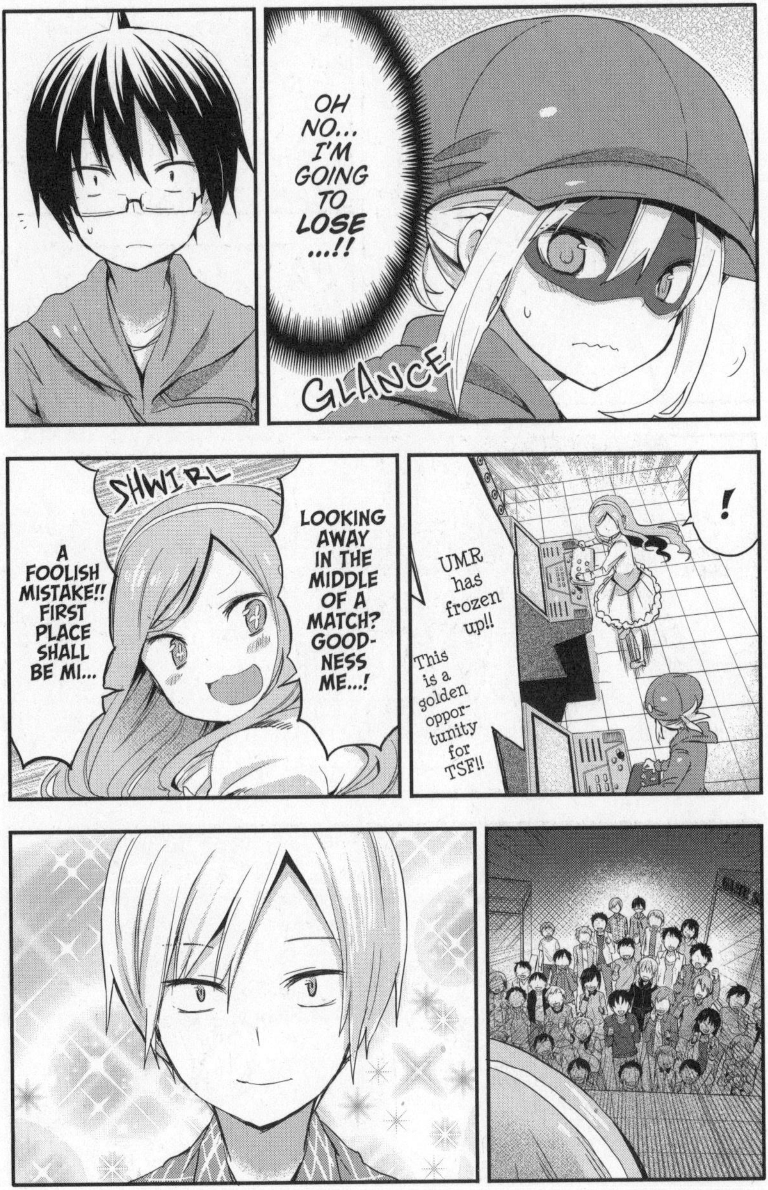
OH NO... I'M GOING TO LOSE ...!!
GLANCE
!
UMR has frozen up!!
This is a golden opportunity for TSF!!
SHWIRL
LOOKING AWAY IN THE MIDDLE OF A MATCH? GOODNESS ME...!
A FOOLISH MISTAKE!! FIRST PLACE SHALL BE MI...

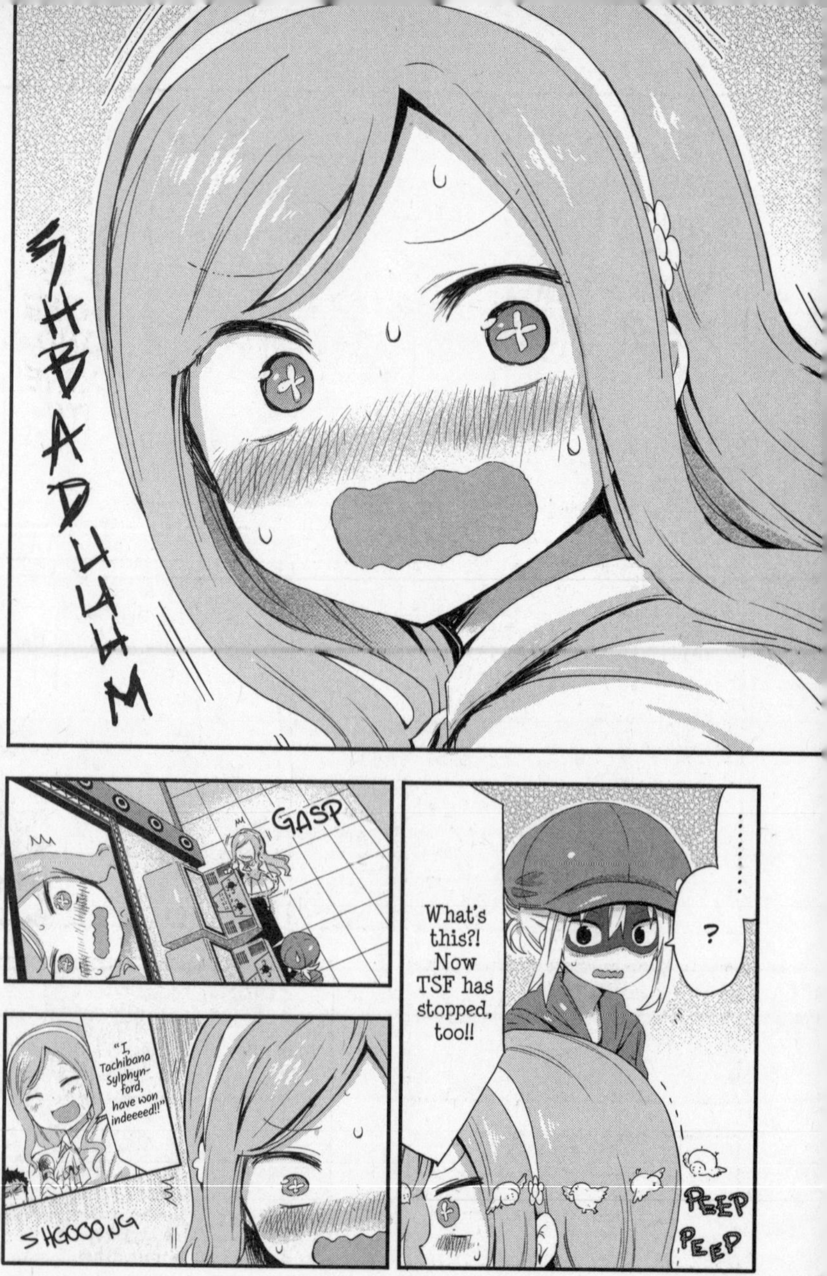
SHBADUHHM
......?
What's this?! Now TSF has stopped, too!!
PEEP PEEP
GASP
"I, Tachibana Sylphynford, have won indeeeed!!"
SHGOOONG

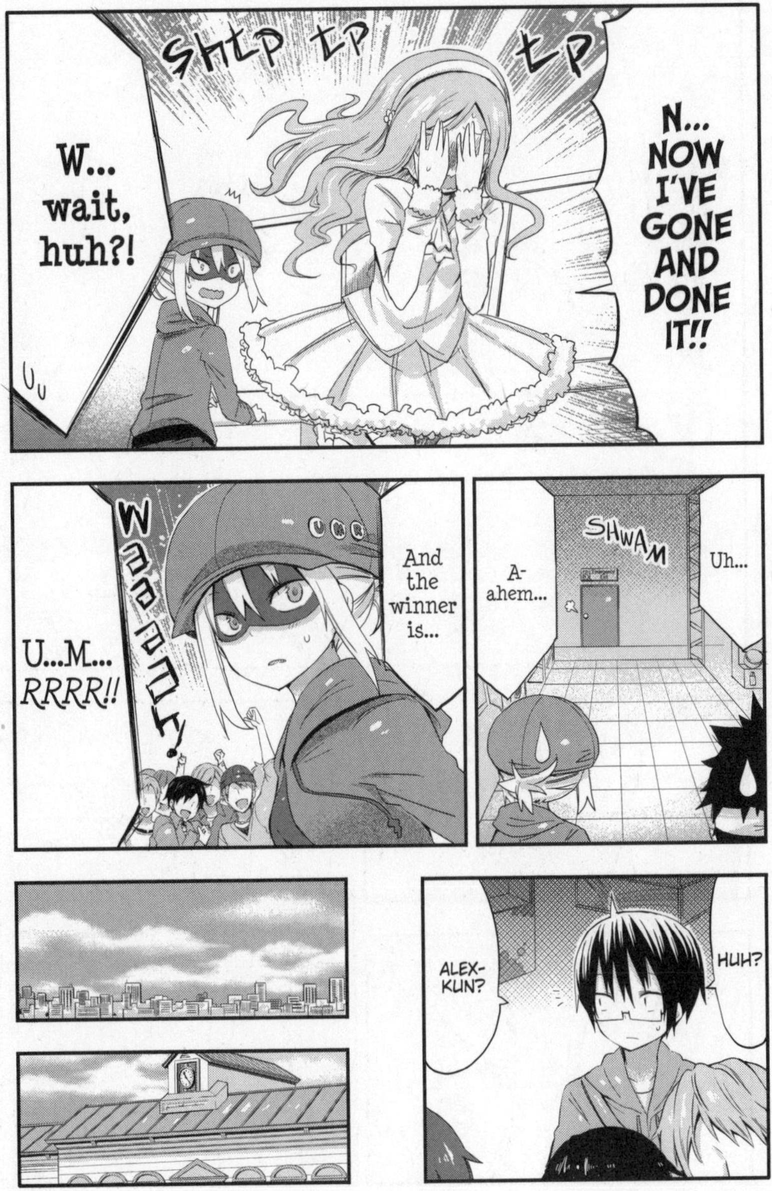
N... NOW I'VE GONE AND DONE IT!!
Shlp tp tp
W... wait, huh?!
Uu
Uh...
SHWAM
A-ahem...
And the winner is...
Waaaah!
U...M... *RRRR!!*
HUH?
ALEX-KUN?

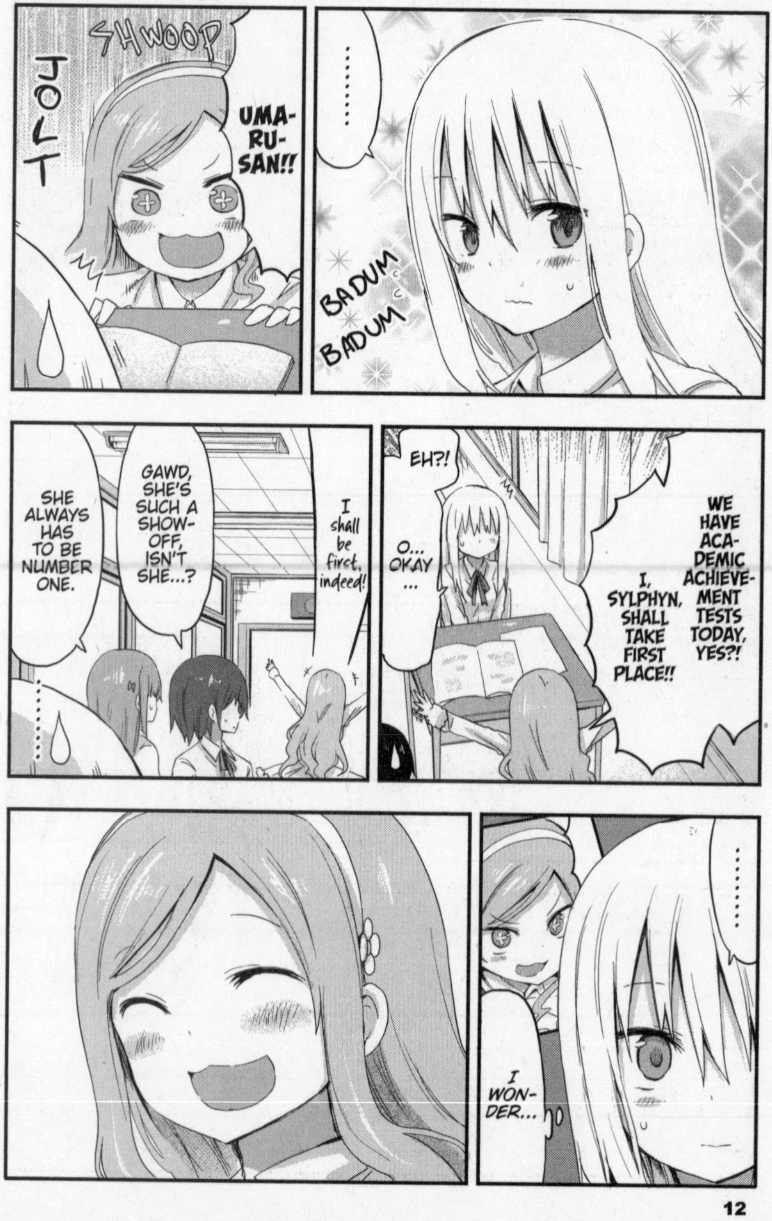
......
BADUM BADUM
SHWOOP
JOLT
UMA-RU-SAN!!
WE HAVE ACA-DEMIC ACHIEVE-MENT TESTS TODAY, YES?!
I, SYLPHYN, SHALL TAKE FIRST PLACE!!
EH?!
O... OKAY...
I shall be first, indeed!
GAWD, SHE'S SUCH A SHOW-OFF, ISN'T SHE...?
SHE ALWAYS HAS TO BE NUMBER ONE.
......
......
I WON-DER...

No. 54 Umaru & Anime

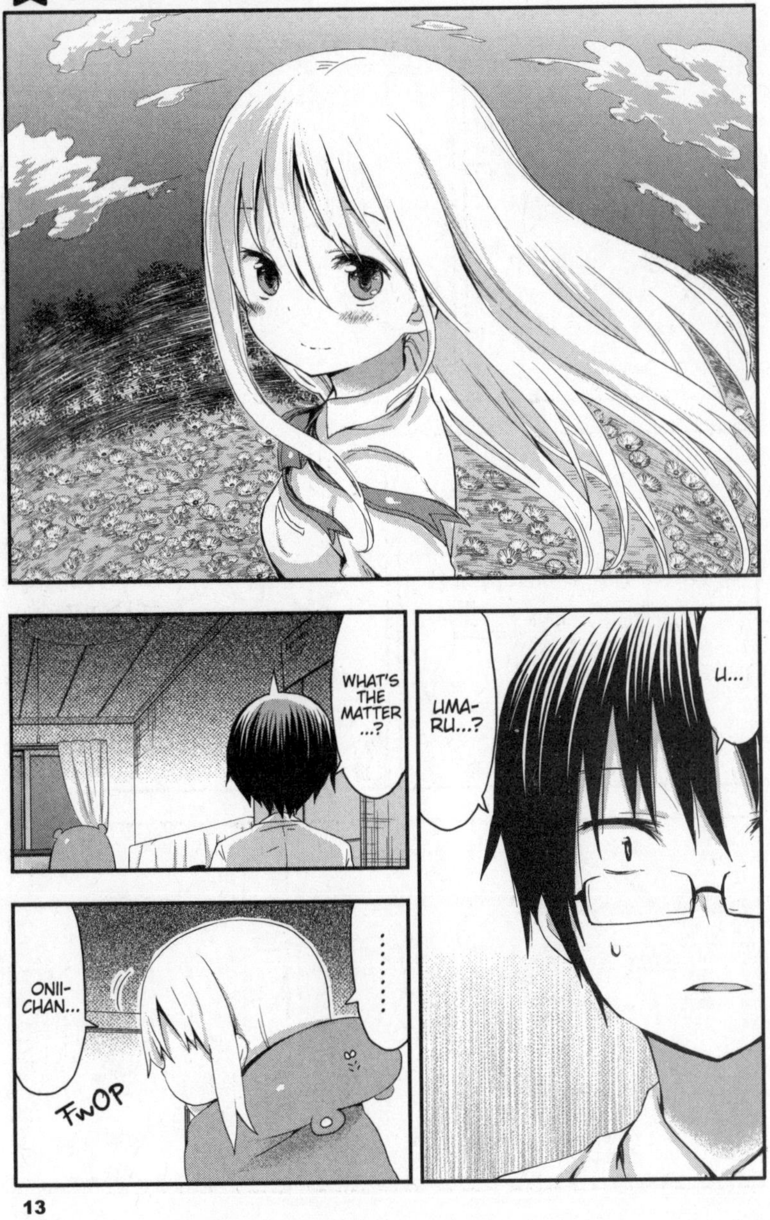

U...
UMA-RU...?
WHAT'S THE MATTER ...?
......
ONII-CHAN...
FWOP

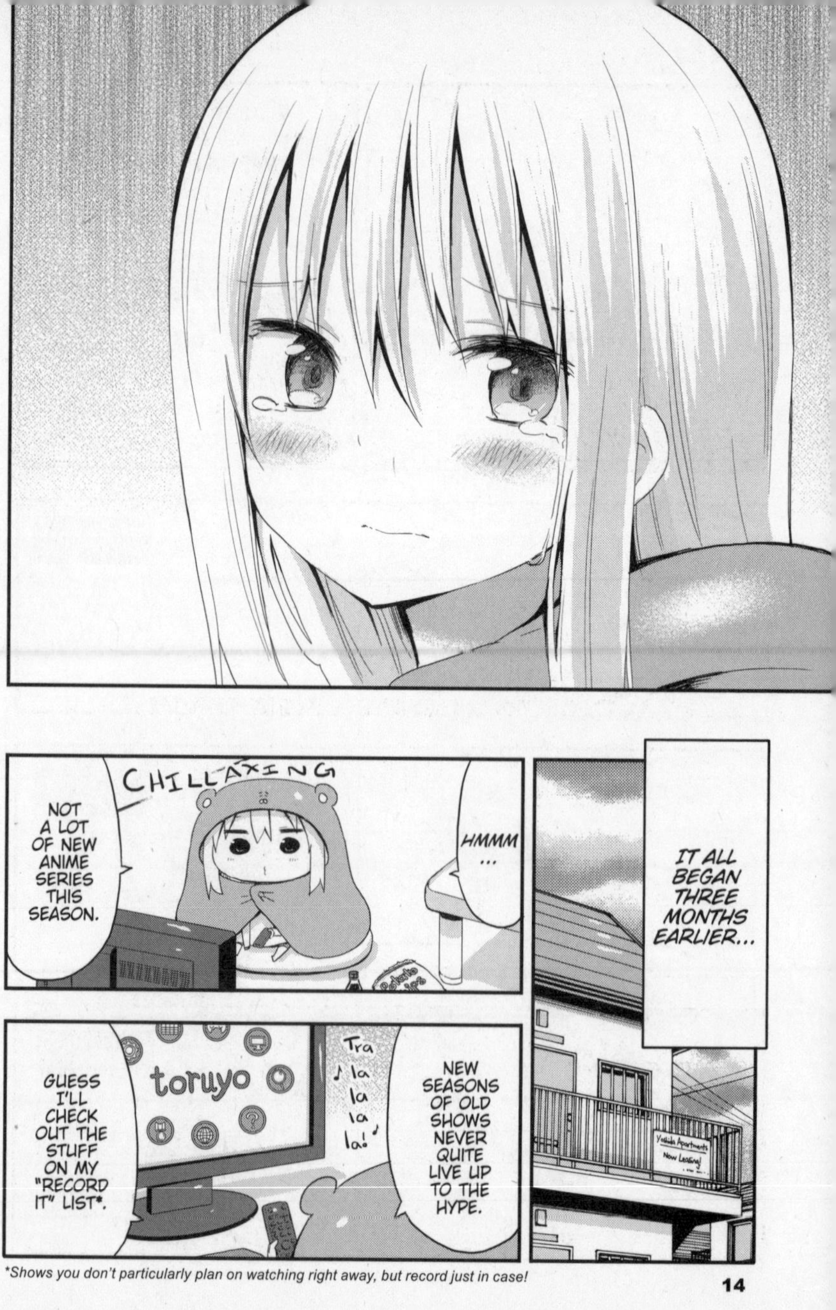
IT ALL BEGAN THREE MONTHS EARLIER...
Yoshida Apartments
Now Leasing!
HMMM ...
CHILLAXING
NOT A LOT OF NEW ANIME SERIES THIS SEASON.
NEW SEASONS OF OLD SHOWS NEVER QUITE LIVE UP TO THE HYPE.
Tra la la la la!
toruyo
GUESS I'LL CHECK OUT THE STUFF ON MY "RECORD IT" LIST*.

*Shows you don't particularly plan on watching right away, but record just in case!

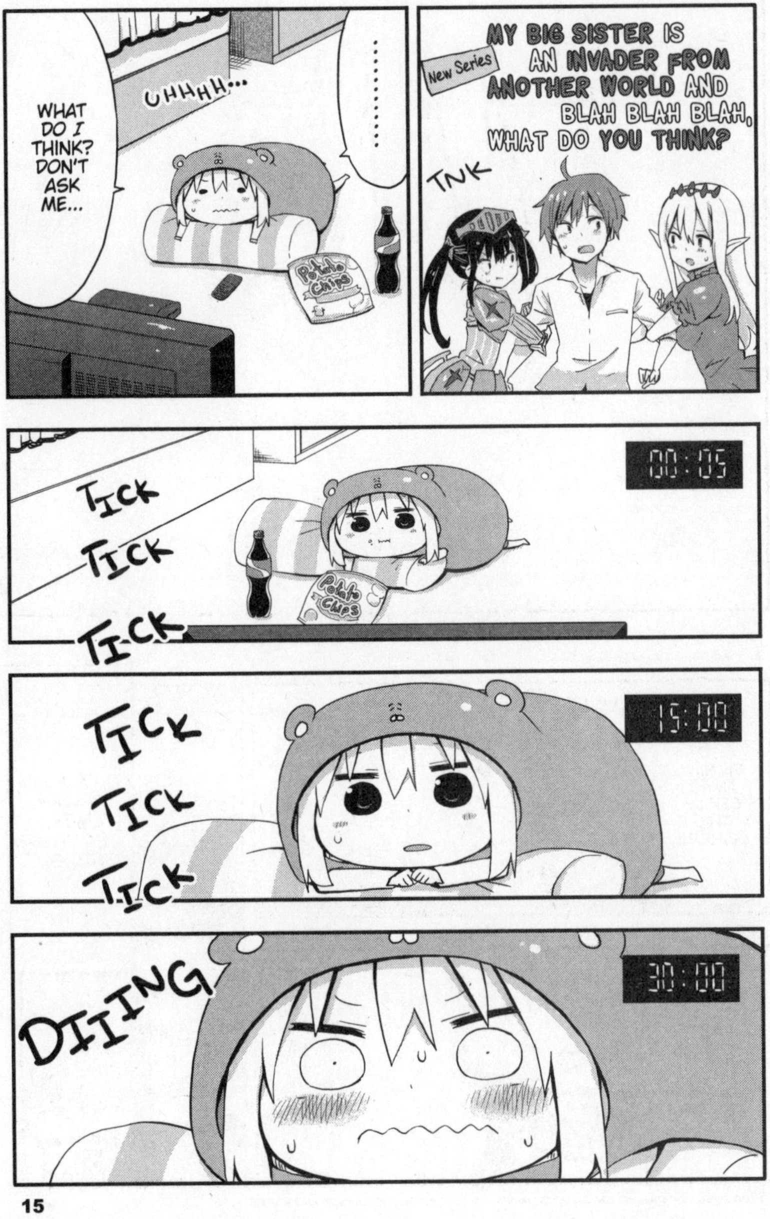
New Series
MY BIG SISTER IS AN INVADER FROM ANOTHER WORLD AND BLAH BLAH BLAH, WHAT DO YOU THINK?
TNK
......
UHHHH...
WHAT DO I THINK? DON'T ASK ME...
Potato Chips
00:05
TICK
TICK
TICK
Potato Chips
15:00
TICK
TICK
TICK
30:00
DIIING

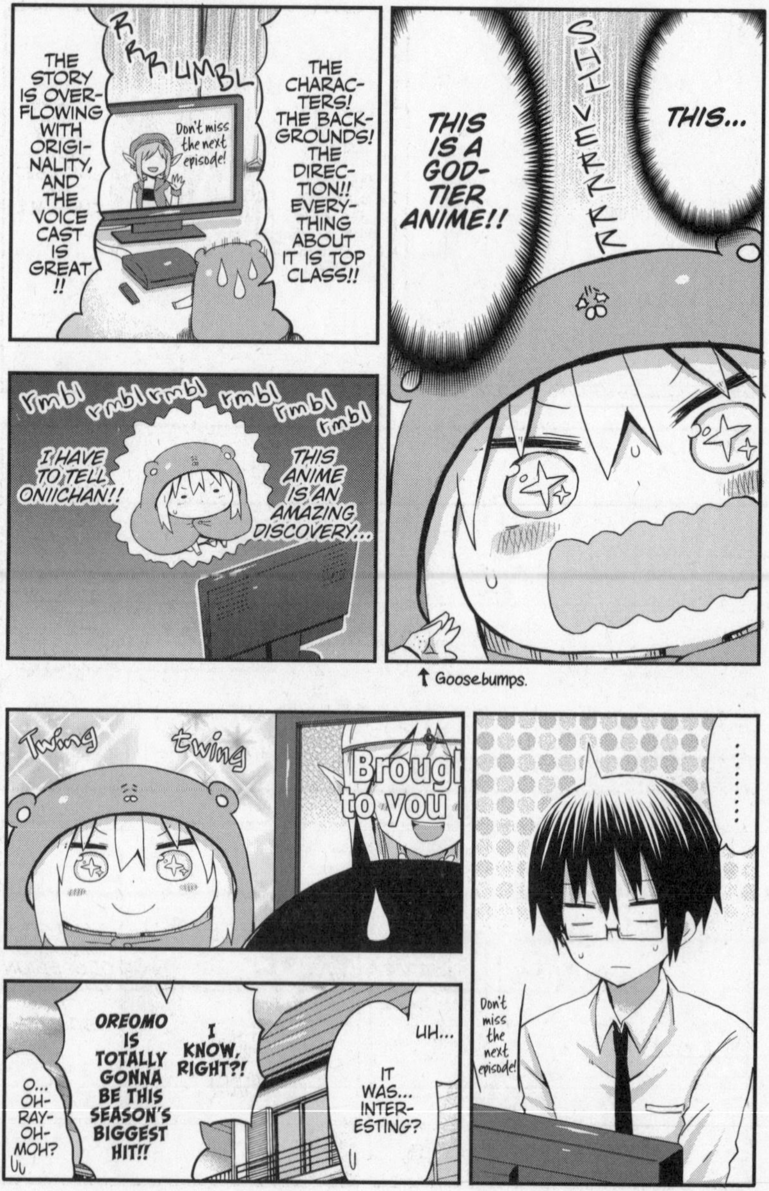
THIS...
SHIVERRRRR
THIS IS A GOD-TIER ANIME!!
↑ Goosebumps.
RRRUMBL
THE CHARACTERS! THE BACKGROUNDS! THE DIRECTION!! EVERYTHING ABOUT IT IS TOP CLASS!!
THE STORY IS OVERFLOWING WITH ORIGINALITY, AND THE VOICE CAST IS GREAT!!
Don't miss the next episode!
rmbl rmbl rmbl rmbl rmbl rmbl rmbl
THIS ANIME IS AN AMAZING DISCOVERY...
I HAVE TO TELL ONIICHAN!!
......
Don't miss the next episode!
twing
Twing
UH...
IT WAS... INTERESTING?
I KNOW, RIGHT?!
OREOMO IS TOTALLY GONNA BE THIS SEASON'S BIGGEST HIT!!
O... OH-RAY-OH-MOH?

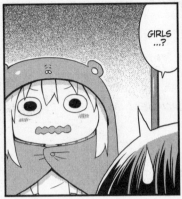

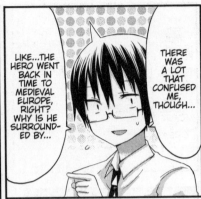

THERE WAS A LOT THAT CONFUSED ME, THOUGH...
LIKE...THE HERO WENT BACK IN TIME TO MEDIEVAL EUROPE, RIGHT? WHY IS HE SURROUND-ED BY...
GIRLS ...?
IT'S NOT EUROPE, IT'S ANOTHER WORLD!! GET WITH THE PROGRAM, ONIICHAN!!
H... HUUUH ?!
DUUN
JEEZ, ONIICHAN. YOU NEED TO WATCH IT AGAIN.
WE'RE SERI-OUSLY GONNA REWATCH THE EPISODE WE JUST SAW?!
BWEEP
AND SO, UMARU'S OBSESSION CONTINUED TO ESCALATE.
Klaka klaka
SHE'S CHECK-ING THE OFFICIAL WEBSITE AGAIN...
MERCHAN-DISE. THE ORIGINAL NOVELS. THE MANGA ADAPTATION. PREORDER-ING THE BLU-RAYS. AND ON TOP OF ALL THAT...
OreOmo Talk Show
Because... I'm... a half-elp...
Hey, every-bodyyy!! What do you think of OreOmo?!

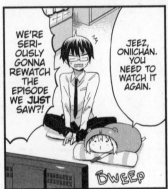

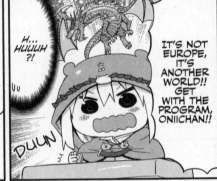

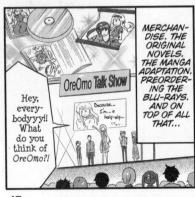

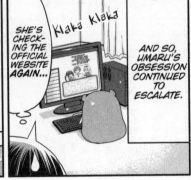

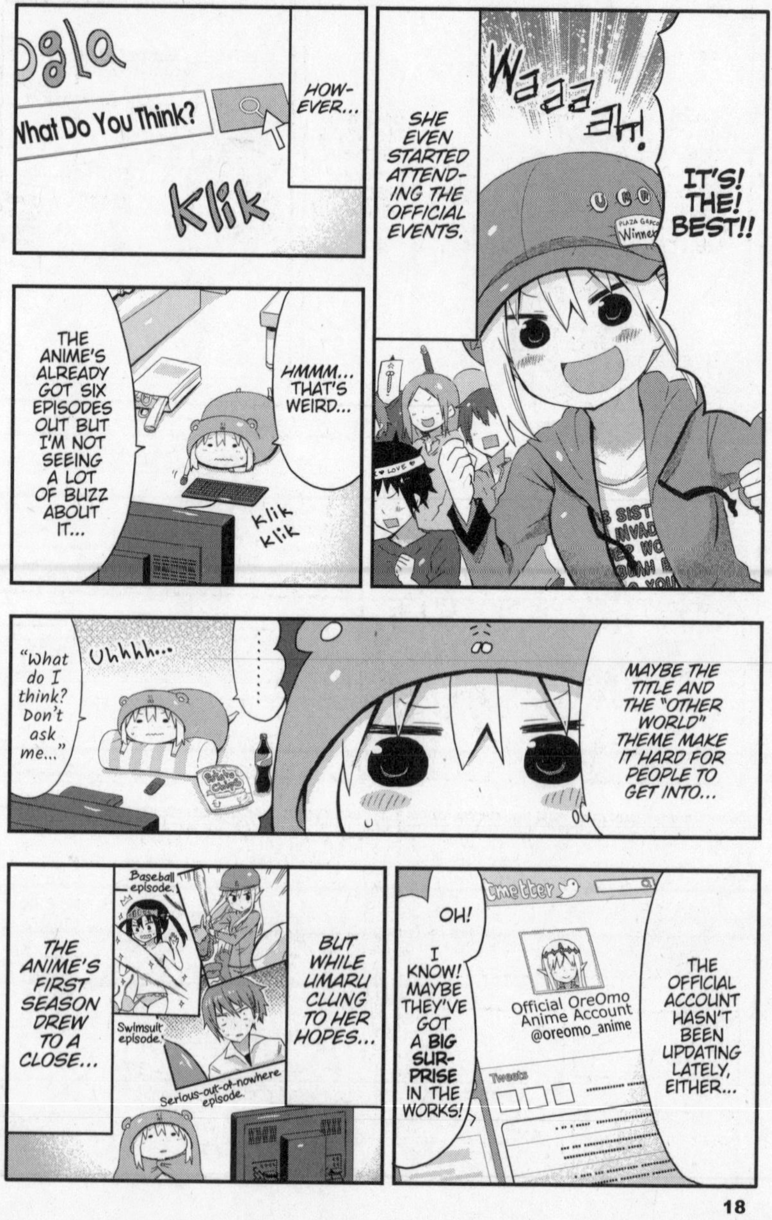

SHE EVEN STARTED ATTENDING THE OFFICIAL EVENTS.
Waaaah!
IT'S! THE! BEST!!
PLAZA GAPCO Winner
HOW-EVER...
What Do You Think?
Klik
HMMM... THAT'S WEIRD...
THE ANIME'S ALREADY GOT SIX EPISODES OUT BUT I'M NOT SEEING A LOT OF BUZZ ABOUT IT...
klik klik
MAYBE THE TITLE AND THE "OTHER WORLD" THEME MAKE IT HARD FOR PEOPLE TO GET INTO...
......
Uhhhh...
"What do I think? Don't ask me..."
THE OFFICIAL ACCOUNT HASN'T BEEN UPDATING LATELY, EITHER...
Official OreOmo Anime Account
@oreomo_anime
Tweets
OH!
I KNOW! MAYBE THEY'VE GOT A **BIG SURPRISE** IN THE WORKS!
BUT WHILE UMARU CLUNG TO HER HOPES...
Baseball episode.
THE ANIME'S FIRST SEASON DREW TO A CLOSE...
Swimsuit episode.
Serious-out-of-nowhere episode.

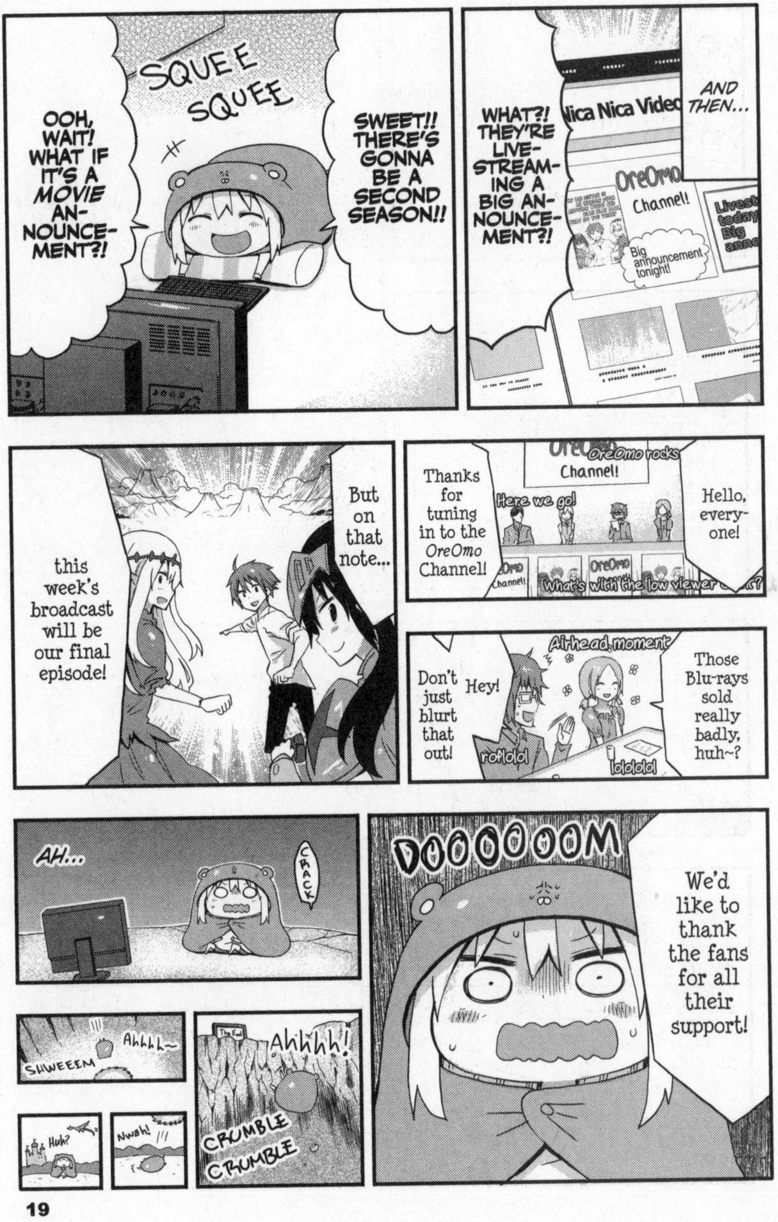
AND THEN...
WHAT?! THEY'RE LIVE-STREAMING A BIG ANNOUNCEMENT?!
OreOmo
Channel!
Big announcement tonight!
SWEET!! THERE'S GONNA BE A SECOND SEASON!!
SQUEE SQUEE
OOH, WAIT! WHAT IF IT'S A *MOVIE* ANNOUNCEMENT?!
OreOmo rocks
Channel!
Hello, everyone!
Here we go!
Thanks for tuning in to the *OreOmo* Channel!
Airhead moment
Those Blu-rays sold really badly, huh~?
lololol
Hey!
Don't just blurt that out!
rofllol
But on that note...
this week's broadcast will be our final episode!
DOOOOOOM
We'd like to thank the fans for all their support!
CRACK
AH...
The End
Ahhhh!
CRUMBLE CRUMBLE
Ahhhh~
SHWEEEM
Nwah!
Huh?

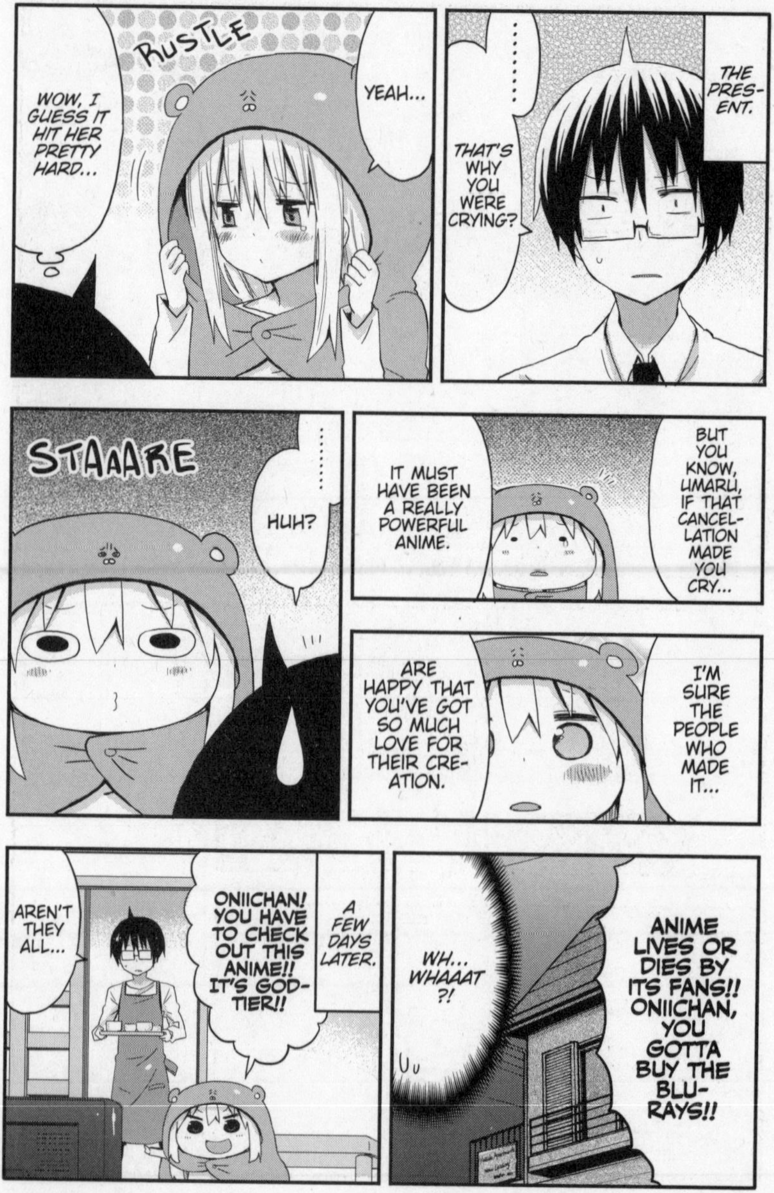
THE PRESENT.
......
THAT'S WHY YOU WERE CRYING?
YEAH...
RUSTLE
WOW, I GUESS IT HIT HER PRETTY HARD...
BUT YOU KNOW, UMARU, IF THAT CANCELLATION MADE YOU CRY...
IT MUST HAVE BEEN A REALLY POWERFUL ANIME.
I'M SURE THE PEOPLE WHO MADE IT...
ARE HAPPY THAT YOU'VE GOT SO MUCH LOVE FOR THEIR CREATION.
......
HUH?
STAAARE
ANIME LIVES OR DIES BY ITS FANS!! ONIICHAN, YOU GOTTA BUY THE BLU-RAYS!!
WH... WHAAAT ?!
A FEW DAYS LATER.
ONIICHAN! YOU HAVE TO CHECK OUT THIS ANIME!! IT'S GOD-TIER!!
AREN'T THEY ALL...

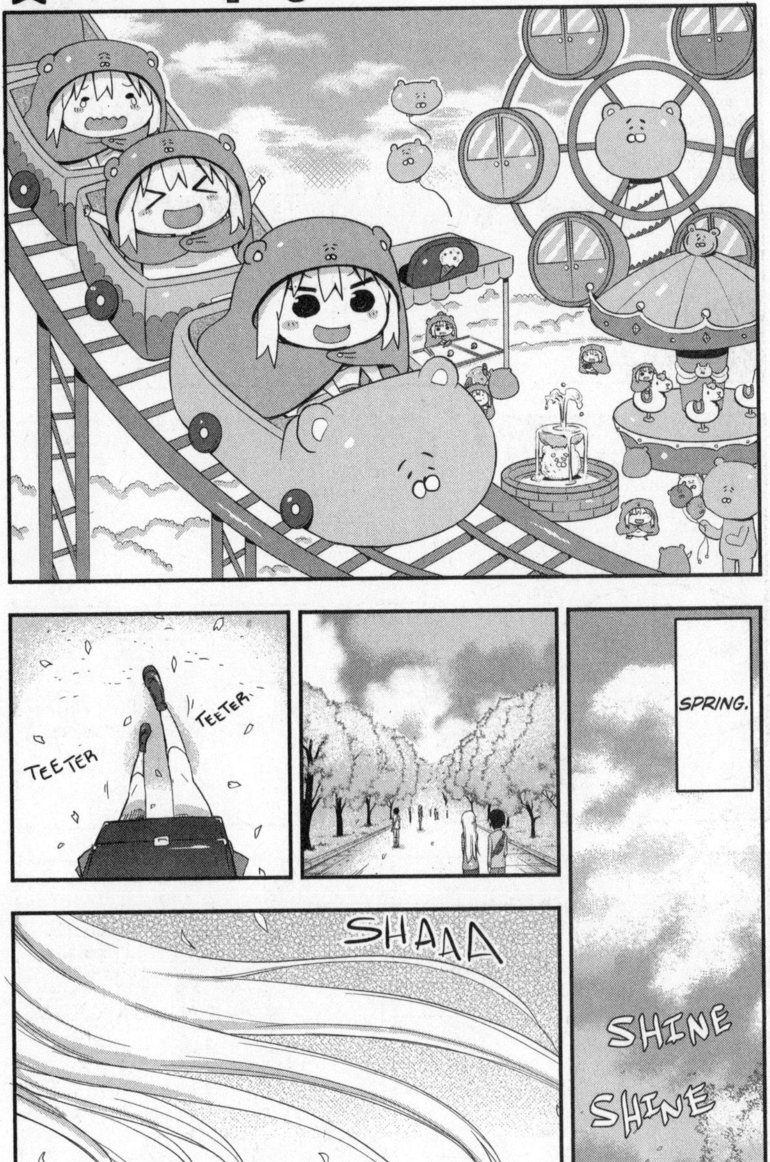
SPRING.
SHINE
SHINE
TEETER
TEETER
SHAAA

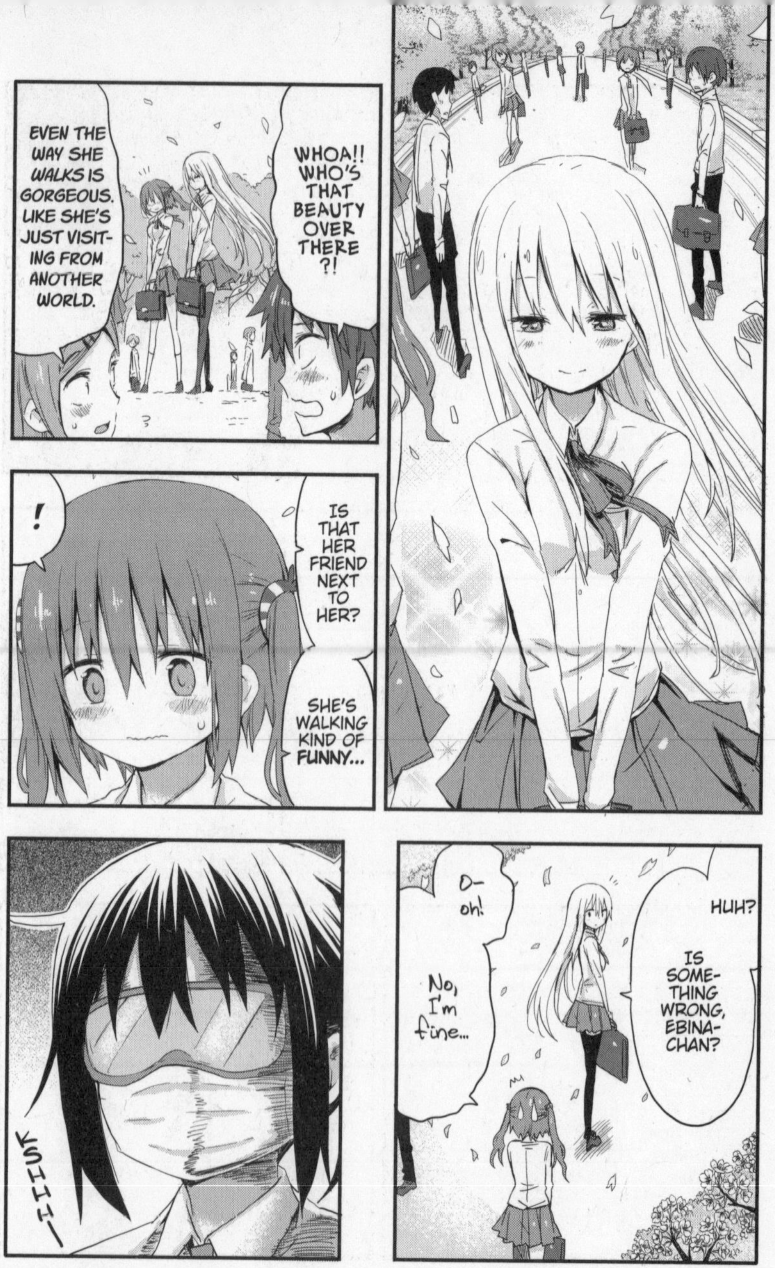
WHOA!! WHO'S THAT BEAUTY OVER THERE?!
EVEN THE WAY SHE WALKS IS GORGEOUS. LIKE SHE'S JUST VISITING FROM ANOTHER WORLD.
IS THAT HER FRIEND NEXT TO HER?
SHE'S WALKING KIND OF FUNNY...
!
HUH?
IS SOMETHING WRONG, EBINA-CHAN?
O-oh!
No, I'm fine...
KSHHH

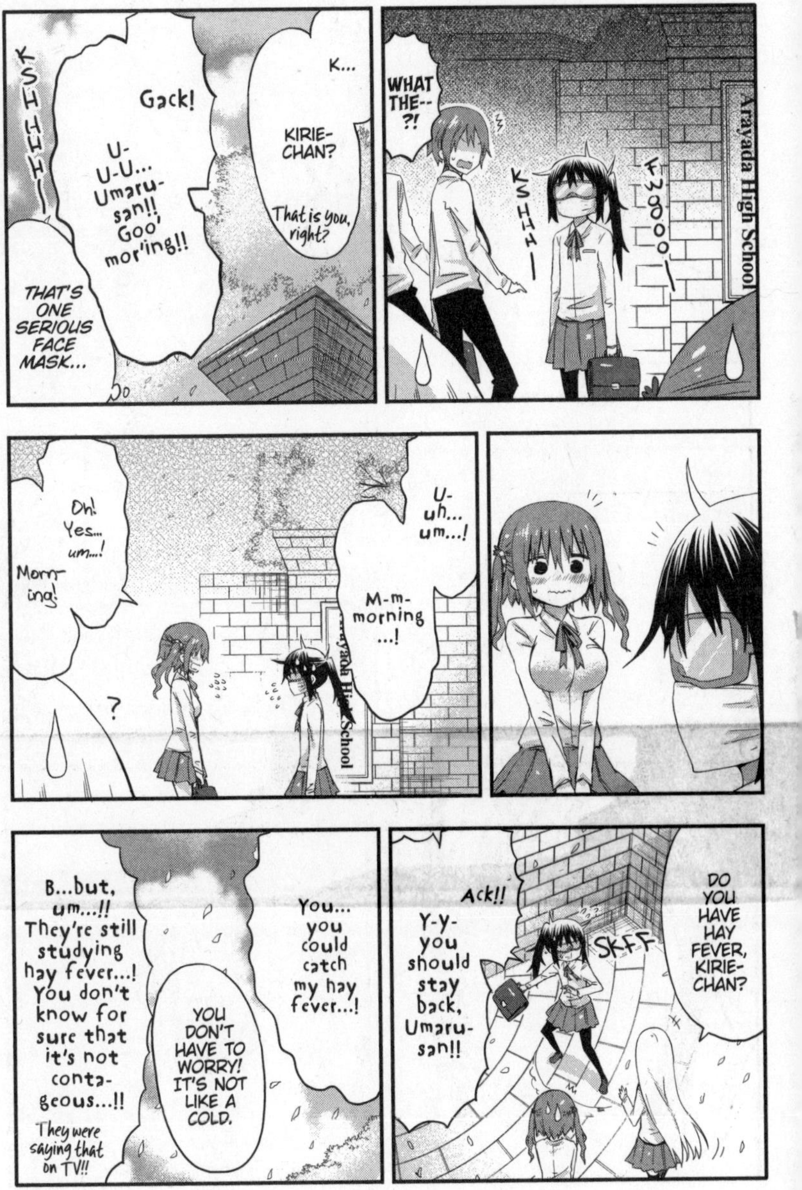
WHAT THE--?!
KSHHHH
FZOOOO
Arayada High School
K...
KIRIE-CHAN?
That is you, right?
Gack!
U-U-U... Umaru-san!! Goo' mor'ing!!
KSHHHH
THAT'S ONE SERIOUS FACE MASK...
U-uh... um...!
M-m-morning...!
Oh! Yes... um...!
Morning!
?
Arayada High School
DO YOU HAVE HAY FEVER, KIRIE-CHAN?
Ack!!
SKFF
Y-y-you should stay back, Umaru-san!!
You... you could catch my hay fever...!
YOU DON'T HAVE TO WORRY! IT'S NOT LIKE A COLD.
B...but, um...!! They're still studying hay fever...! You don't know for sure that it's not conta-geous...!!
They were saying that on TV!!

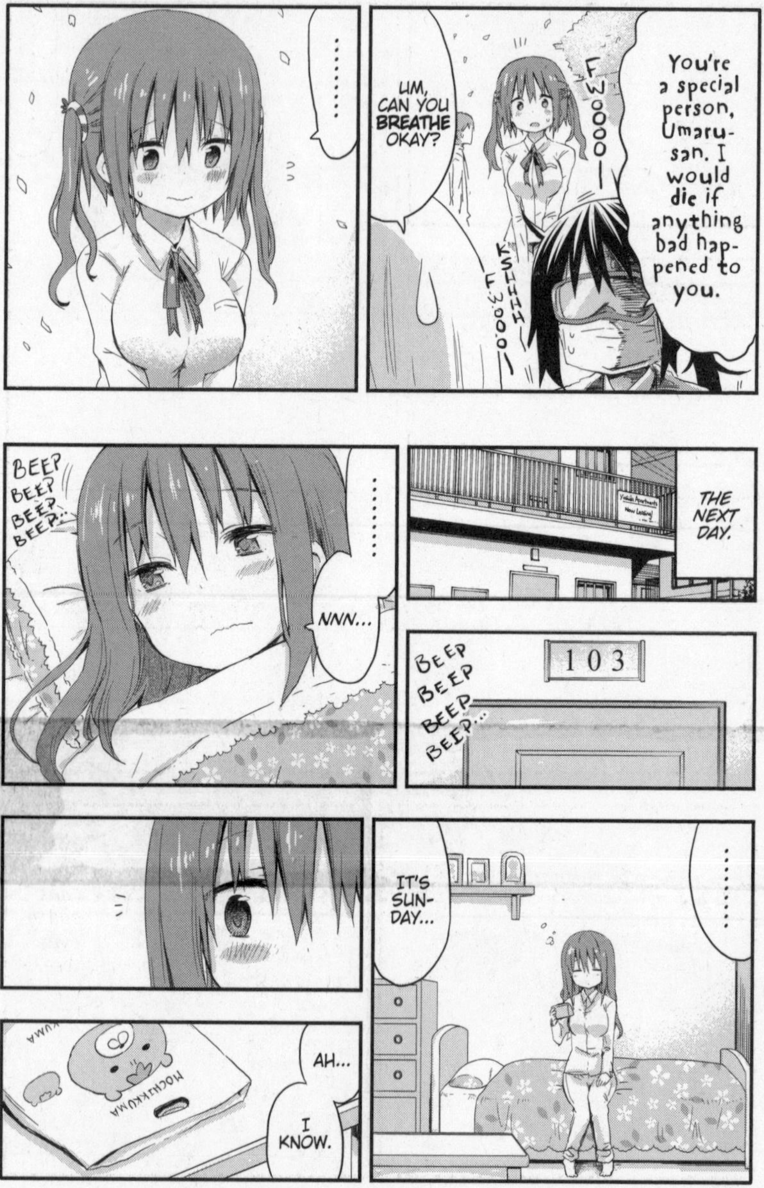
You're a special person, Umaru-san. I would die if anything bad hap-pened to you.
FWOOOO
KSHHHH
FWOOO
UM, CAN YOU BREATHE OKAY?
......
THE NEXT DAY.
103
BEEP BEEP BEEP BEEP...
BEEP BEEP BEEP BEEP...
......
NNN...
......
IT'S SUN-DAY...
MOCHIKKUMA
AH...
I KNOW.

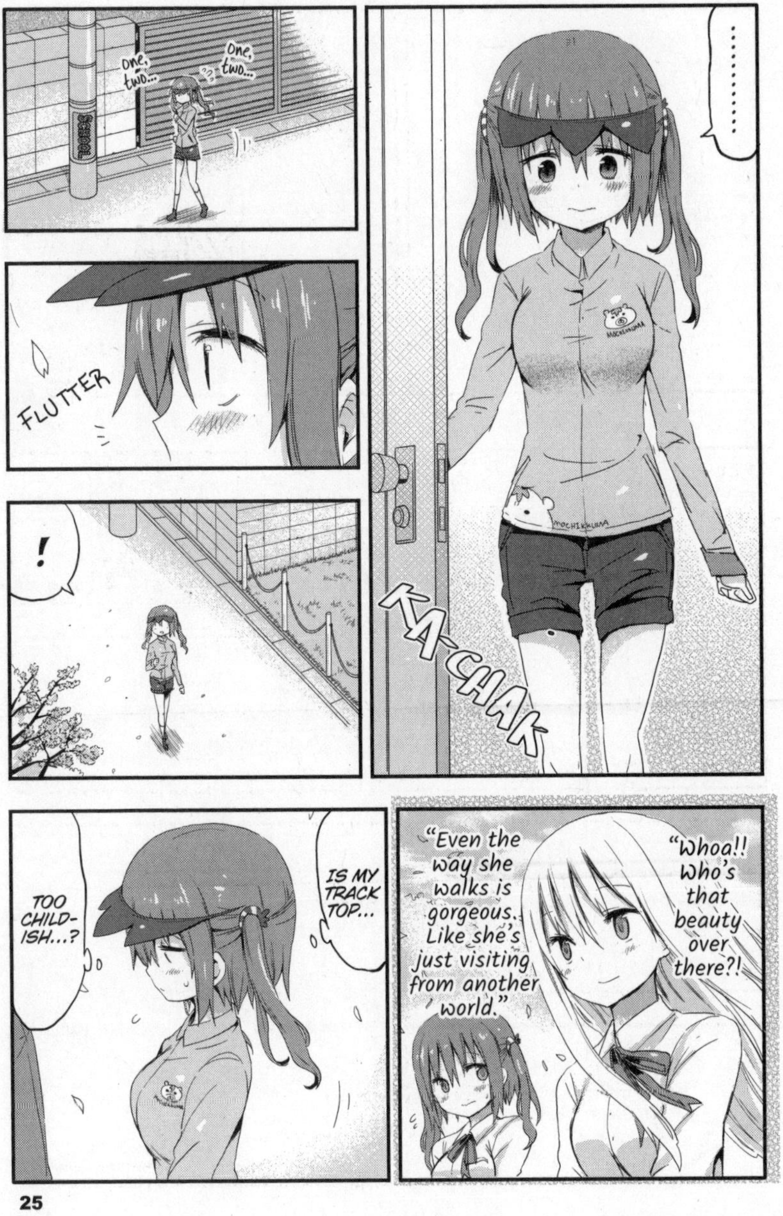
......
KA-CHAK
One, two...
One, two...
SCHOOL
FLUTTER
!
"Whoa!! Who's that beauty over there?!"
"Even the way she walks is gorgeous. Like she's just visiting from another world."
IS MY TRACK TOP...
TOO CHILD-ISH...?

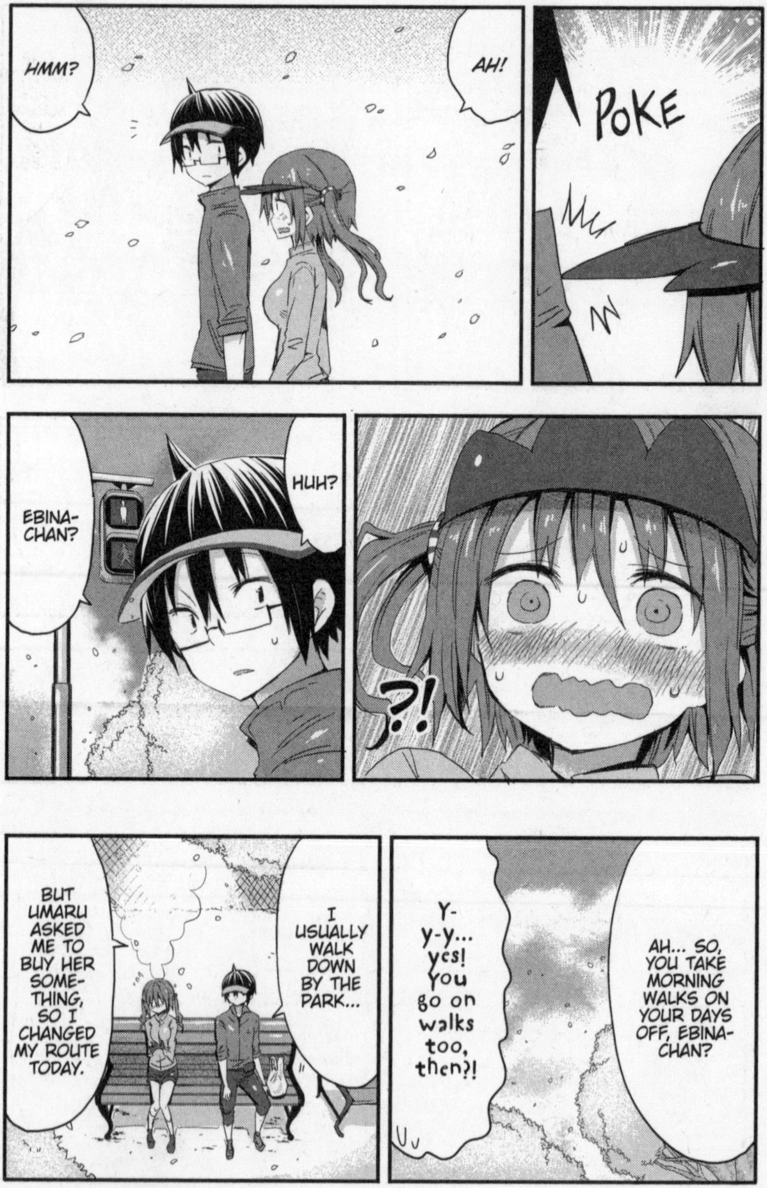
POKE
AH!
HMM?
?!
HUH?
EBINA-CHAN?
AH... SO, YOU TAKE MORNING WALKS ON YOUR DAYS OFF, EBINA-CHAN?
Y-y-y... yes! You go on walks too, then?!
I USUALLY WALK DOWN BY THE PARK...
BUT UMARU ASKED ME TO BUY HER SOMETHING, SO I CHANGED MY ROUTE TODAY.

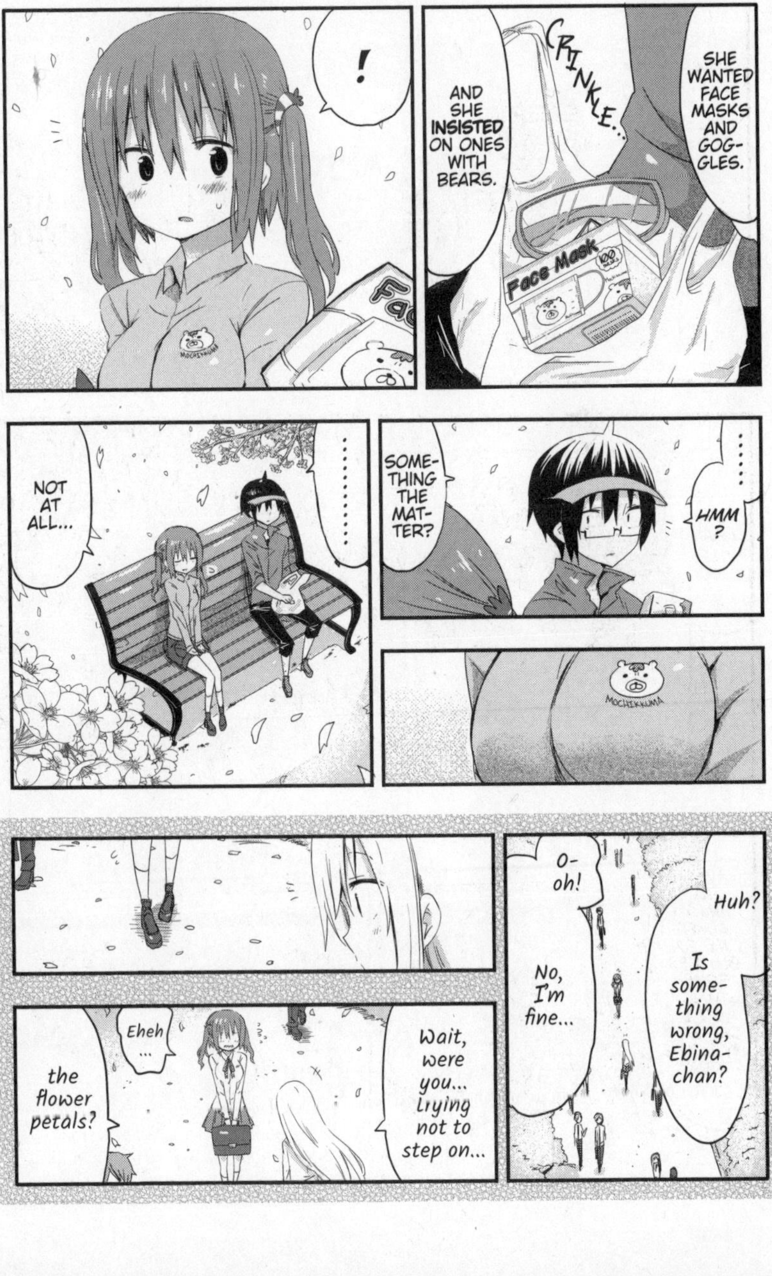
SHE WANTED FACE MASKS AND GOG-GLES.
CRINKLE...
AND SHE INSISTED ON ONES WITH BEARS.
Face Mask
!
......
HMM?
SOME-THING THE MAT-TER?
MOCHIKKUMA
......
NOT AT ALL...
Huh?
Is some-thing wrong, Ebina-chan?
O-oh!
No, I'm fine...
Wait, were you... trying not to step on...
Eheh...
the flower petals?

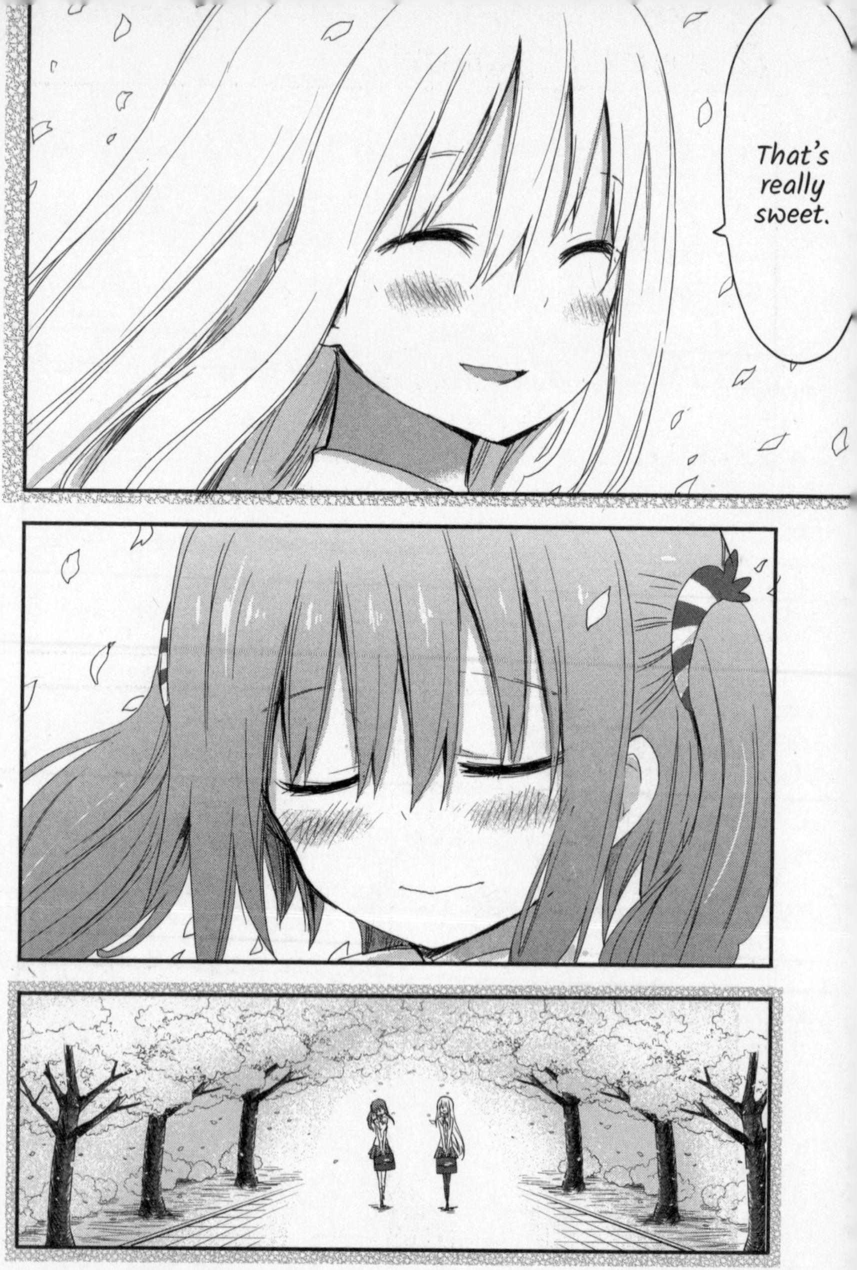
That's really sweet.

No. 56 Umaru & Sylphynford

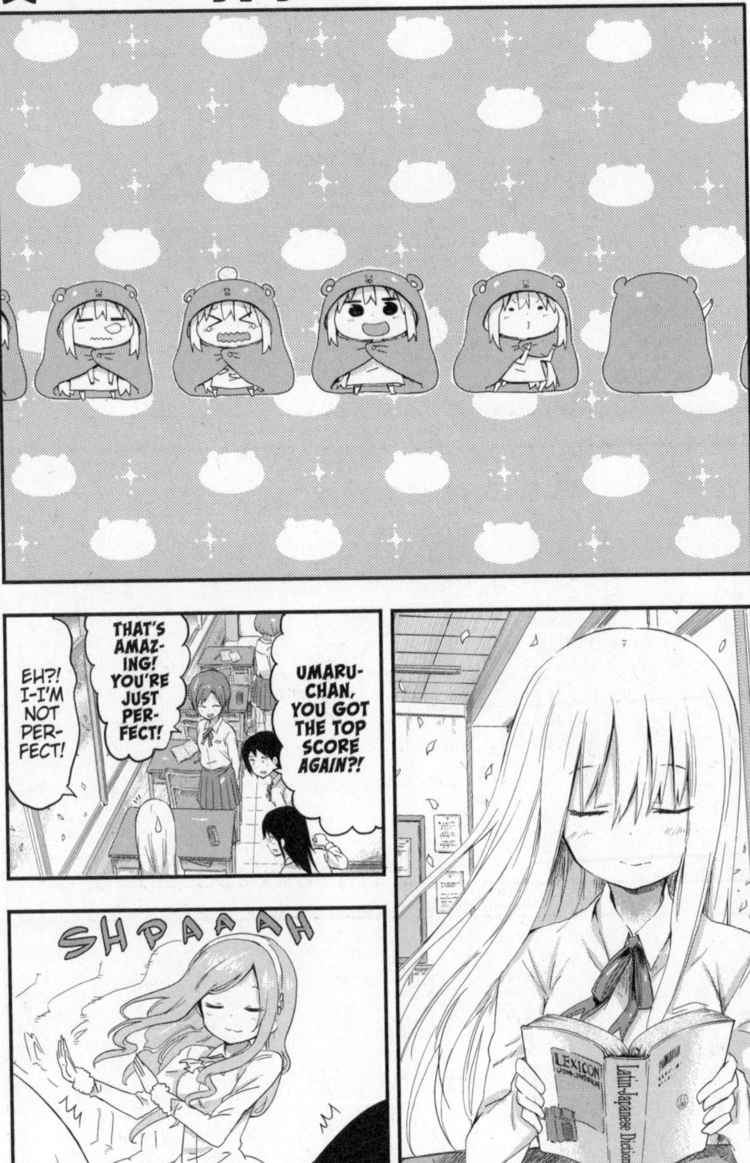
LEXICON
Latin-Japanese Dictionary
UMARU-CHAN, YOU GOT THE TOP SCORE AGAIN?!
THAT'S AMAZING! YOU'RE JUST PERFECT!
EH?! I-I'M NOT PERFECT!
SHPAAAH

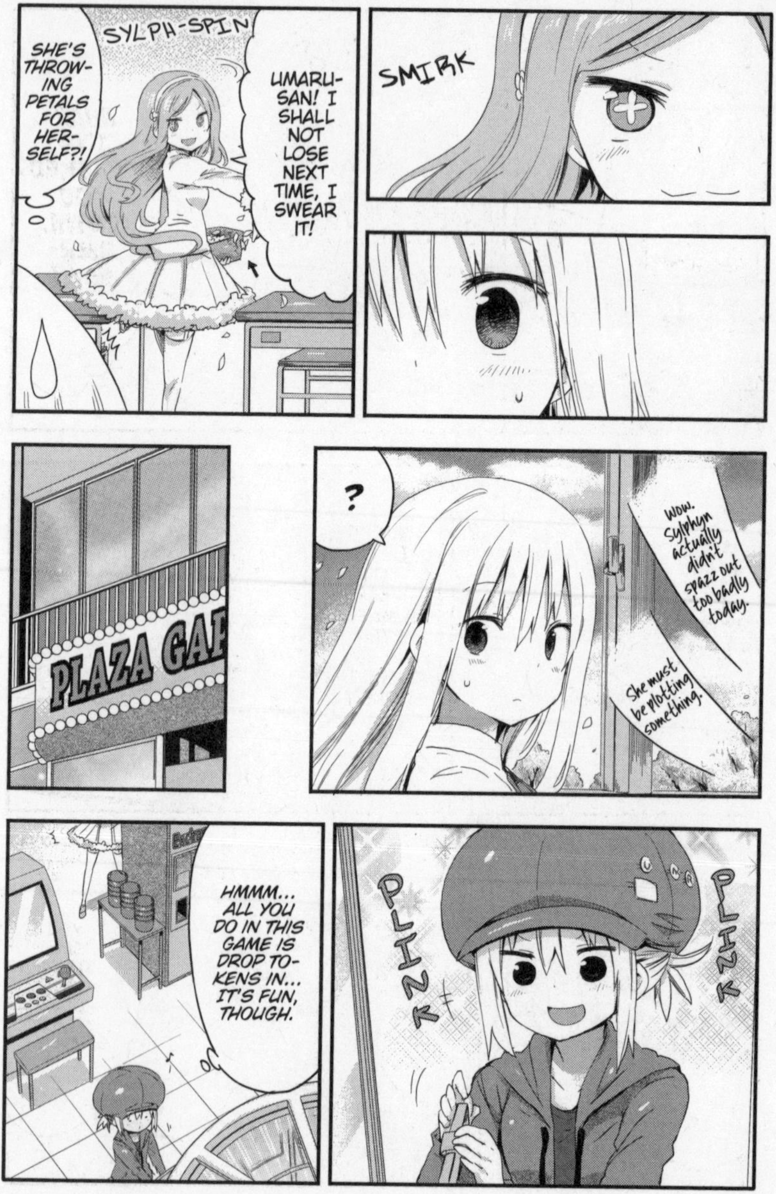

SMIRK
UMARU-SAN! I SHALL NOT LOSE NEXT TIME, I SWEAR IT!
SYLPH-SPIN
SHE'S THROWING PETALS FOR HERSELF?!
Wow. Sylphyn actually didn't spazz out too badly today.
?
She must be plotting something.
PLAZA GA
PLINK
PLINK
HMMM... ALL YOU DO IN THIS GAME IS DROP TOKENS IN... IT'S FUN, THOUGH.

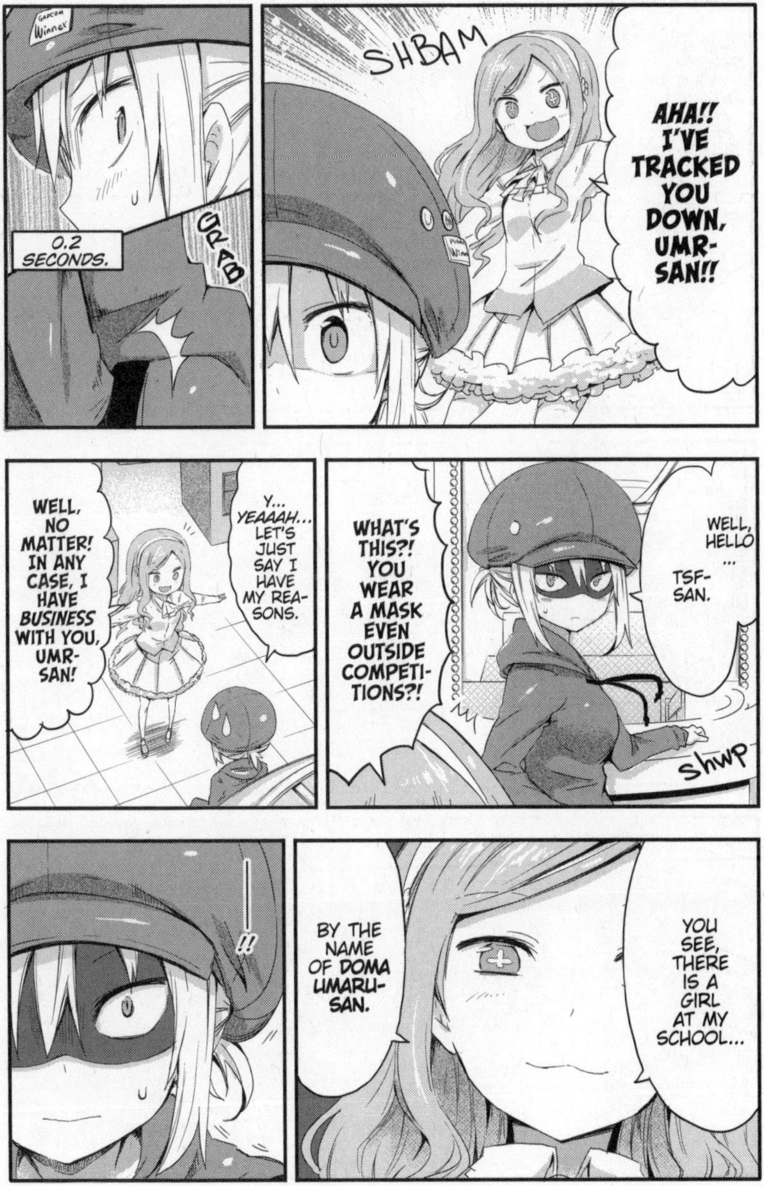
SHBAM
AHA!! I'VE TRACKED YOU DOWN, UMR-SAN!!
GRAB
0.2 SECONDS.
WELL, HELLO... TSF-SAN.
WHAT'S THIS?! YOU WEAR A MASK EVEN OUTSIDE COMPETITIONS?!
shwp
Y... YEAAAH... LET'S JUST SAY I HAVE MY REASONS.
WELL, NO MATTER! IN ANY CASE, I HAVE BUSINESS WITH YOU, UMR-SAN!
YOU SEE, THERE IS A GIRL AT MY SCHOOL...
BY THE NAME OF DOMA UMARU-SAN.
——!!

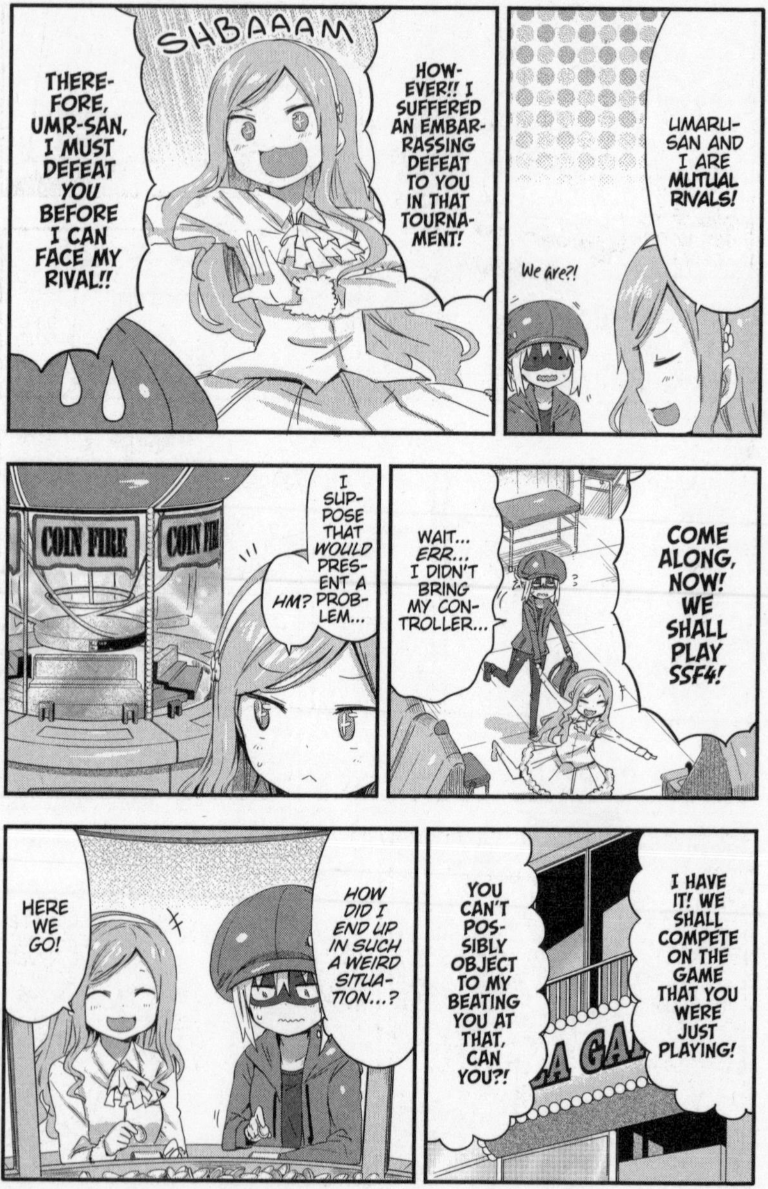
UMARU-SAN AND I ARE MUTUAL RIVALS!
We are?!
HOW-EVER!! I SUFFERED AN EMBARRASSING DEFEAT TO YOU IN THAT TOURNAMENT!
SHBAAAM
THEREFORE, UMR-SAN, I MUST DEFEAT YOU BEFORE I CAN FACE MY RIVAL!!
COME ALONG, NOW! WE SHALL PLAY SSF4!
WAIT... ERR... I DIDN'T BRING MY CONTROLLER...
I SUPPOSE THAT WOULD PRESENT A PROBLEM...
HM?
COIN FIRE
COIN FIRE
I HAVE IT! WE SHALL COMPETE ON THE GAME THAT YOU WERE JUST PLAYING!
YOU CAN'T POSSIBLY OBJECT TO MY BEATING YOU AT THAT, CAN YOU?!
HOW DID I END UP IN SUCH A WEIRD SITUATION...?
HERE WE GO!

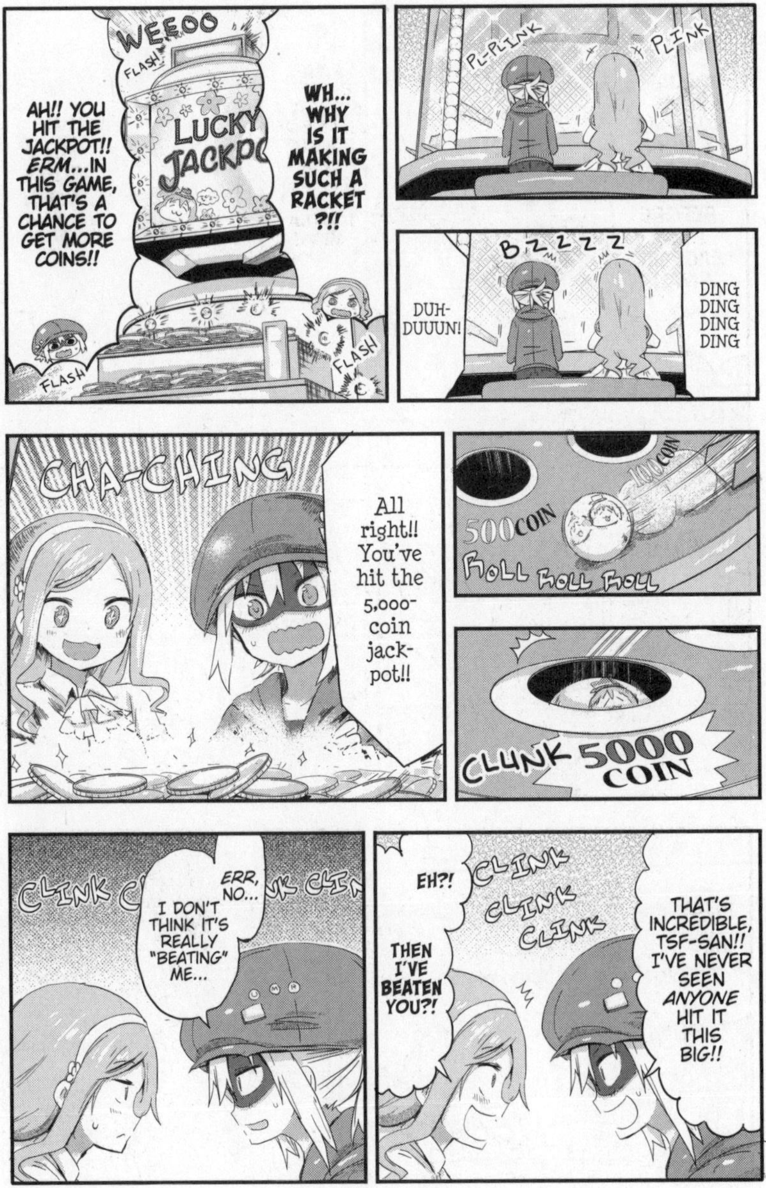
PLINK
PL-PLINK
BZZZZZ
DING DING DING DING
DUH-DUUUN!
WEEOO
FLASH
LUCKY JACKPO
WH... WHY IS IT MAKING SUCH A RACKET?!!
AH!! YOU HIT THE JACKPOT!! *ERM*...IN THIS GAME, THAT'S A CHANCE TO GET MORE COINS!!
FLASH
FLASH
100 COIN
500 COIN
ROLL ROLL ROLL
CLUNK
5000 COIN
All right!! You've hit the 5,000-coin jackpot!!
CHA-CHING
THAT'S INCREDIBLE, TSF-SAN!! I'VE NEVER SEEN *ANYONE* HIT IT THIS BIG!!
CLINK
CLINK
CLINK
EH?!
THEN I'VE BEATEN YOU?!
ERR, NO...
I DON'T THINK IT'S REALLY "BEATING" ME...
CLINK

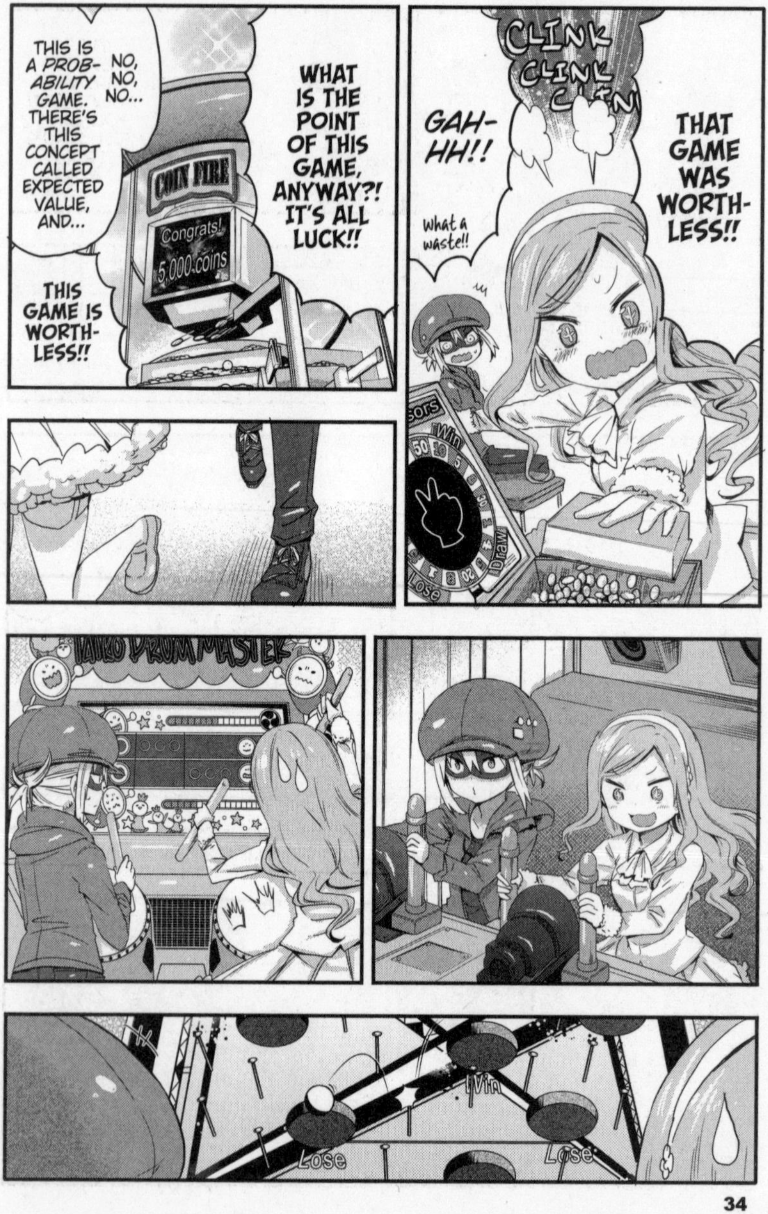
THAT GAME WAS WORTHLESS!!
CLINK CLINK CLINK
GAH-HH!!
What a waste!!
Win
50
Draw
20
30
Lose
WHAT IS THE POINT OF THIS GAME, ANYWAY?! IT'S ALL LUCK!!
NO, NO, NO...
THIS IS A *PROBABILITY* GAME. THERE'S THIS CONCEPT CALLED EXPECTED VALUE, AND...
COIN FIRE
Congrats! 5,000 coins
THIS GAME IS WORTHLESS!!
TAIKO DRUM MASTER
Win
Lose
Lose

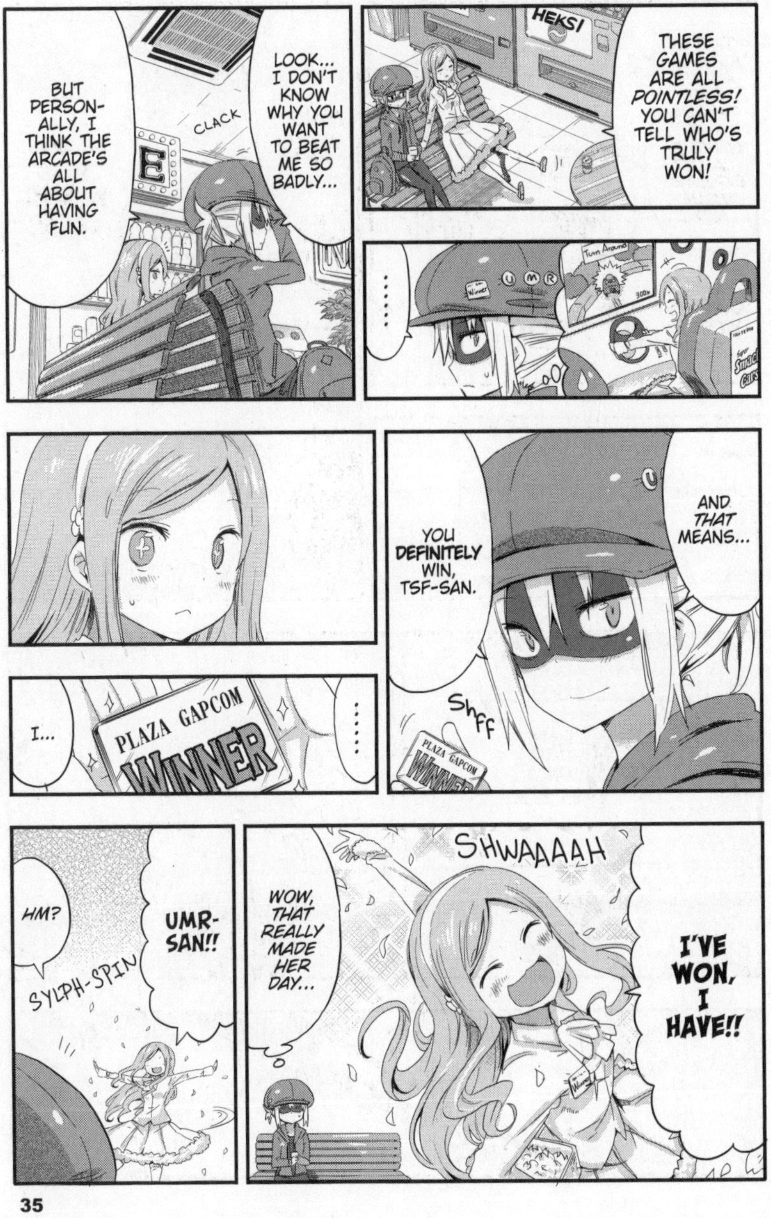
HEKSI
THESE GAMES ARE ALL *POINTLESS!* YOU CAN'T TELL WHO'S TRULY WON!
Turn Around
Winner
UMR
......
LOOK... I DON'T KNOW WHY YOU WANT TO BEAT ME SO BADLY...
CLACK
BUT PERSONALLY, I THINK THE ARCADE'S ALL ABOUT HAVING FUN.
AND *THAT* MEANS...
YOU **DEFINITELY** WIN, TSF-SAN.
Shfff
PLAZA GAPCOM WINNER
......
I...
PLAZA GAPCOM WINNER
SHWAAAAH
I'VE WON, I HAVE!!
WOW, THAT REALLY MADE HER DAY...
UMR-SAN!!
HM?
SYLPH-SPIN

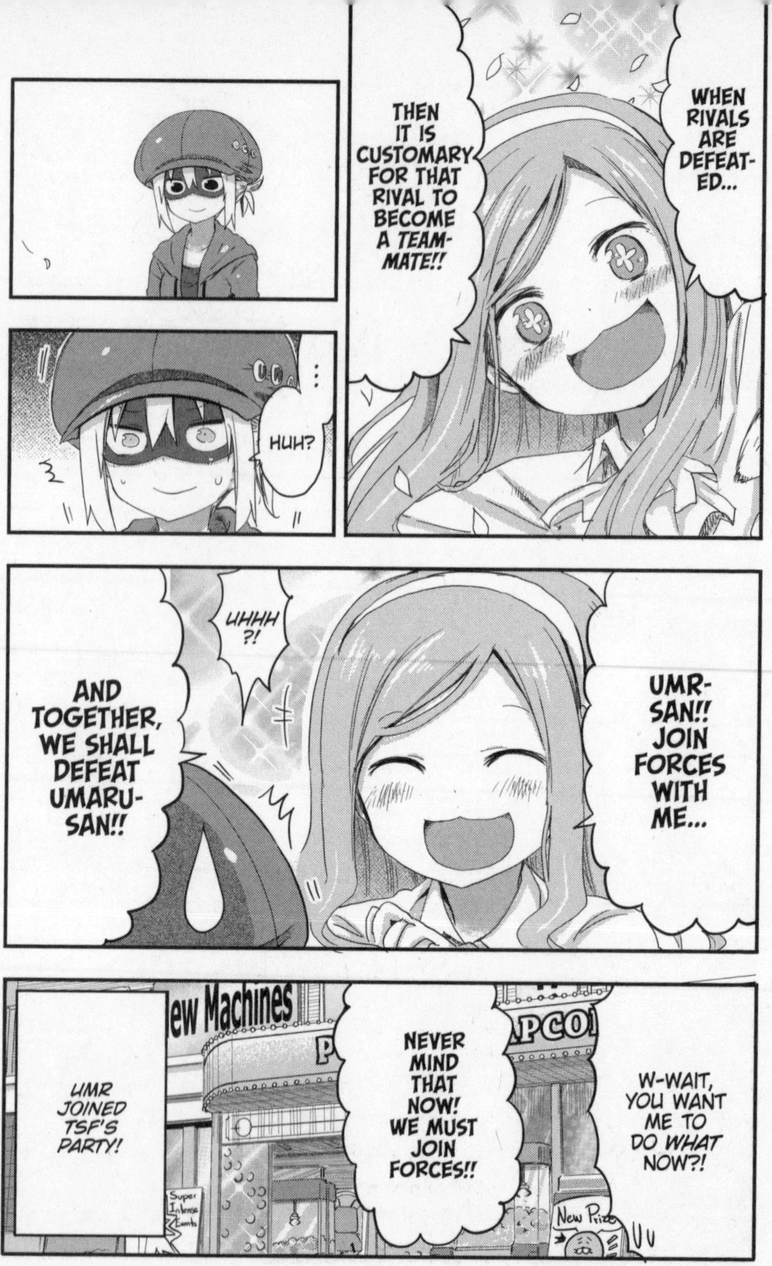
WHEN RIVALS ARE DEFEAT-ED...
THEN IT IS CUSTOMARY FOR THAT RIVAL TO BECOME A *TEAM-MATE!!*
...
HUH?
UMR-SAN!! JOIN FORCES WITH ME...
AND TOGETHER, WE SHALL DEFEAT UMARU-SAN!!
UHHH ?!
W-WAIT, YOU WANT ME TO DO *WHAT* NOW?!
NEVER MIND THAT NOW! WE MUST JOIN FORCES!!
New Machines
Super Intense Events
New Prize
UMR JOINED TSF'S PARTY!

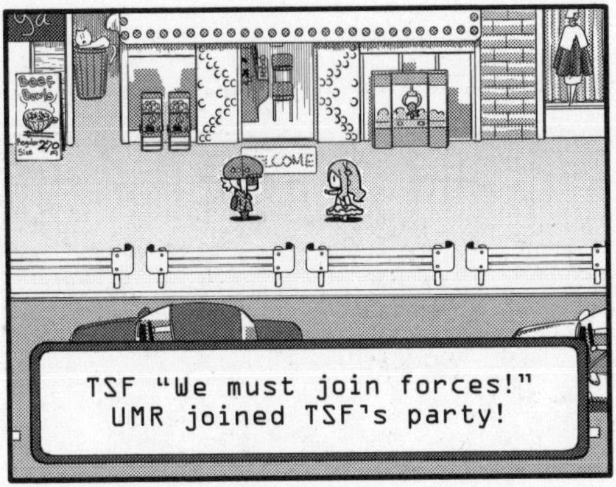
TSF "We must join forces!"
UMR joined TSF's party!

HIMOUTO! UMARU-CHAN

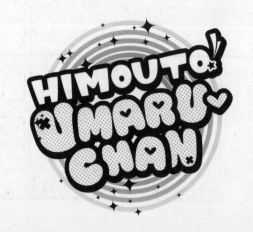

No. 57 Umaru & Cup Noodles

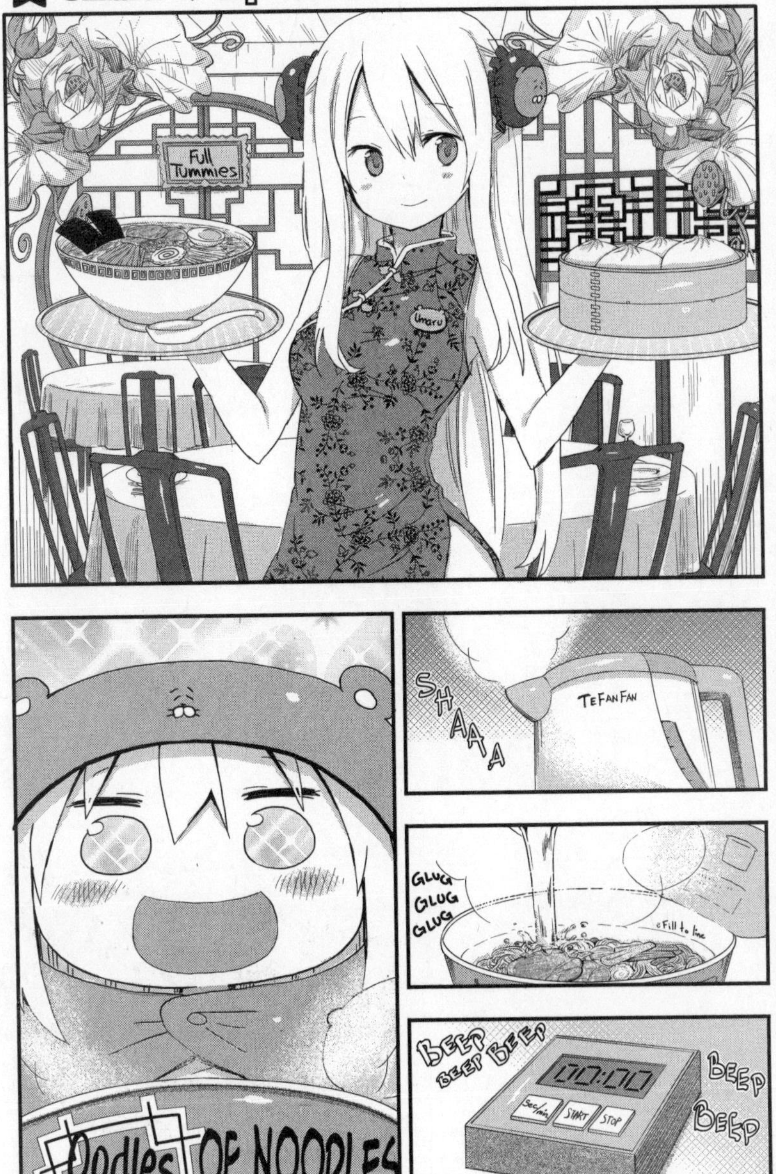
Full Tummies
Umaru
SHAAAA
TEFANFAN
GLUG GLUG GLUG
Fill to line
BEEP BEEP BEEP
BEEP BEEP
00:00
Sec/min START STOP
Oodles OF NOODLES

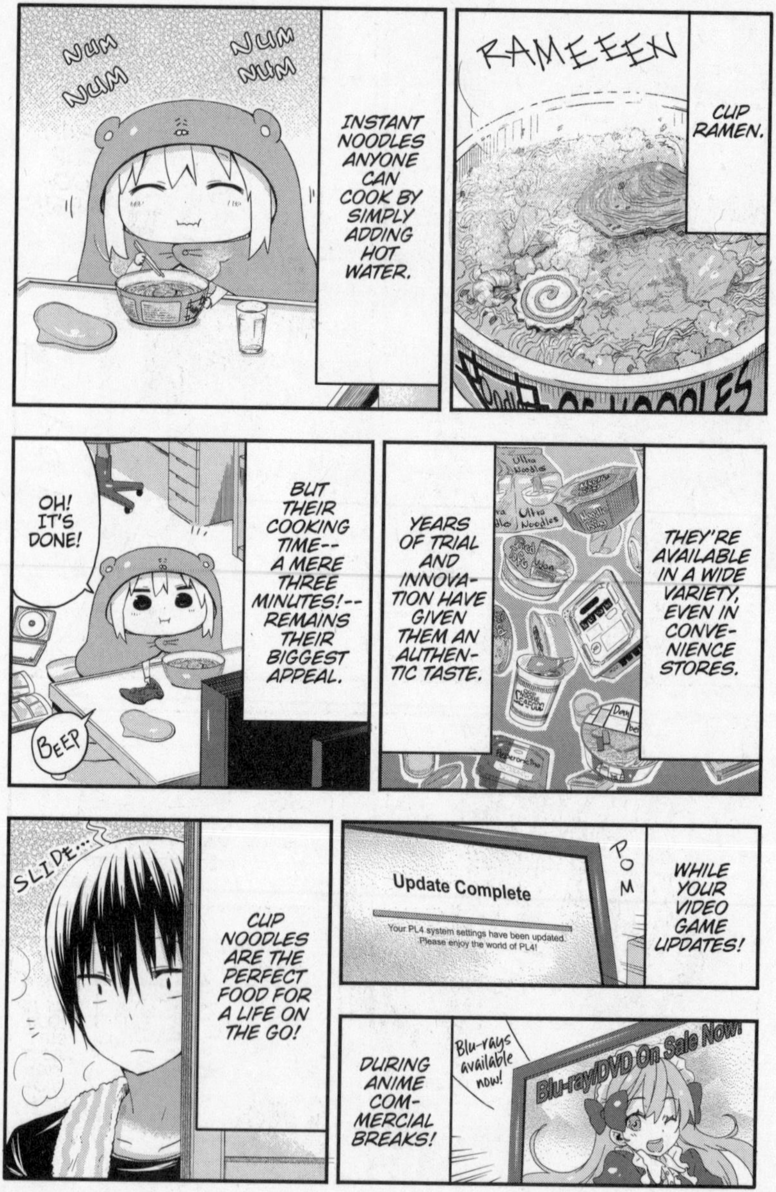
RAMEEEN
CUP RAMEN.
INSTANT NOODLES ANYONE CAN COOK BY SIMPLY ADDING HOT WATER.
NUM NUM
NUM NUM
THEY'RE AVAILABLE IN A WIDE VARIETY, EVEN IN CONVE-NIENCE STORES.
YEARS OF TRIAL AND INNOVA-TION HAVE GIVEN THEM AN AUTHEN-TIC TASTE.
BUT THEIR COOKING TIME-- A MERE THREE MINUTES!-- REMAINS THEIR BIGGEST APPEAL.
OH! IT'S DONE!
BEEP
WHILE YOUR VIDEO GAME UPDATES!
POM
Update Complete
Your PL4 system settings have been updated.
Please enjoy the world of PL4!
DURING ANIME COM-MERCIAL BREAKS!
Blu-rays available now!
Blu-ray/DVD On Sale Now!
CUP NOODLES ARE THE PERFECT FOOD FOR A LIFE ON THE GO!
SLIDE...

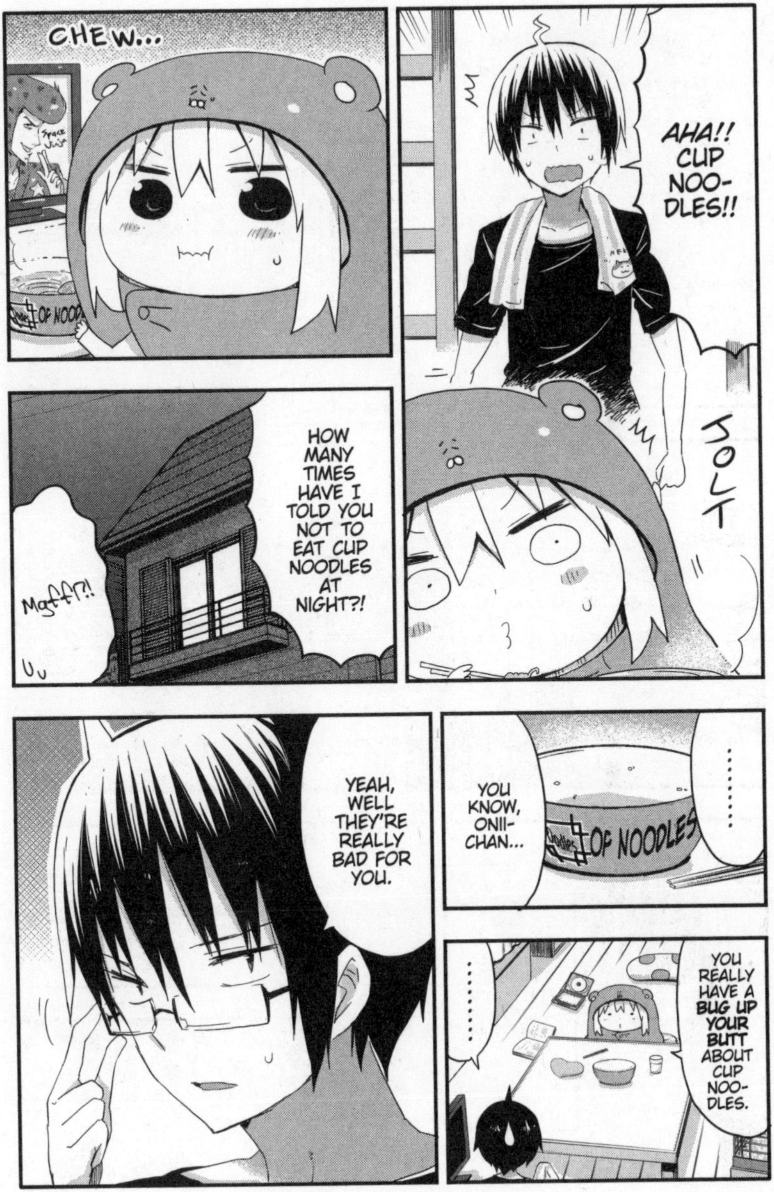
AHA!! CUP NOO-DLES!!
JOLT
CHEW...
HOW MANY TIMES HAVE I TOLD YOU NOT TO EAT CUP NOODLES AT NIGHT?!
Maff?!
......
YOU KNOW, ONII-CHAN...
YOU REALLY HAVE A BUG UP YOUR BUTT ABOUT CUP NOO-DLES.
......
YEAH, WELL THEY'RE REALLY BAD FOR YOU.

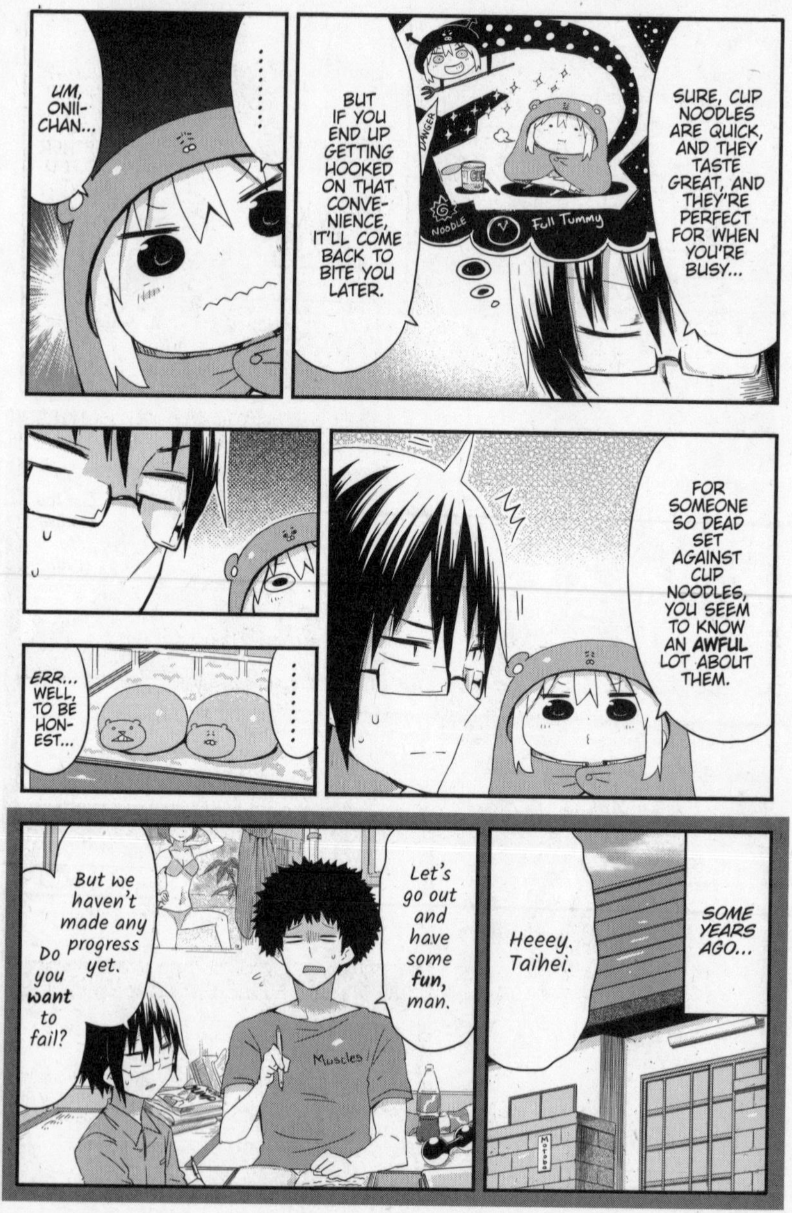
SURE, CUP NOODLES ARE QUICK, AND THEY TASTE GREAT, AND THEY'RE PERFECT FOR WHEN YOU'RE BUSY...
BUT IF YOU END UP GETTING HOOKED ON THAT CONVENIENCE, IT'LL COME BACK TO BITE YOU LATER.
DANGER
NOODLE
Full Tummy
......
UM, ONII-CHAN...
FOR SOMEONE SO DEAD SET AGAINST CUP NOODLES, YOU SEEM TO KNOW AN AWFUL LOT ABOUT THEM.
......
ERR... WELL, TO BE HONEST...
SOME YEARS AGO...
Heeey. Taihei.
Motoba
Let's go out and have some fun, man.
But we haven't made any progress yet. Do you want to fail?
Muscles

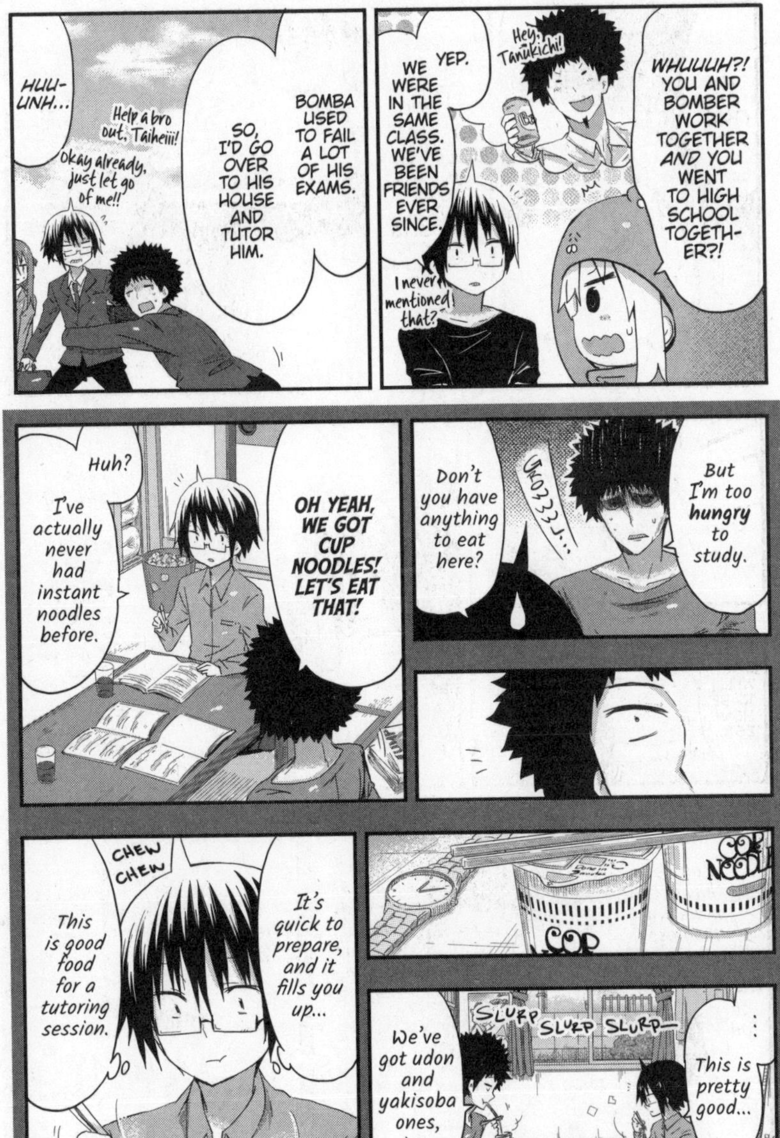
WHUUUH?! YOU AND BOMBER WORK TOGETHER AND YOU WENT TO HIGH SCHOOL TOGETHER?!
Hey, Tanukichi!
YEP.
WE WERE IN THE SAME CLASS. WE'VE BEEN FRIENDS EVER SINCE.
I never mentioned that?
BOMBA USED TO FAIL A LOT OF HIS EXAMS.
SO, I'D GO OVER TO HIS HOUSE AND TUTOR HIM.
Help a bro out, Taiheiii!
Okay already, just let go of me!!
HUU-UNH...
But I'm too **hungry** to study.
GROWWWL...
Don't you have anything to eat here?
OH YEAH, WE GOT CUP NOODLES! LET'S EAT THAT!
Huh?
I've actually never had instant noodles before.
...
This is pretty good...
SLURP SLURP SLURP—
We've got udon and yakisoba ones, too.
It's quick to prepare, and it fills you up...
CHEW CHEW
This is good food for a tutoring session.

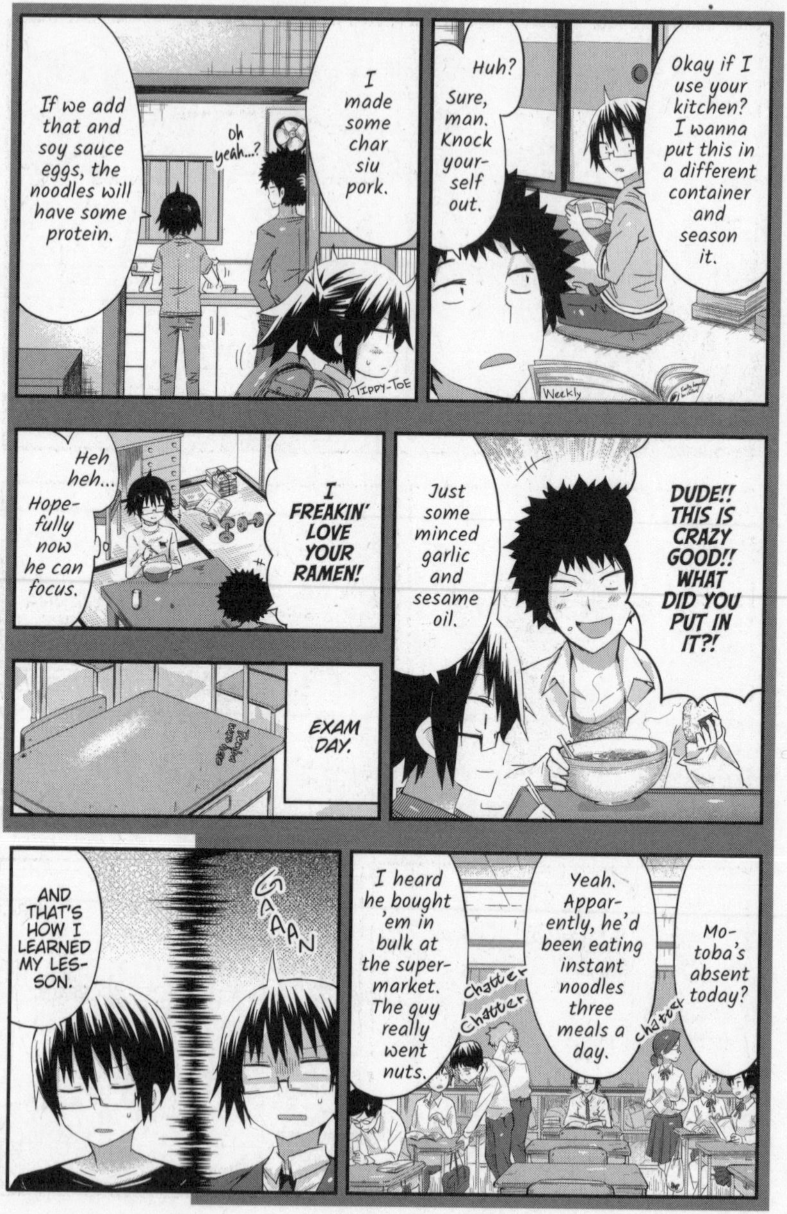
Okay if I use your kitchen? I wanna put this in a different container and season it.
Huh? Sure, man. Knock yourself out.
Weekly
I made some char siu pork.
Oh yeah...?
If we add that and soy sauce eggs, the noodles will have some protein.
TIPPY-TOE
DUDE!! THIS IS CRAZY GOOD!! WHAT DID YOU PUT IN IT?!
Just some minced garlic and sesame oil.
I FREAKIN' LOVE YOUR RAMEN!
Heh heh... Hopefully now he can focus.
EXAM DAY.
Motoba's absent today?
Yeah. Apparently, he'd been eating instant noodles three meals a day.
I heard he bought 'em in bulk at the supermarket. The guy really went nuts.
Chatter
Chatter
Chatter
GAAAN
AND THAT'S HOW I LEARNED MY LESSON.

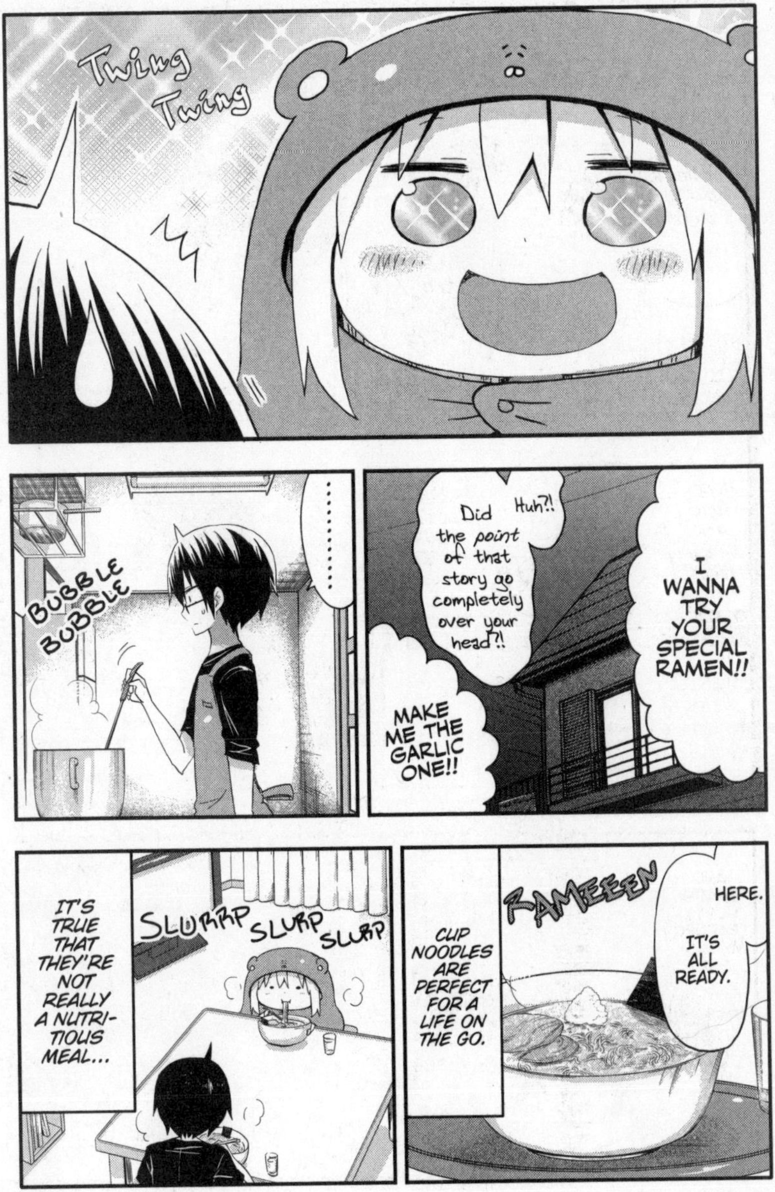
Twing Twing
I WANNA TRY YOUR SPECIAL RAMEN!!
Huh?!
Did the point of that story go completely over your head?!
MAKE ME THE GARLIC ONE!!
BUBBLE BUBBLE
……
HERE.
IT'S ALL READY.
RAMEEEN
CUP NOODLES ARE PERFECT FOR A LIFE ON THE GO.
SLURRP SLURP SLURP
IT'S TRUE THAT THEY'RE NOT REALLY A NUTRI-TIOUS MEAL…

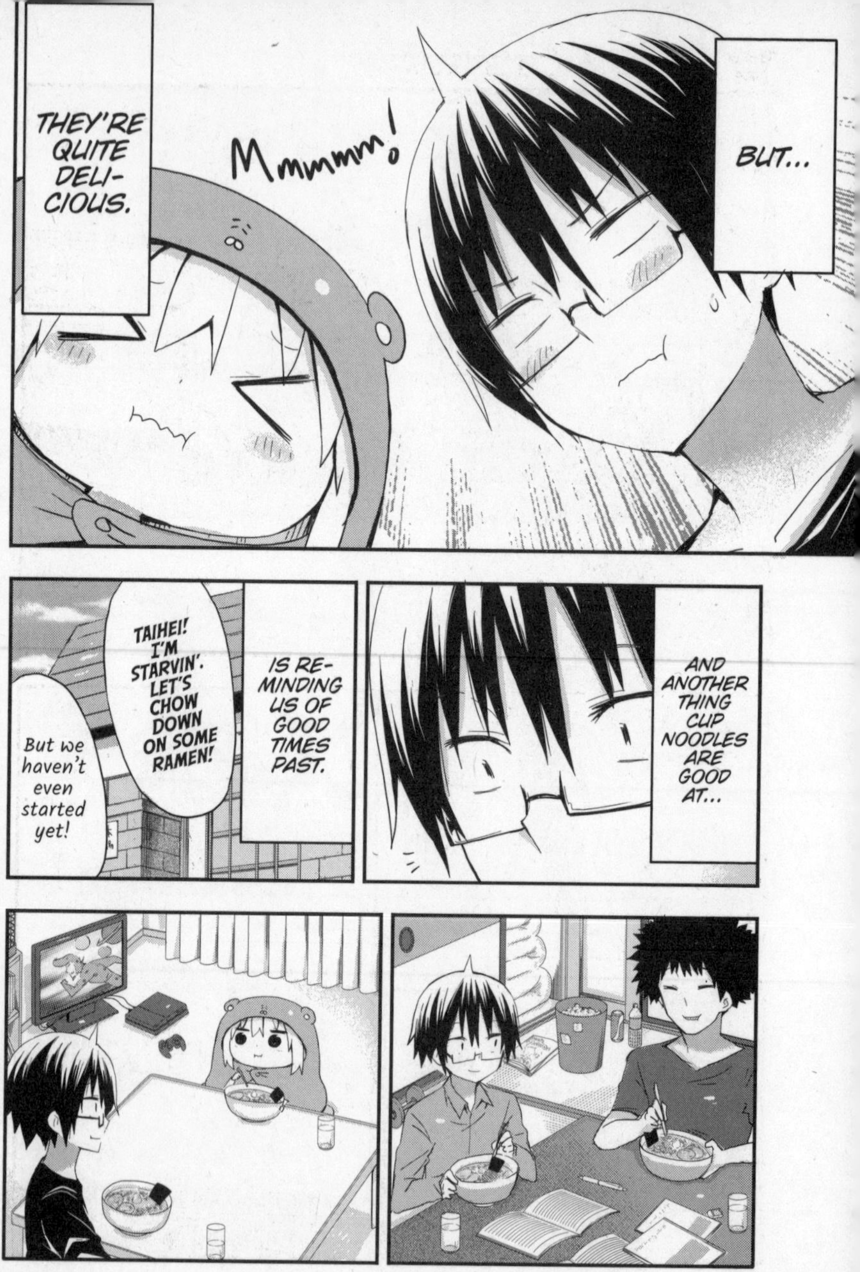
BUT...
Mmmmm!
THEY'RE QUITE DELI-CIOUS.
AND ANOTHER THING CUP NOODLES ARE GOOD AT...
IS RE-MINDING US OF GOOD TIMES PAST.
TAIHEI! I'M STARVIN'. LET'S CHOW DOWN ON SOME RAMEN!
But we haven't even started yet!

No. 58 Umaru & the Lottery

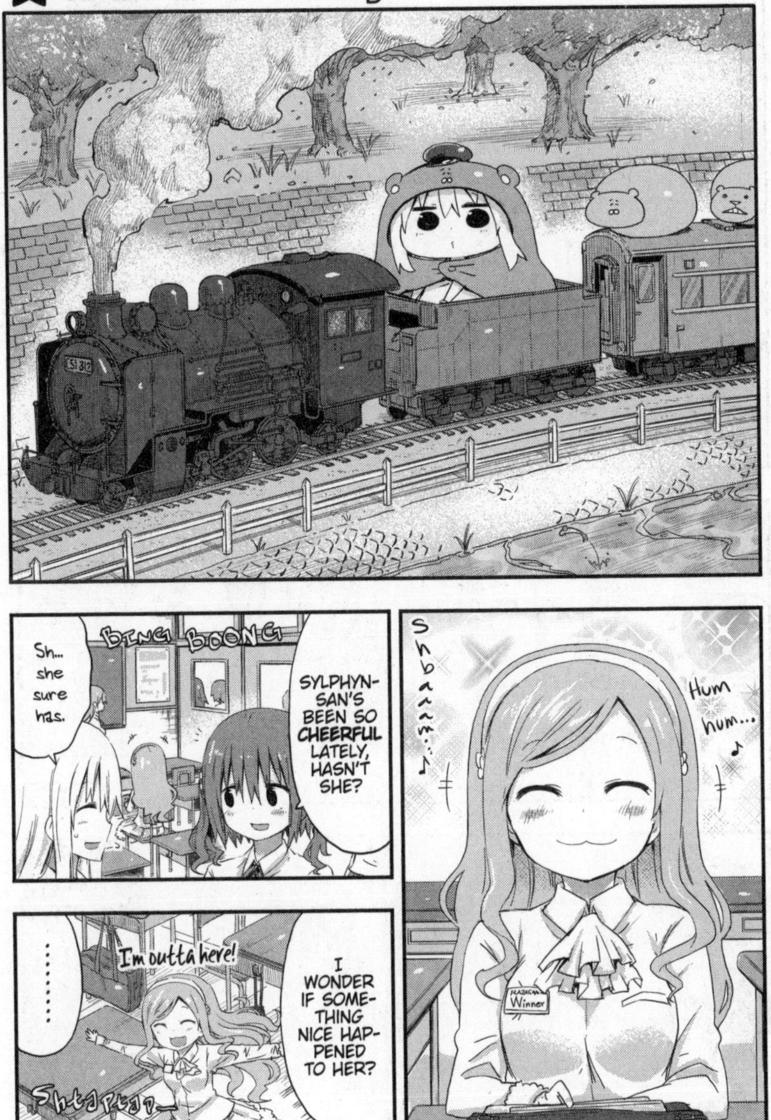

Shbaaam...♪
Hum hum...♪
Winner
SYLPHYN-SAN'S BEEN SO CHEERFUL LATELY, HASN'T SHE?
BING BOONG
Sh... she sure has.
I WONDER IF SOMETHING NICE HAPPENED TO HER?
......
I'm outta here!
Shtaptap—

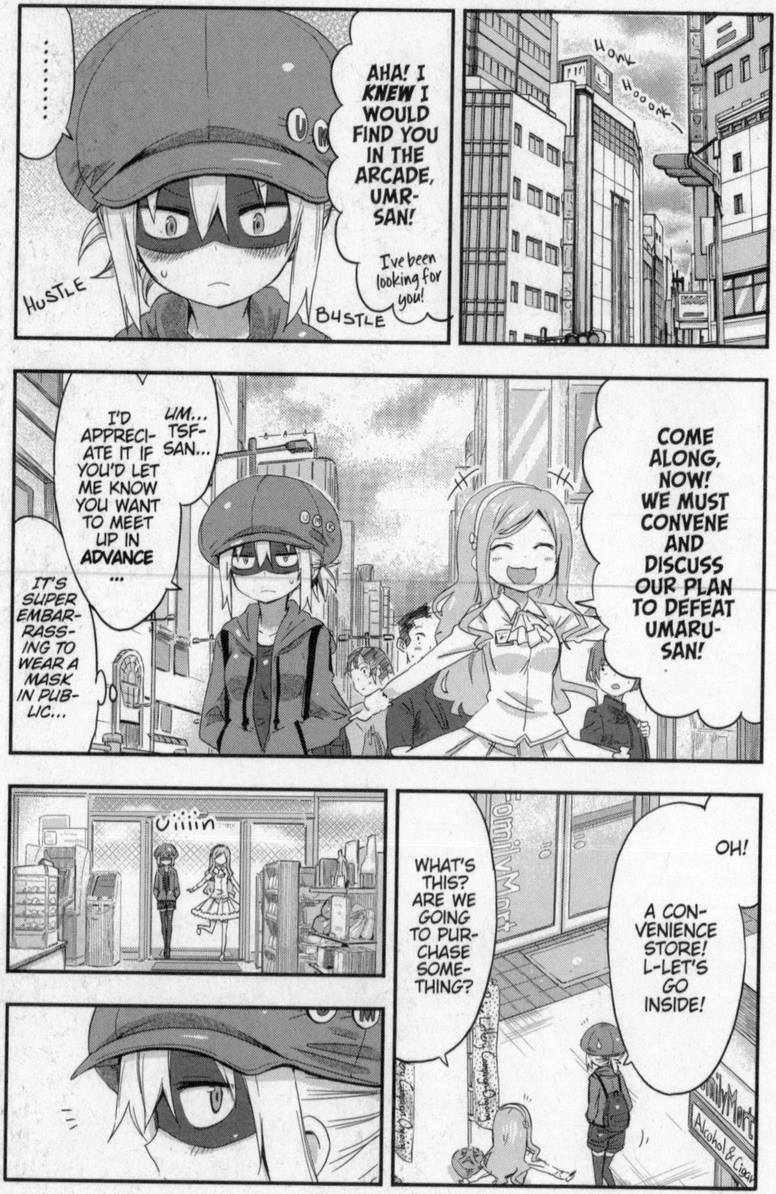
HONK
HOOOONK—
AHA! I **KNEW** I WOULD FIND YOU IN THE ARCADE, UMR-SAN!
I've been looking for you!
......
HUSTLE
BUSTLE
COME ALONG, NOW! WE MUST CONVENE AND DISCUSS OUR PLAN TO DEFEAT UMARU-SAN!
UM... TSF-SAN...
I'D APPRECIATE IT IF YOU'D LET ME KNOW YOU WANT TO MEET UP IN **ADVANCE**...
IT'S SUPER EMBARRASSING TO WEAR A MASK IN PUBLIC...
OH!
A CONVENIENCE STORE! L-LET'S GO INSIDE!
WHAT'S THIS? ARE WE GOING TO PURCHASE SOMETHING?
Uiiiin

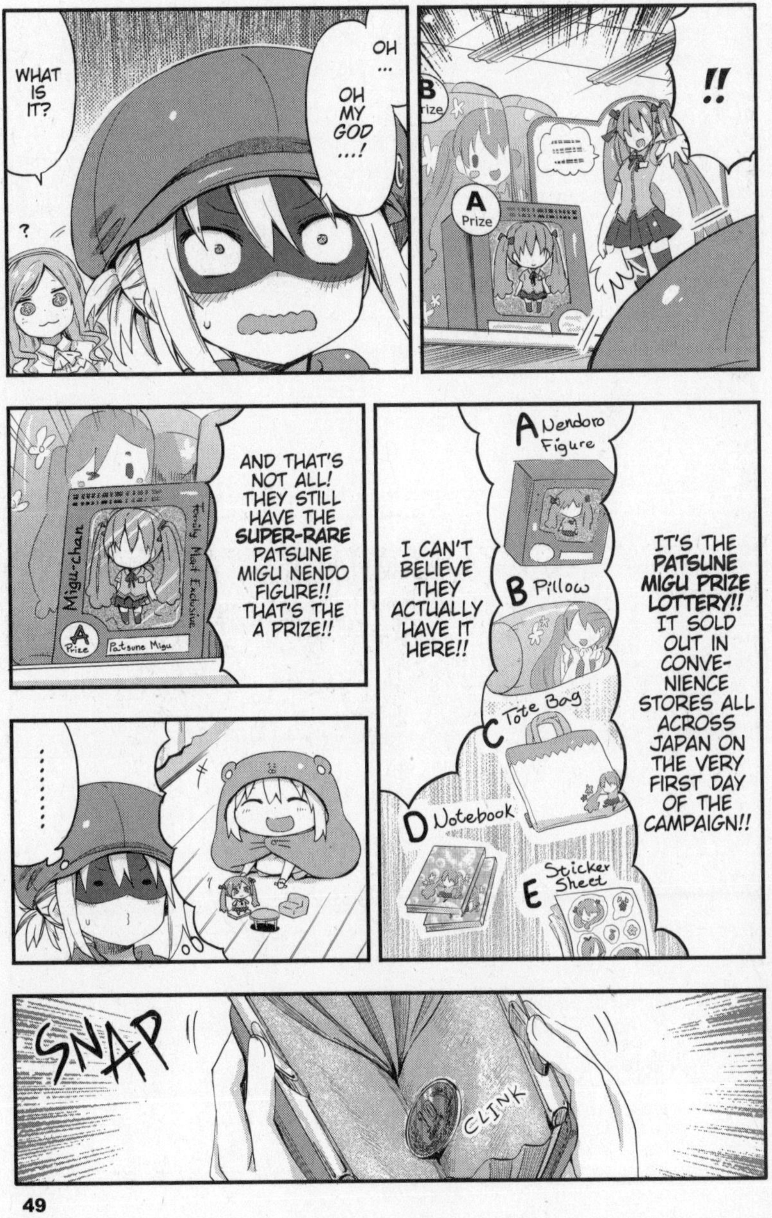

B
Prize
!!
A
Prize
OH ... OH MY GOD ...!
WHAT IS IT?
?
IT'S THE PATSUNE MIGU PRIZE LOTTERY!! IT SOLD OUT IN CONVE-NIENCE STORES ALL ACROSS JAPAN ON THE VERY FIRST DAY OF THE CAMPAIGN!!
A Nendoro Figure
B Pillow
C Tote Bag
D Notebook
E Sticker Sheet
I CAN'T BELIEVE THEY ACTUALLY HAVE IT HERE!!
AND THAT'S NOT ALL! THEY STILL HAVE THE SUPER-RARE PATSUNE MIGU NENDO FIGURE!! THAT'S THE A PRIZE!!
Family Mart Exclusive
Migu-chan
A
Prize
Patsune Migu
......
SNAP
CLINK

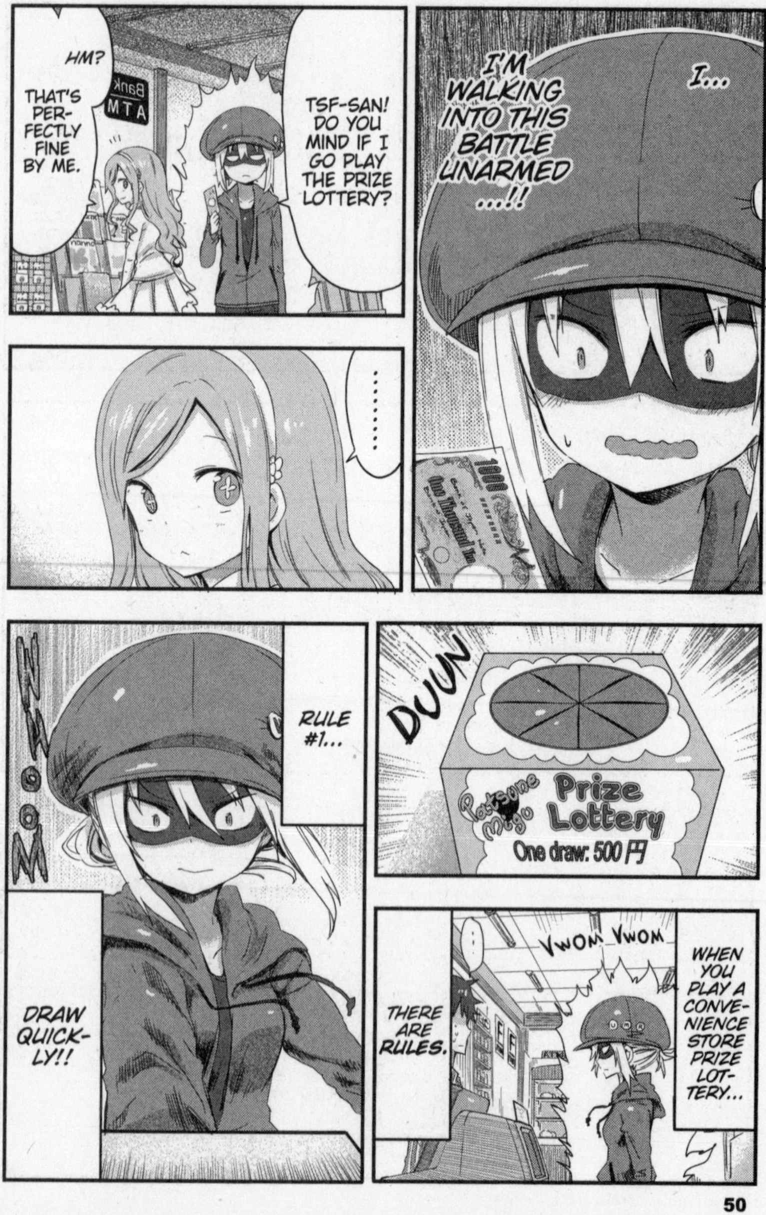
I...
I'M WALKING INTO THIS BATTLE UNARMED ...!!
TSF-SAN! DO YOU MIND IF I GO PLAY THE PRIZE LOTTERY?
HM?
THAT'S PERFECTLY FINE BY ME.
......
DUUN
Patsune Migo Prize Lottery
One draw: 500 円
VWOM VWOM
WHEN YOU PLAY A CONVENIENCE STORE PRIZE LOTTERY...
THERE ARE RULES.
...
ZOOM
RULE #1...
DRAW QUICKLY!!

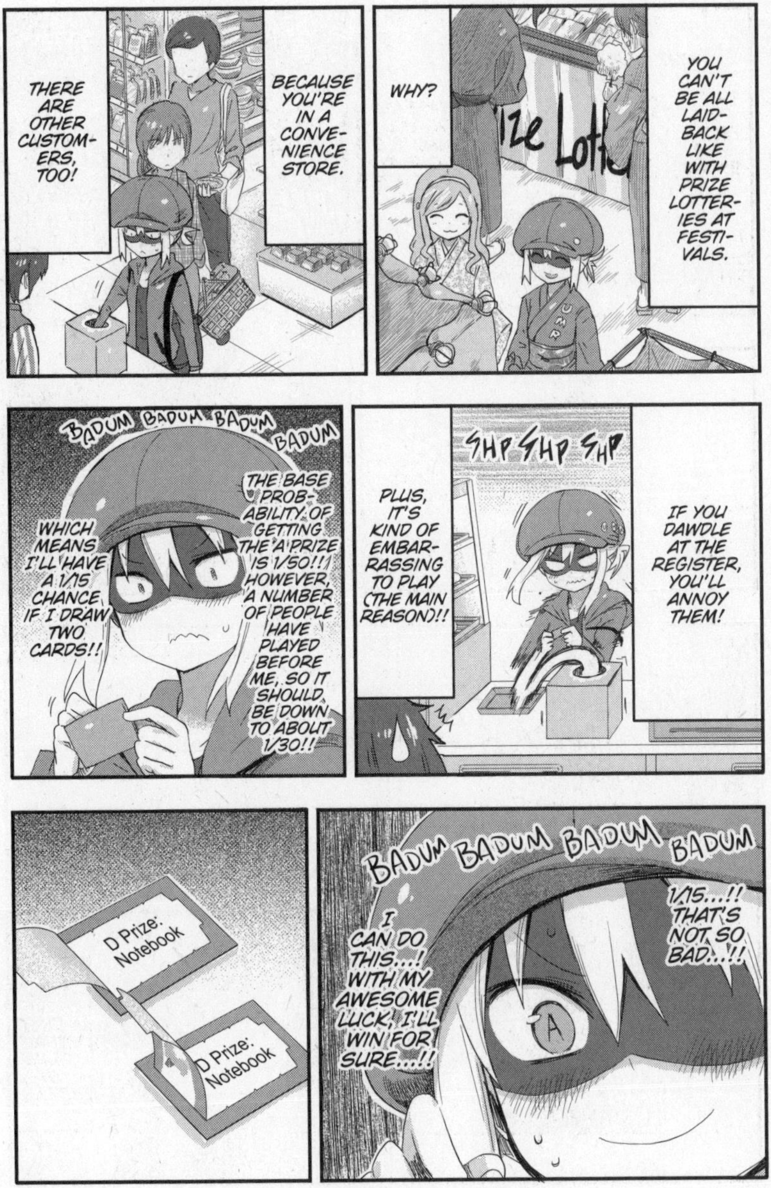
YOU CAN'T BE ALL LAID-BACK LIKE WITH PRIZE LOTTERIES AT FESTIVALS.
WHY?
BECAUSE YOU'RE IN A CONVENIENCE STORE.
THERE ARE OTHER CUSTOMERS, TOO!
SHP SHP SHP
IF YOU DAWDLE AT THE REGISTER, YOU'LL ANNOY THEM!
PLUS, IT'S KIND OF EMBARRASSING TO PLAY (THE MAIN REASON)!!
BADUM BADUM BADUM BADUM
THE BASE PROBABILITY OF GETTING THE A PRIZE IS 1/50!! HOWEVER, A NUMBER OF PEOPLE HAVE PLAYED BEFORE ME, SO IT SHOULD BE DOWN TO ABOUT 1/30!!
WHICH MEANS I'LL HAVE A 1/15 CHANCE IF I DRAW TWO CARDS!!
BADUM BADUM BADUM BADUM
1/15...!! THAT'S NOT SO BAD...!!
I CAN DO THIS...! WITH MY AWESOME LUCK, I'LL WIN FOR SURE...!!
D Prize: Notebook
D Prize: Notebook

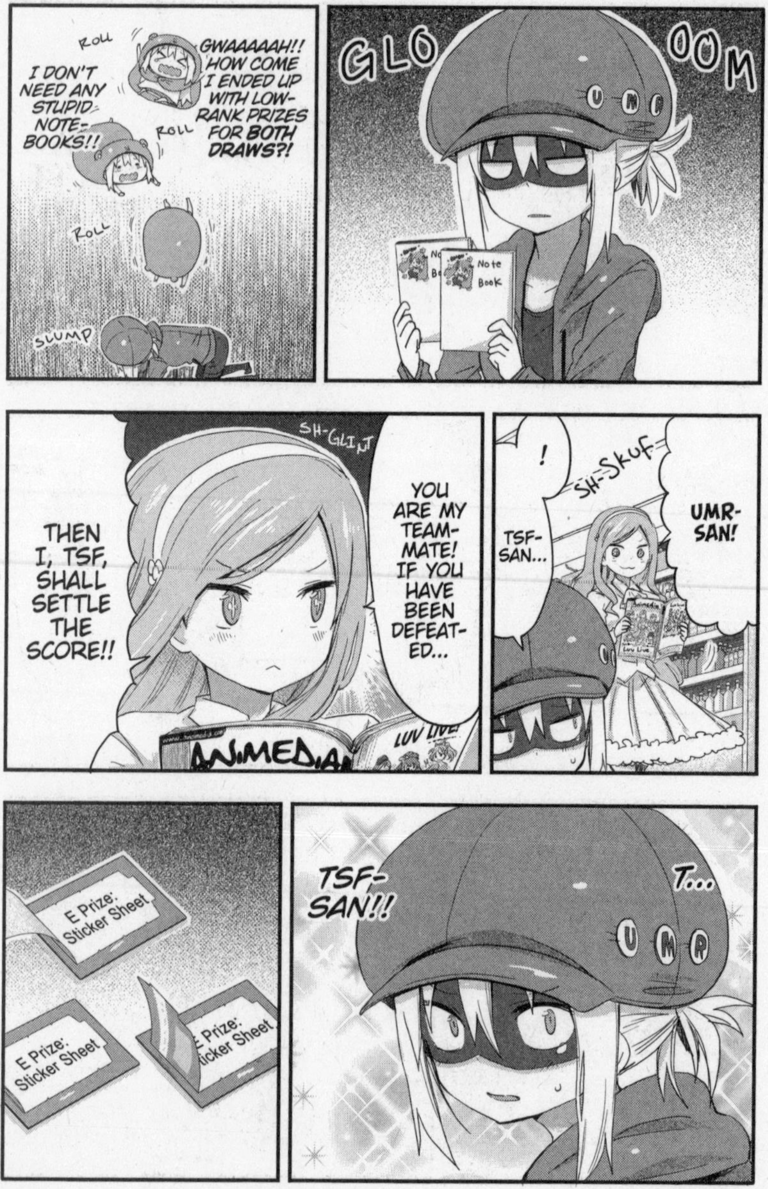
GLO OOM
Note Book
Note Book
GWAAAAAH!! HOW COME I ENDED UP WITH LOW-RANK PRIZES FOR BOTH DRAWS?!
ROLL
I DON'T NEED ANY STUPID NOTE-BOOKS!!
ROLL
ROLL
SLUMP
UMR-SAN!
SH-SKUF
!
TSF-SAN...
SH-GLINT
YOU ARE MY TEAM-MATE! IF YOU HAVE BEEN DEFEAT-ED...
THEN I, TSF, SHALL SETTLE THE SCORE!!
LUV LIVE!
ANIMEDIA
T...
TSF-SAN!!
E Prize: Sticker Sheet
E Prize: Sticker Sheet
E Prize: Sticker Sheet

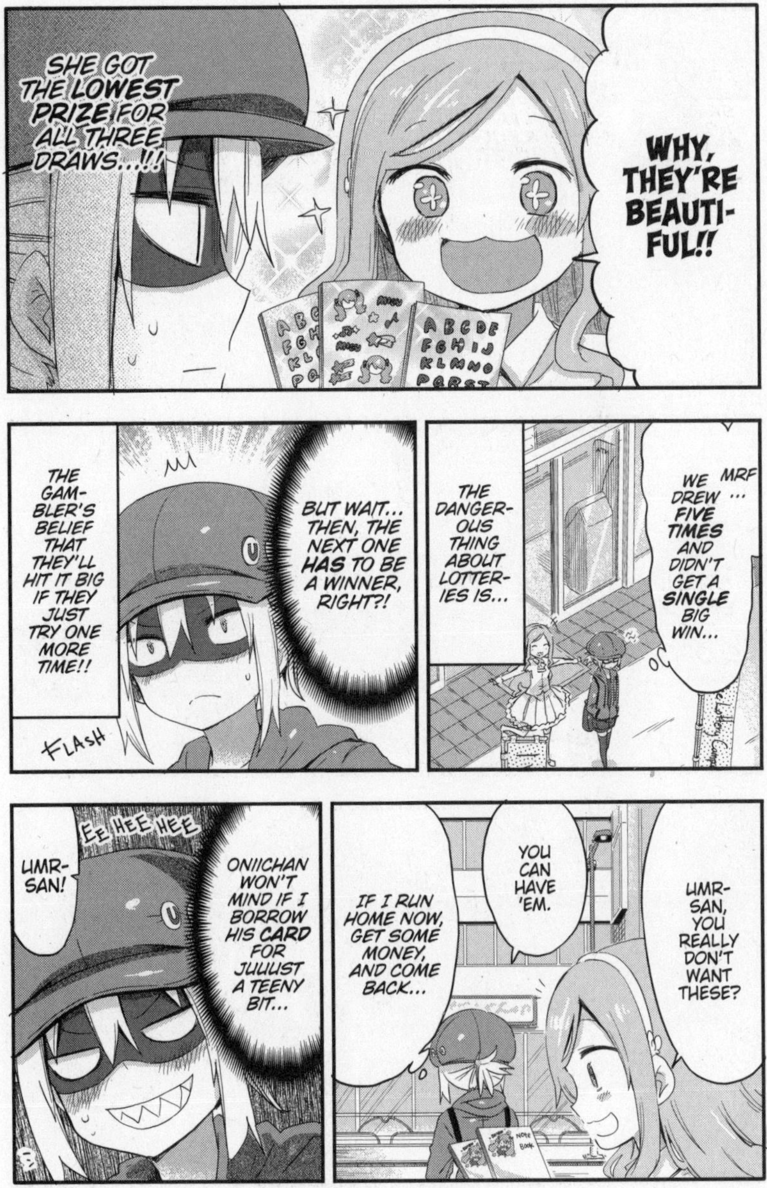
WHY, THEY'RE BEAUTIFUL!!
SHE GOT THE LOWEST PRIZE FOR ALL THREE DRAWS...!!
MRF...
WE DREW FIVE TIMES AND DIDN'T GET A SINGLE BIG WIN...
THE DANGEROUS THING ABOUT LOTTERIES IS...
BUT WAIT... THEN, THE NEXT ONE HAS TO BE A WINNER, RIGHT?!
THE GAMBLER'S BELIEF THAT THEY'LL HIT IT BIG IF THEY JUST TRY ONE MORE TIME!!
FLASH
UMR-SAN, YOU REALLY DON'T WANT THESE?
YOU CAN HAVE 'EM.
IF I RUN HOME NOW, GET SOME MONEY, AND COME BACK...
Note Book
UMR-SAN!
EE HEE HEE
ONIICHAN WON'T MIND IF I BORROW HIS CARD FOR JUUUST A TEENY BIT...

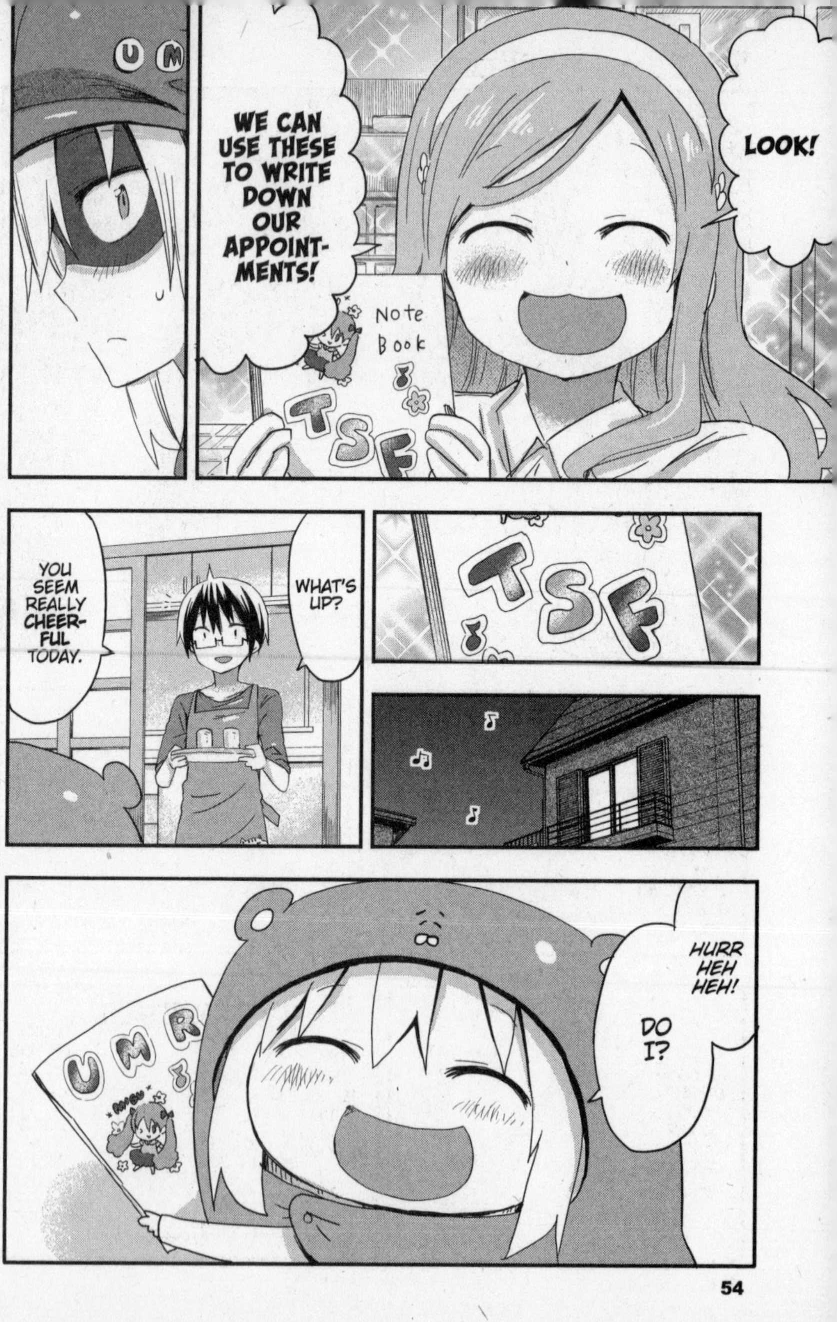
LOOK!
WE CAN USE THESE TO WRITE DOWN OUR APPOINTMENTS!
Note Book
TSF
UM
TSF
WHAT'S UP?
YOU SEEM REALLY CHEERFUL TODAY.
HURR HEH HEH!
DO I?
UMR

No. 59 Umaru & Pillows

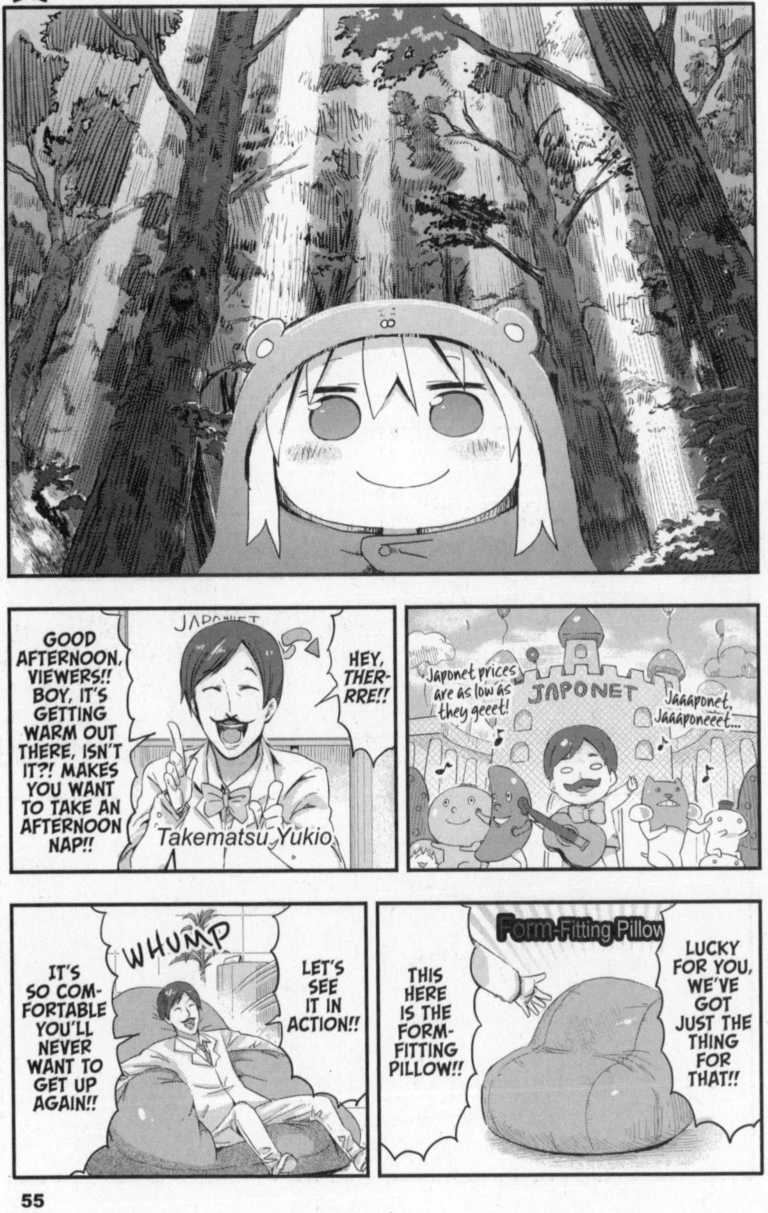

JAPONET
Jaaaponet, Jaaaponeeet...
Japonet prices are as low as they geeet!
HEY, THERRE!!
GOOD AFTERNOON, VIEWERS!! BOY, IT'S GETTING WARM OUT THERE, ISN'T IT?! MAKES YOU WANT TO TAKE AN AFTERNOON NAP!!
Takematsu Yukio
Form-Fitting Pillow
LUCKY FOR YOU, WE'VE GOT JUST THE THING FOR THAT!!
THIS HERE IS THE FORM-FITTING PILLOW!!
LET'S SEE IT IN ACTION!!
WHUMP
IT'S SO COMFORTABLE YOU'LL NEVER WANT TO GET UP AGAIN!!

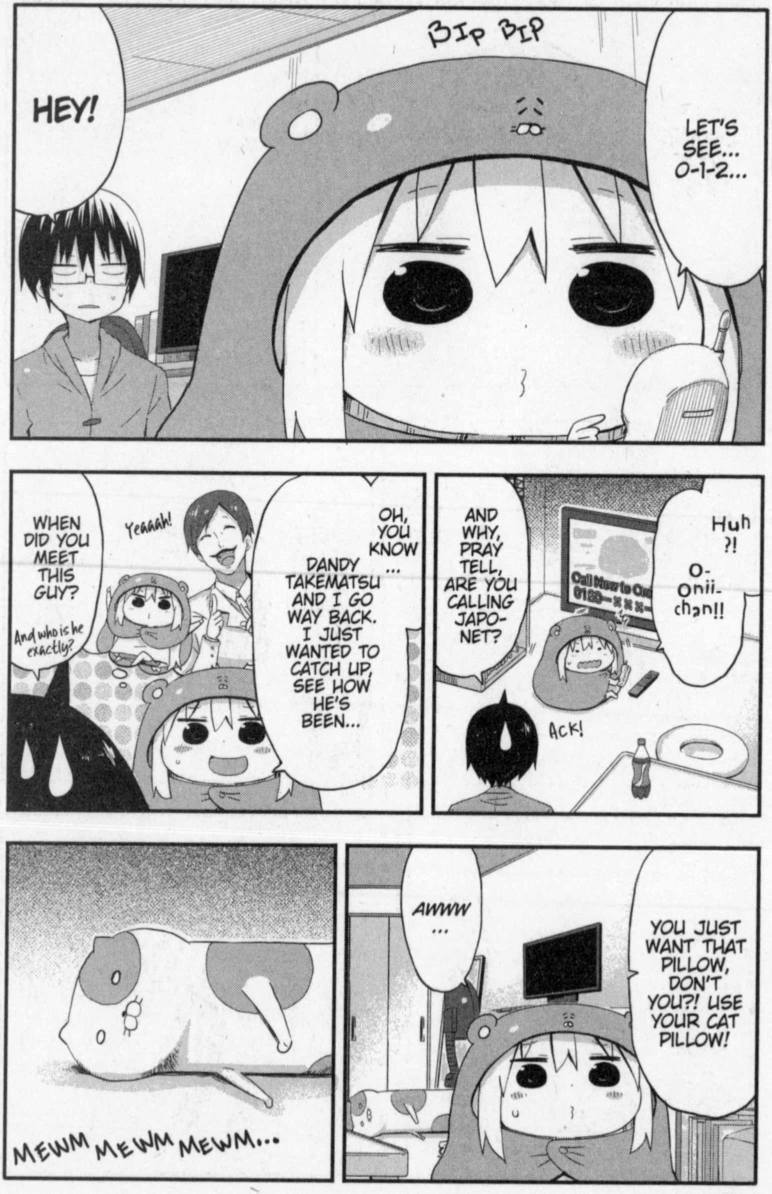
LET'S SEE... 0-1-2...
BIP BIP
HEY!
Huh?! O-Onii-chan!!
AND WHY, PRAY TELL, ARE YOU CALLING JAPONET?
ACK!
OH, YOU KNOW ... DANDY TAKEMATSU AND I GO WAY BACK. I JUST WANTED TO CATCH UP, SEE HOW HE'S BEEN...
Yeaaah!
WHEN DID YOU MEET THIS GUY?
And who is he exactly?
YOU JUST WANT THAT PILLOW, DON'T YOU?! USE YOUR CAT PILLOW!
AWWW ...
MEWM MEWM MEWM...

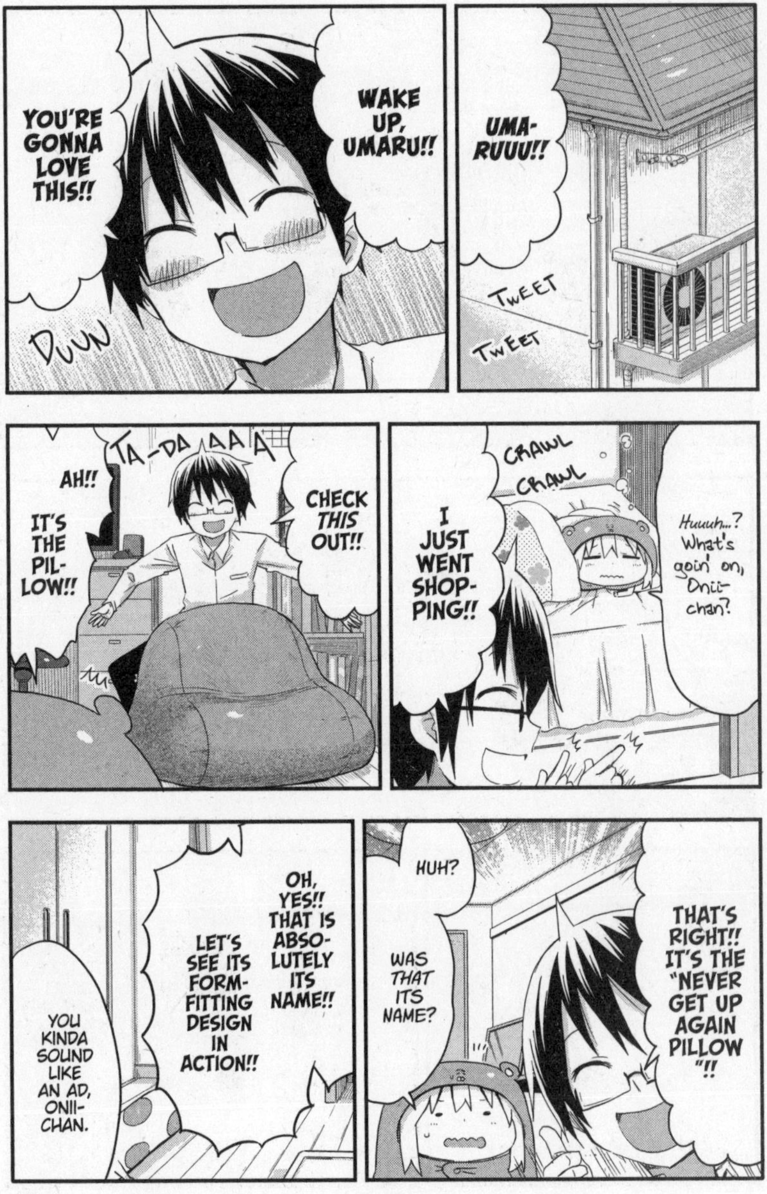
UMA-RUUU!!
TWEET
TWEET
WAKE UP, UMARU!!
YOU'RE GONNA LOVE THIS!!
DUUN
Huuuh...? What's goin' on, Onii-chan?
CRAWL
CRAWL
I JUST WENT SHOP-PING!!
CHECK THIS OUT!!
TA-DAAAAA
AH!! IT'S THE PIL-LOW!!
THAT'S RIGHT!! IT'S THE "NEVER GET UP AGAIN PILLOW"!!
HUH?
WAS THAT ITS NAME?
OH, YES!! THAT IS ABSO-LUTELY ITS NAME!!
LET'S SEE ITS FORM-FITTING DESIGN IN ACTION!!
YOU KINDA SOUND LIKE AN AD, ONII-CHAN.

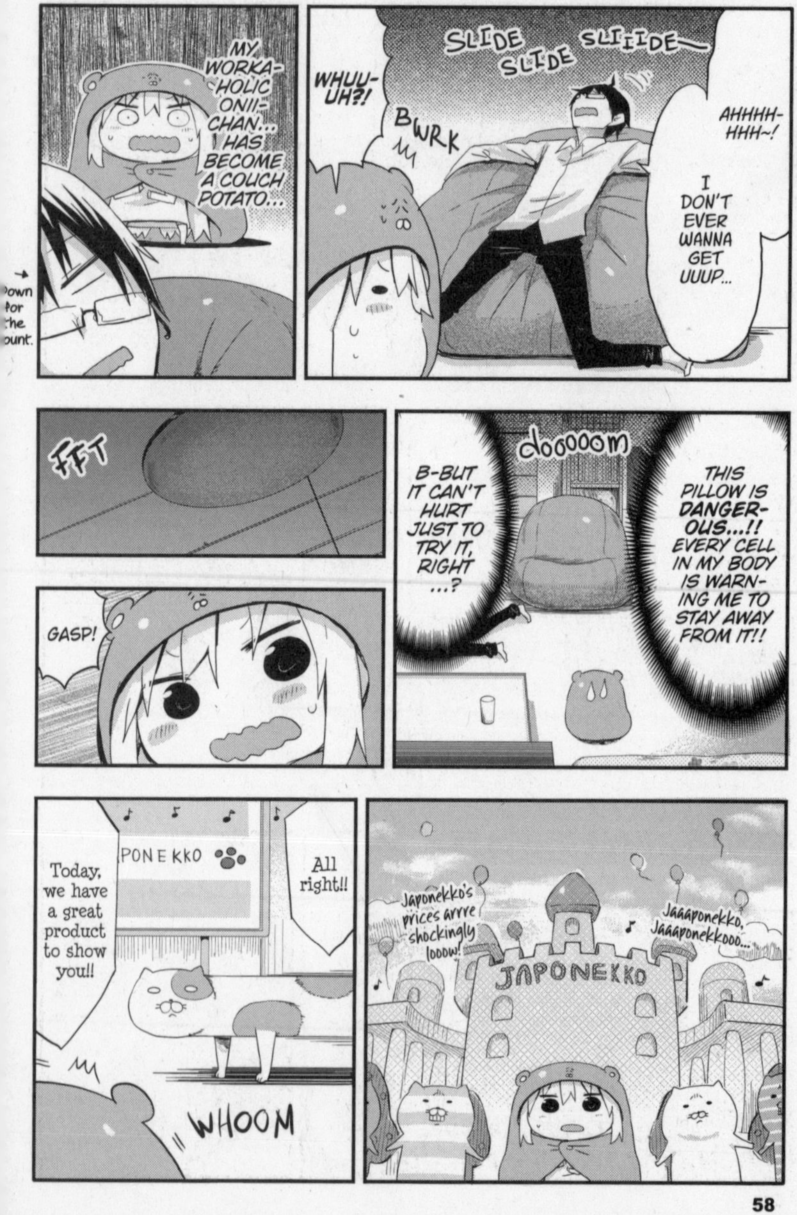
AHHHH-HHH~!
I DON'T EVER WANNA GET UUUP...
SLIDE SLIDE SLIIIDE—
WHUUU-UH?!
BWRK
MY WORKA-HOLIC ONII-CHAN... HAS BECOME A COUCH POTATO...
Down for the count.
doooom
THIS PILLOW IS DANGER-OUS...!! EVERY CELL IN MY BODY IS WARN-ING ME TO STAY AWAY FROM IT!!
B-BUT IT CAN'T HURT JUST TO TRY IT, RIGHT ...?
FFT
GASP!
Jaaaponekko, Jaaaponekkooo...
Japonekko's prices arrre shockingly looow!
JAPONEKKO
All right!!
Today, we have a great product to show you!!
PONEKKO
WHOOM

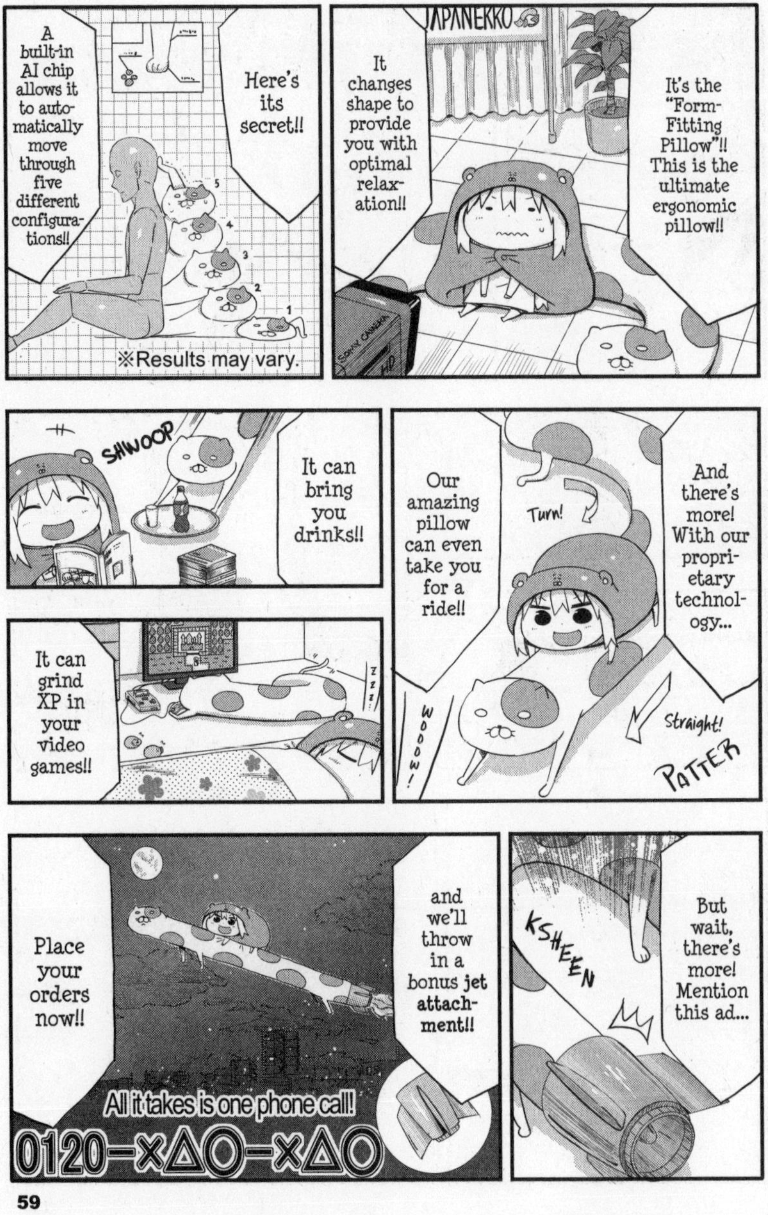
JAPANEKKO
It's the "Form-Fitting Pillow"!! This is the ultimate ergonomic pillow!!
It changes shape to provide you with optimal relaxation!!
SONY CAMERA HD
Here's its secret!!
A built-in AI chip allows it to automatically move through five different configurations!!
5
4
3
2
1
※Results may vary.
And there's more! With our proprietary technology...
Our amazing pillow can even take you for a ride!!
Turn!
Straight!
PATTER
WOOOOW!
It can bring you drinks!!
SHWOOP
It can grind XP in your video games!!
ZZZ...
But wait, there's more! Mention this ad...
KSHEEN
and we'll throw in a bonus **jet attachment!!**
Place your orders now!!
All it takes is one phone call!
0120-×△○-×△○

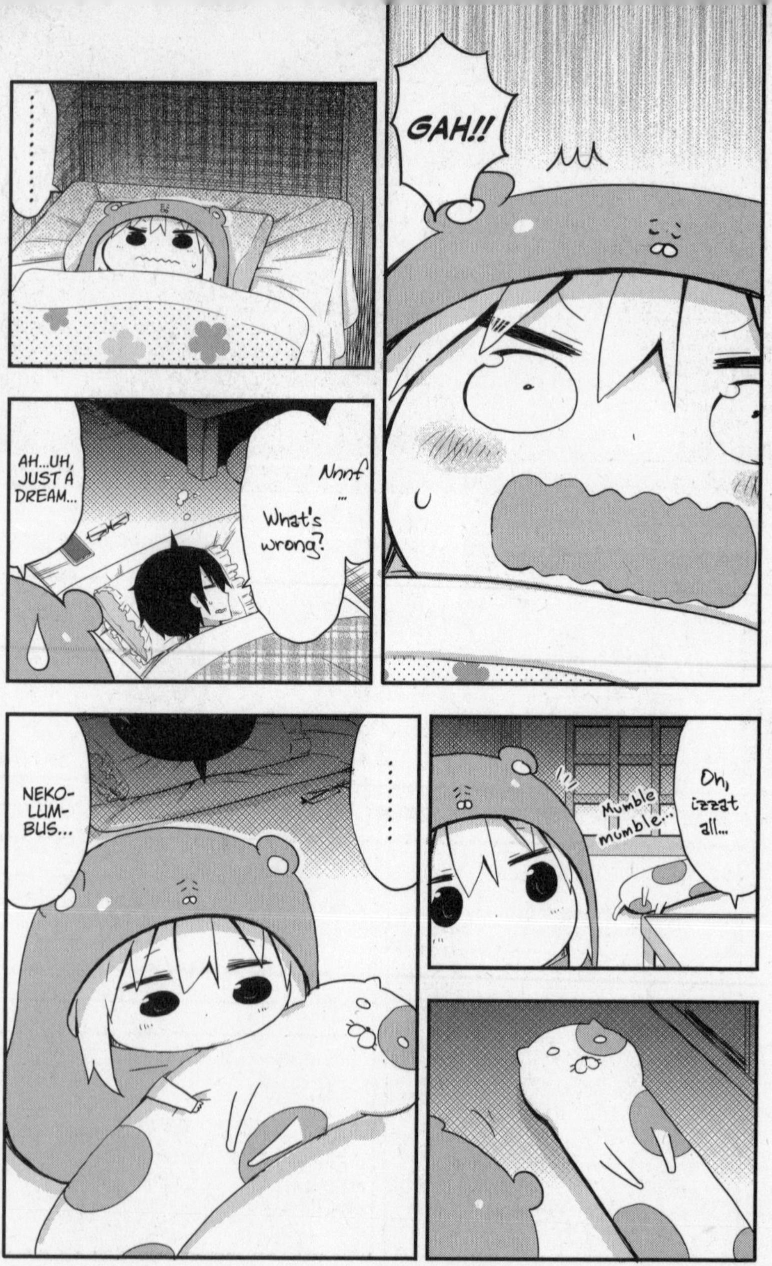
GAH!!
......
Nnnf ... What's wrong?
AH...UH, JUST A DREAM...
Oh, izzat all...
Mumble mumble...
......
NEKO-LUMBUS...

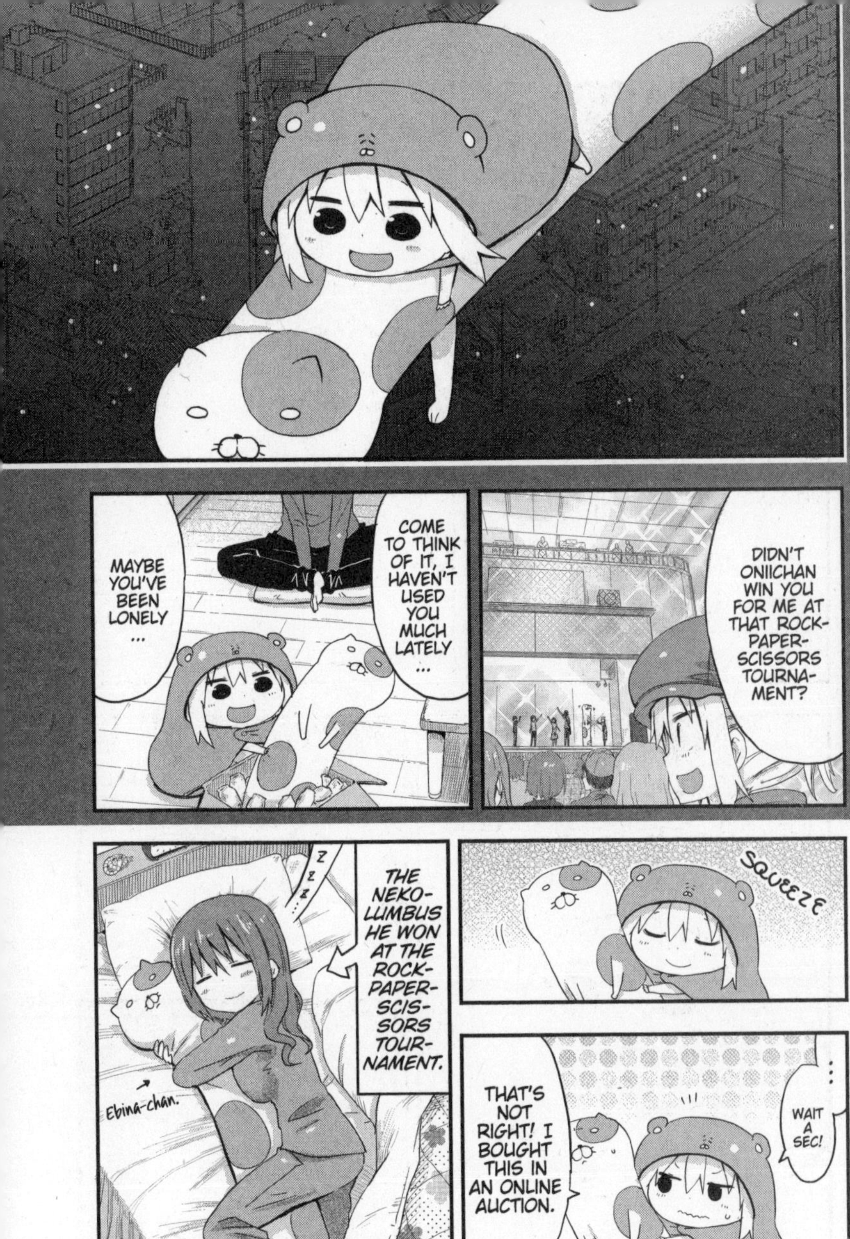
DIDN'T ONIICHAN WIN YOU FOR ME AT THAT ROCK-PAPER-SCISSORS TOURNAMENT?
COME TO THINK OF IT, I HAVEN'T USED YOU MUCH LATELY ...
MAYBE YOU'VE BEEN LONELY ...
SQUEEZE
...
WAIT A SEC!
THAT'S NOT RIGHT! I BOUGHT THIS IN AN ONLINE AUCTION.
ZZZ...
THE NEKO-LUMBUS HE WON AT THE ROCK-PAPER-SCISSORS TOURNAMENT.
Ebina-chan.

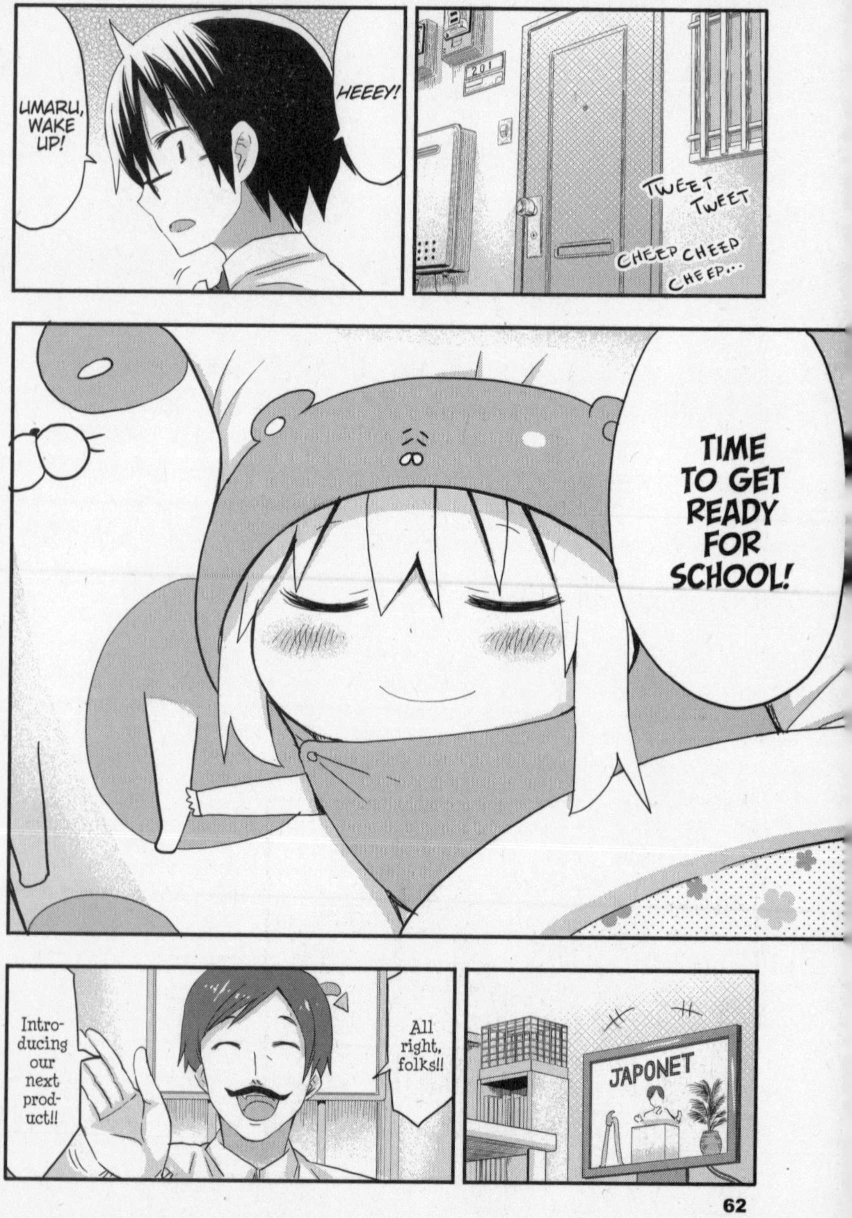
TWEET TWEET
CHEEP CHEEP CHEEP...
HEEEY!
UMARU, WAKE UP!
TIME TO GET READY FOR SCHOOL!
JAPONET
All right, folks!!
Intro-ducing our next prod-uct!!

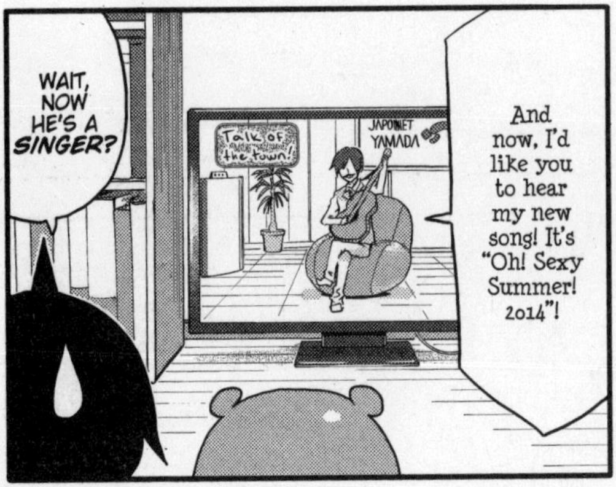
And now, I'd like you to hear my new song! It's "Oh! Sexy Summer! 2014"!
Talk of the town!
WAIT, NOW HE'S A SINGER?

HIMOUTO! UMARU-CHAN

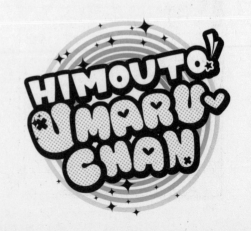

No. 60 Umaru & the Meeting

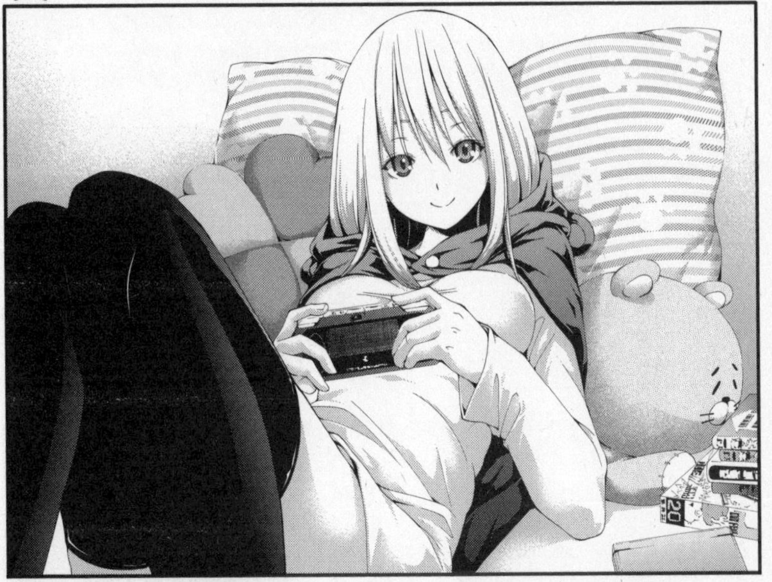

Guest Illustrator: Nao Akinari

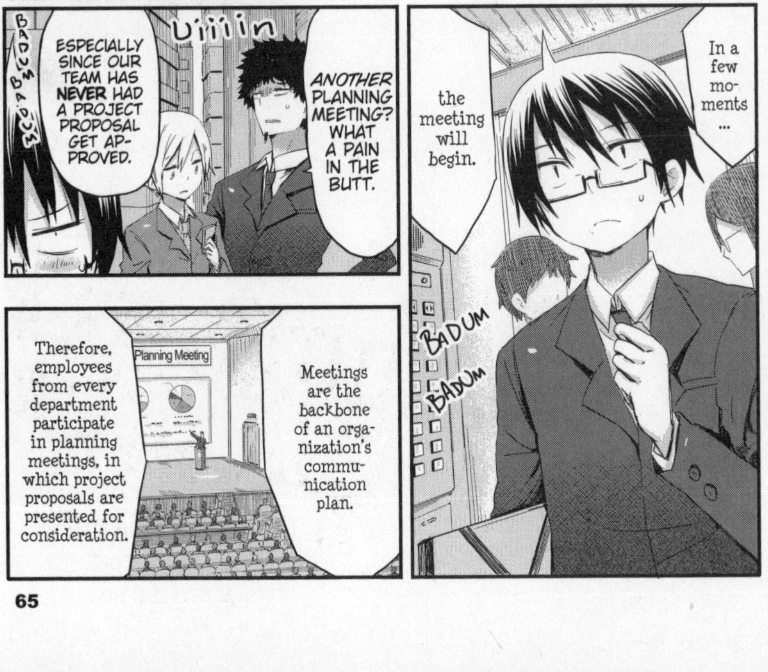

In a few moments...
the meeting will begin.
BADUM
BADUM
ANOTHER PLANNING MEETING? WHAT A PAIN IN THE BUTT.
Uiiin
ESPECIALLY SINCE OUR TEAM HAS NEVER HAD A PROJECT PROPOSAL GET APPROVED.
BADUM BADUM BADUM
Meetings are the backbone of an organization's communication plan.
Planning Meeting
Therefore, employees from every department participate in planning meetings, in which project proposals are presented for consideration.

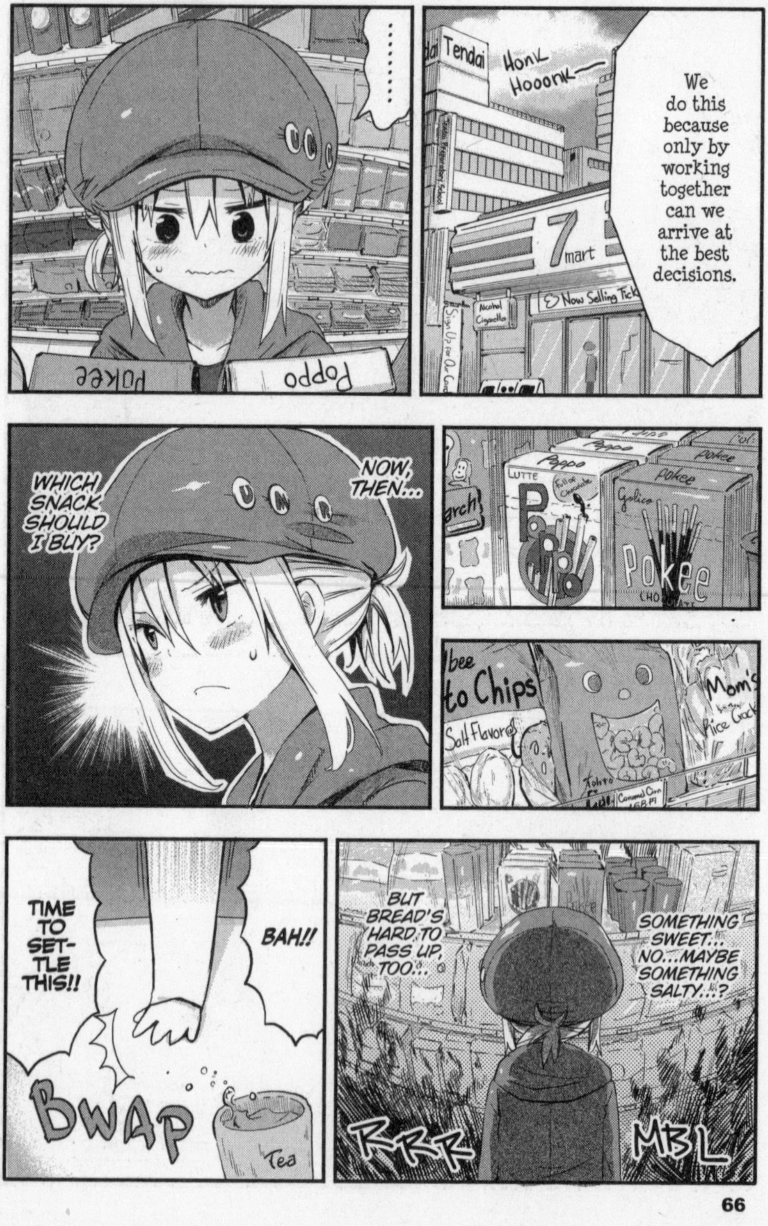
We do this because only by working together can we arrive at the best decisions.
HONK Hooonk—
Tendai
7 mart
Now Selling Tick
Alcohol Cigarettes
Sign Up for Our Card
……
Pokee
Poppo
Poppo
Pokee
LUTTE
Full of Chocolate
Glico
Pokee
to Chips
Salt Flavor
Mom's
Rice Crack
NOW, THEN...
WHICH SNACK SHOULD I BUY?
SOMETHING SWEET... NO...MAYBE SOMETHING SALTY...?
BUT BREAD'S HARD TO PASS UP, TOO...
RRR
MBL
BAH!!
TIME TO SET-TLE THIS!!
BWAP
Tea

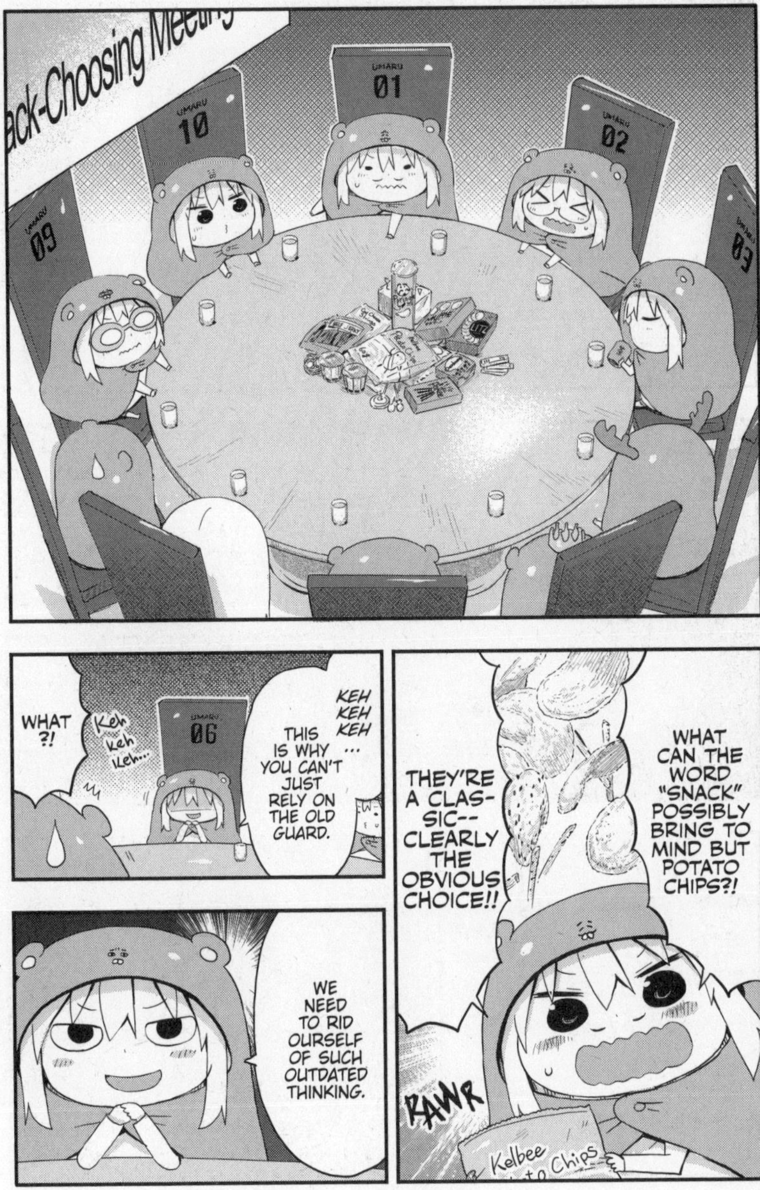
ack-Choosing Meetin
UMARU 01
UMARU 02
UMARU 10
UMARU 03
UMARU 09
WHAT CAN THE WORD "SNACK" POSSIBLY BRING TO MIND BUT POTATO CHIPS?!
THEY'RE A CLAS-SIC--CLEARLY THE OBVIOUS CHOICE!!
RAWR
Kelbee
to Chips
KEH KEH KEH ...
THIS IS WHY YOU CAN'T JUST RELY ON THE OLD GUARD.
UMARU 06
Keh keh keh...
WHAT ?!
WE NEED TO RID OURSELF OF SUCH OUTDATED THINKING.

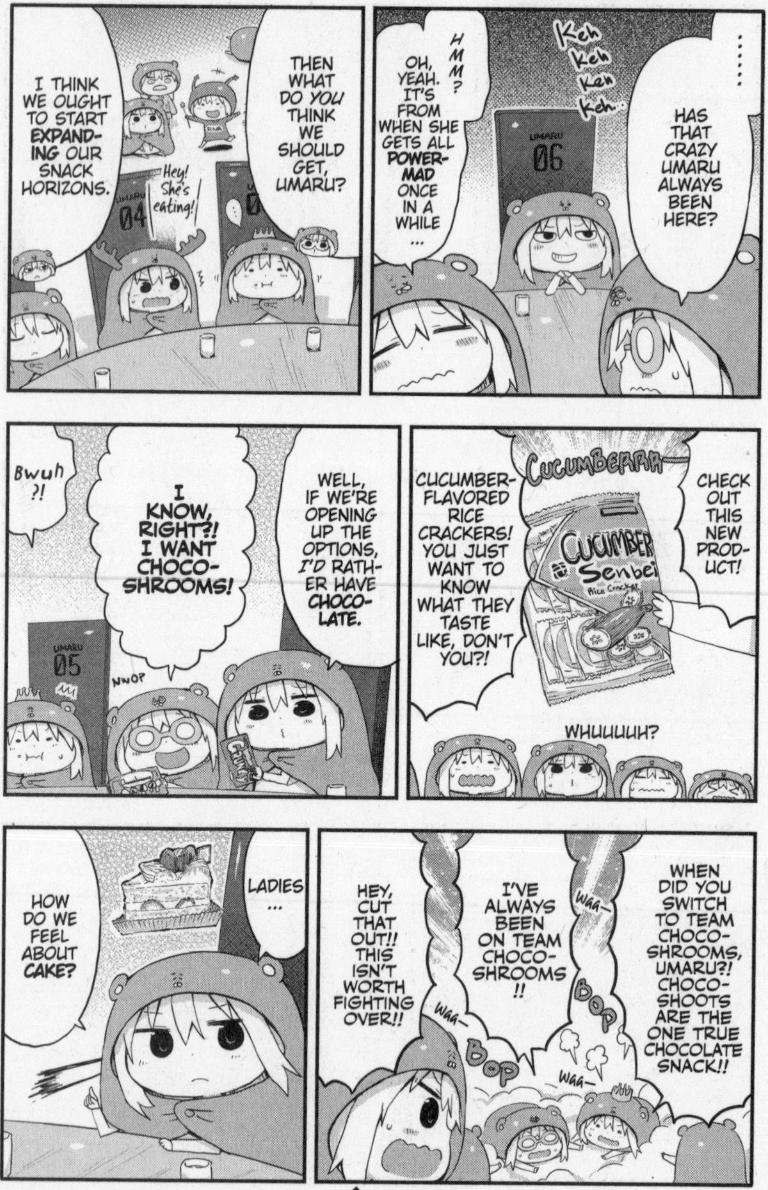
......
HAS THAT CRAZY UMARU ALWAYS BEEN HERE?
Keh Keh Keh Keh...
UMARU 06
HMMM? OH, YEAH. IT'S FROM WHEN SHE GETS ALL POWER-MAD ONCE IN A WHILE ...
THEN WHAT DO YOU THINK WE SHOULD GET, UMARU?
Hey! She's eating!
UMARU 04
I THINK WE OUGHT TO START EXPANDING OUR SNACK HORIZONS.
CUCUMBERRR—
CHECK OUT THIS NEW PRODUCT!
CUCUMBER Senbei Rice Cracker
CUCUMBER-FLAVORED RICE CRACKERS! YOU JUST WANT TO KNOW WHAT THEY TASTE LIKE, DON'T YOU?!
WHUUUUH?
WELL, IF WE'RE OPENING UP THE OPTIONS, I'D RATHER HAVE CHOCOLATE.
I KNOW, RIGHT?! I WANT CHOCO-SHROOMS!
Bwuh?!
UMARU 05
NWOP
WHEN DID YOU SWITCH TO TEAM CHOCO-SHROOMS, UMARU?! CHOCO-SHOOTS ARE THE ONE TRUE CHOCOLATE SNACK!!
Waa—
BOP
I'VE ALWAYS BEEN ON TEAM CHOCO-SHROOMS!!
HEY, CUT THAT OUT!! THIS ISN'T WORTH FIGHTING OVER!!
Waa—
Bop
Waa—
LADIES ...
HOW DO WE FEEL ABOUT CAKE?

↑ Team Chocopines.

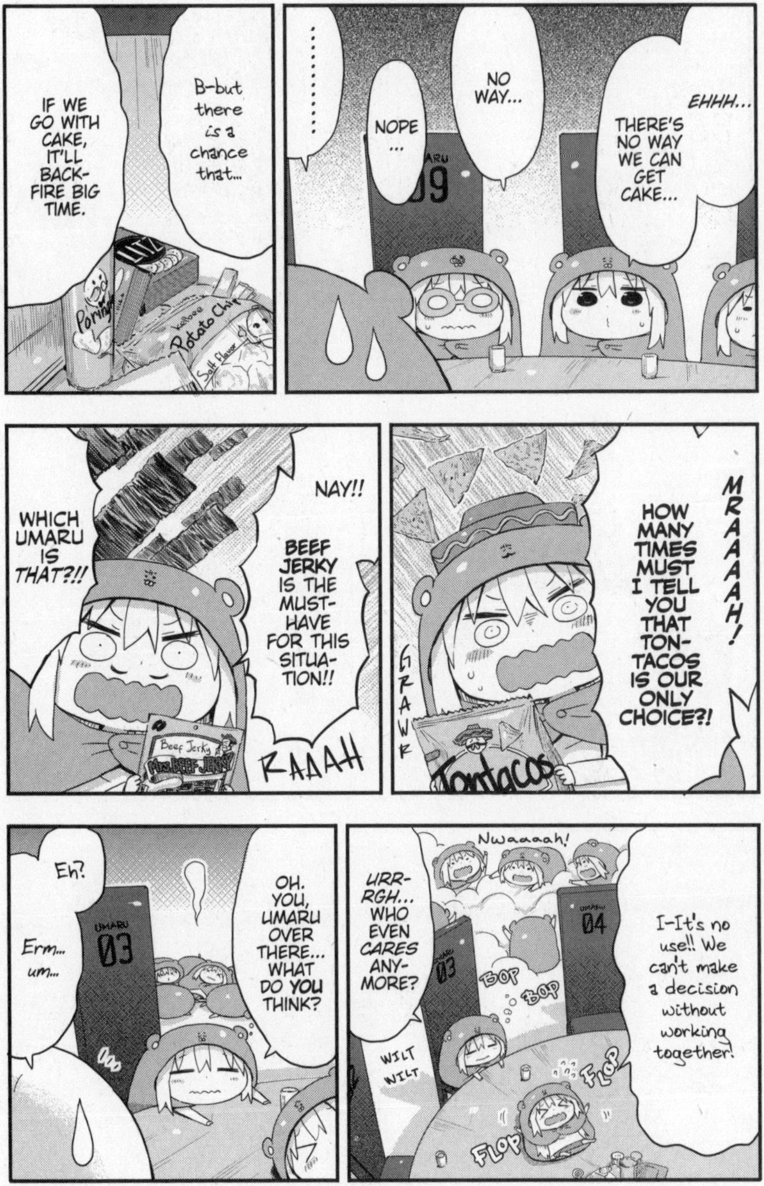
EHHH...
THERE'S NO WAY WE CAN GET CAKE...
NO WAY...
NOPE ...
......
B-but there is a chance that...
IF WE GO WITH CAKE, IT'LL BACK-FIRE BIG TIME.
MRAAAAAH!
HOW MANY TIMES MUST I TELL YOU THAT TON-TACOS IS OUR ONLY CHOICE?!
GRAWR
Tontacos
NAY!!
BEEF JERKY IS THE MUST-HAVE FOR THIS SITUA-TION!!
WHICH UMARU IS THAT?!!
RAAAH
Beef Jerky
I-It's no use!! We can't make a decision without working together!
Nwaaaah!
URRRGH... WHO EVEN CARES ANY-MORE?
BOP
BOP
WILT WILT
FLOP
FLOP
OH. YOU, UMARU OVER THERE... WHAT DO YOU THINK?
Eh?
Erm... um...

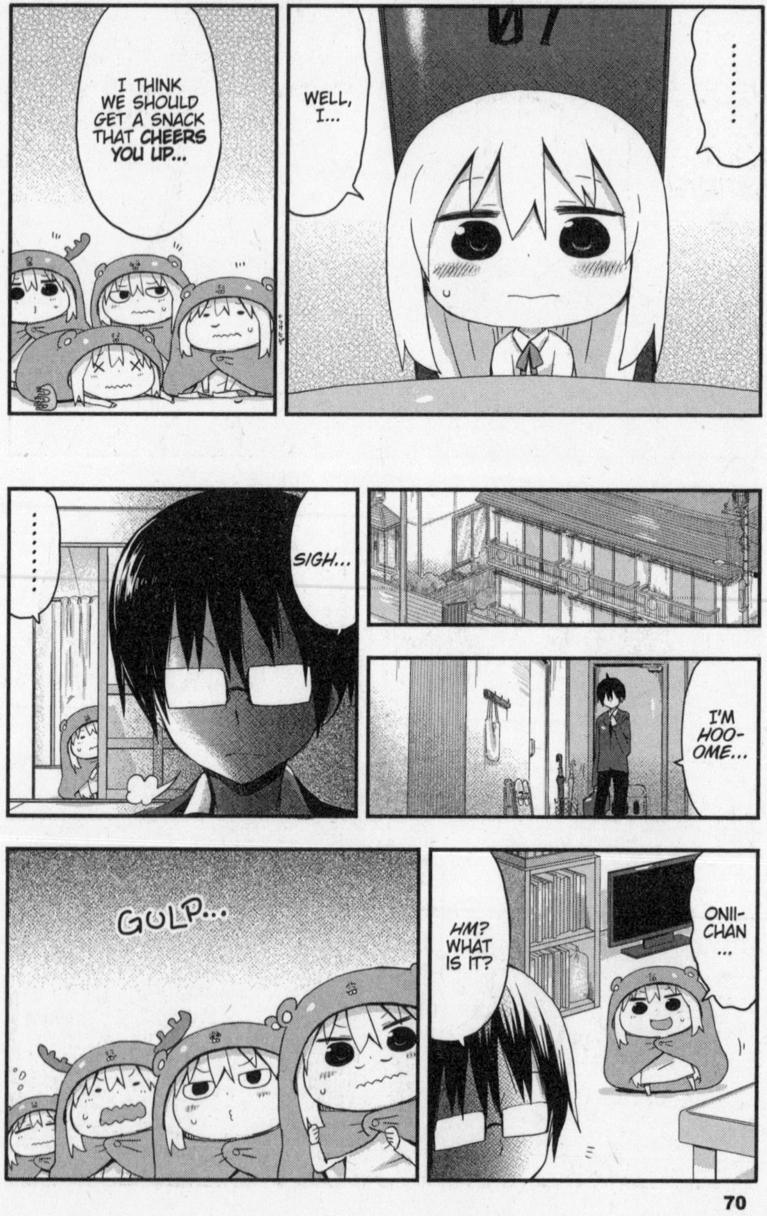
......
WELL, I...
I THINK WE SHOULD GET A SNACK THAT CHEERS YOU UP...
I'M HOO-OME...
SIGH...
......
ONII-CHAN ...
HM? WHAT IS IT?
GULP...

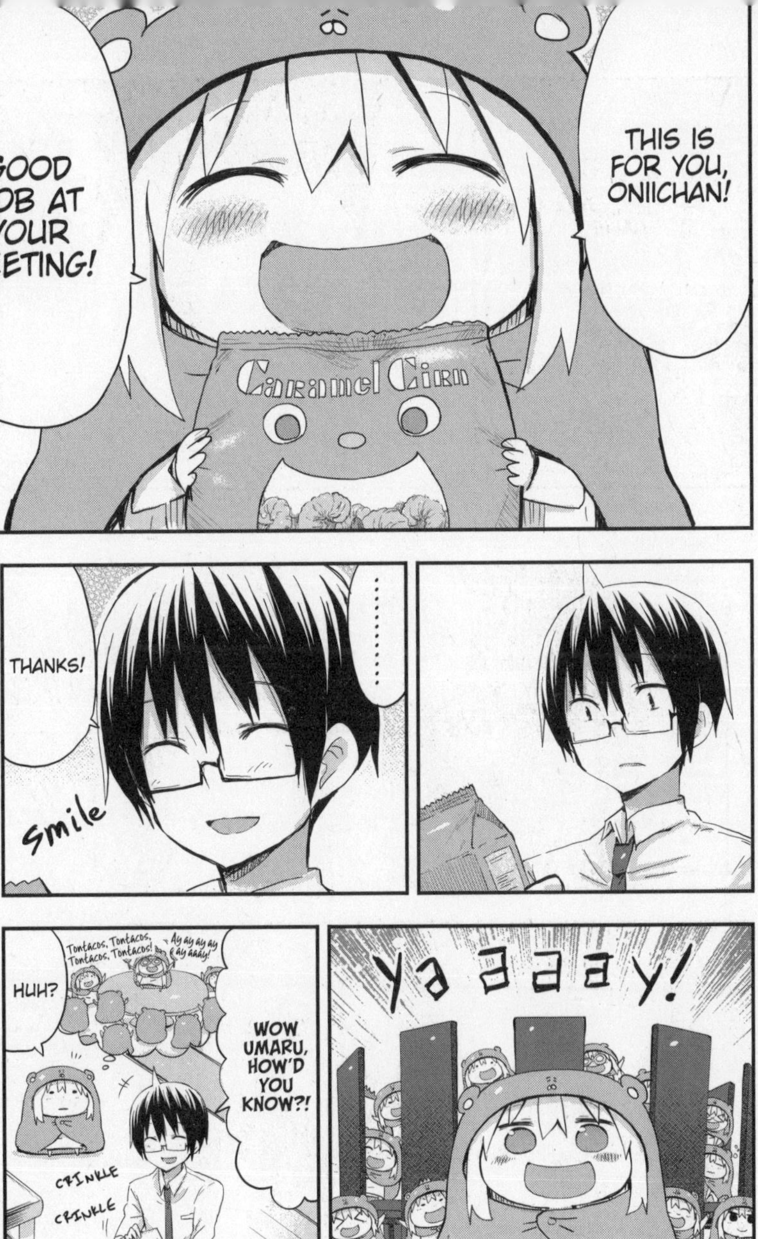
THIS IS FOR YOU, ONIICHAN!
GOOD JOB AT YOUR MEETING!
......
THANKS!
smile
yaaaay!
WOW UMARU, HOW'D YOU KNOW?!
Ay ay ay ay ay aaay!
Tontacos, Tontacos, Tontacos, Tontacos!
HUH?
CRINKLE
CRINKLE

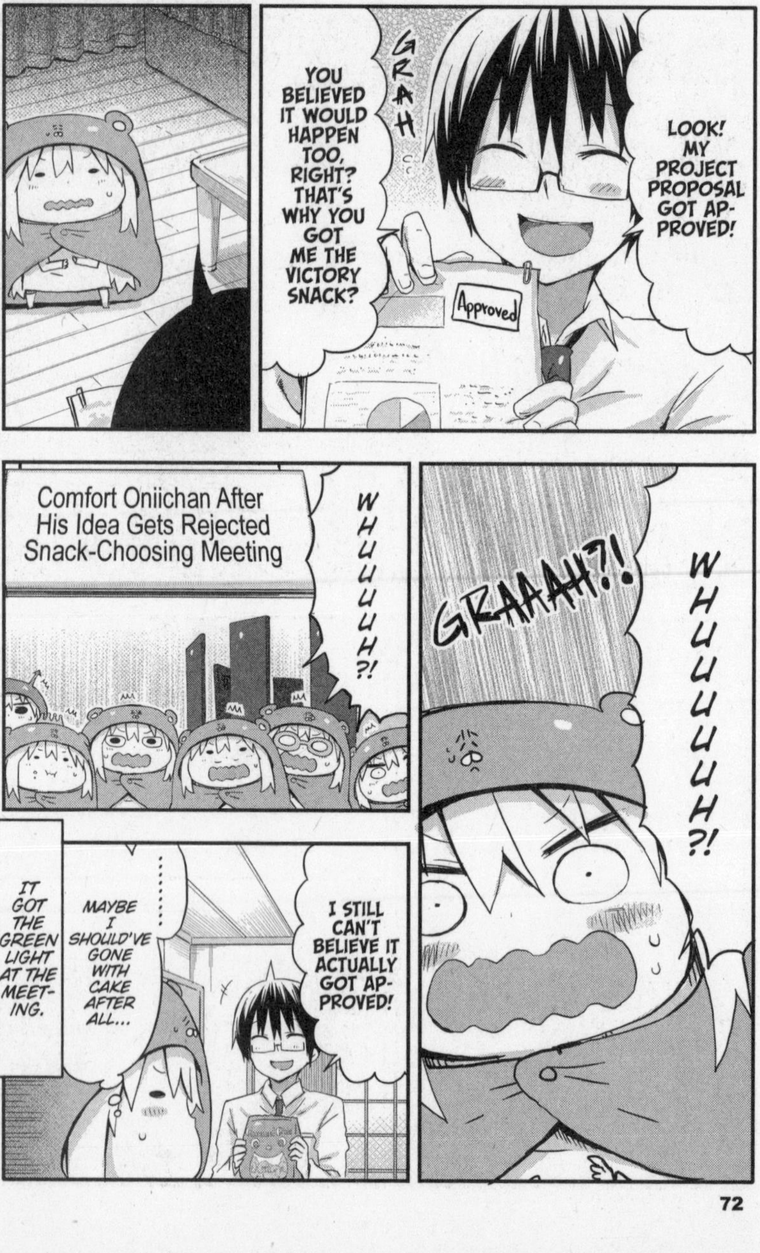
LOOK! MY PROJECT PROPOSAL GOT APPROVED!
GRAH
YOU BELIEVED IT WOULD HAPPEN TOO, RIGHT? THAT'S WHY YOU GOT ME THE VICTORY SNACK?
Approved
WHUUUUUUUH?!
GRAAAH?!
WHUUUUUUH?!
Comfort Oniichan After His Idea Gets Rejected Snack-Choosing Meeting
I STILL CAN'T BELIEVE IT ACTUALLY GOT APPROVED!
......
MAYBE I SHOULD'VE GONE WITH CAKE AFTER ALL...
IT GOT THE GREEN LIGHT AT THE MEETING.

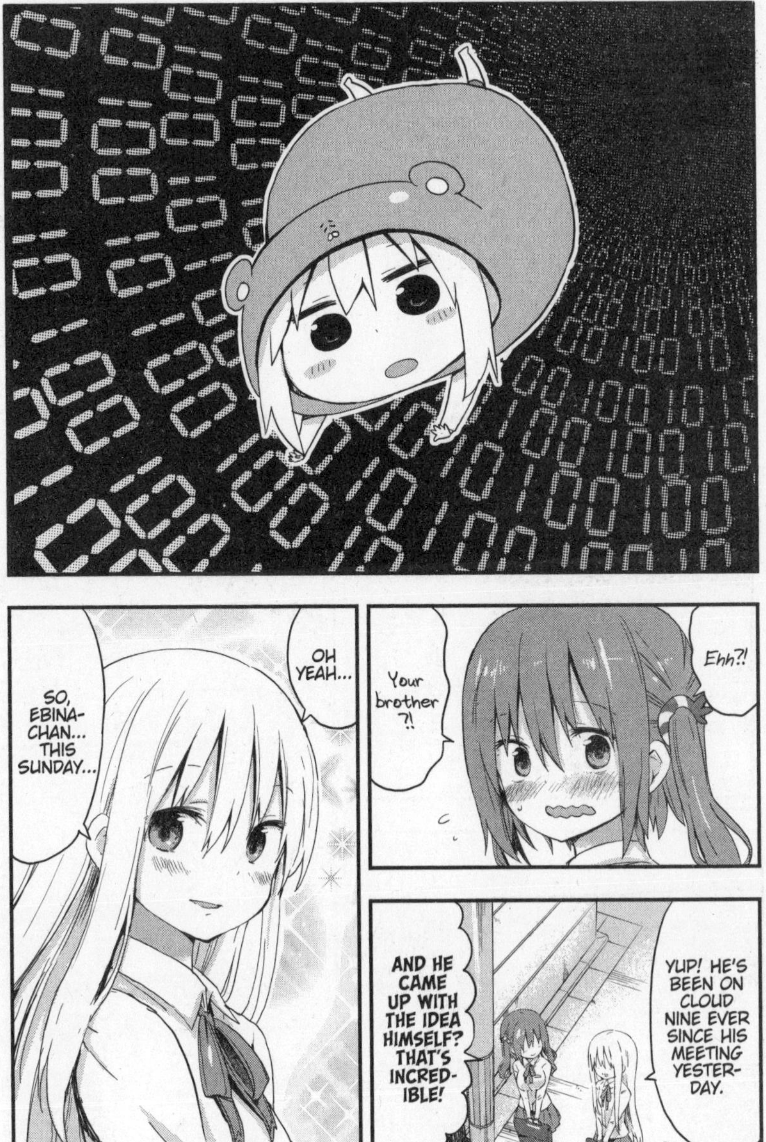
Ehh?!
Your brother?!
YUP! HE'S BEEN ON CLOUD NINE EVER SINCE HIS MEETING YESTER-DAY.
AND HE CAME UP WITH THE IDEA HIMSELF? THAT'S INCRED-IBLE!
OH YEAH...
SO, EBINA-CHAN... THIS SUNDAY...

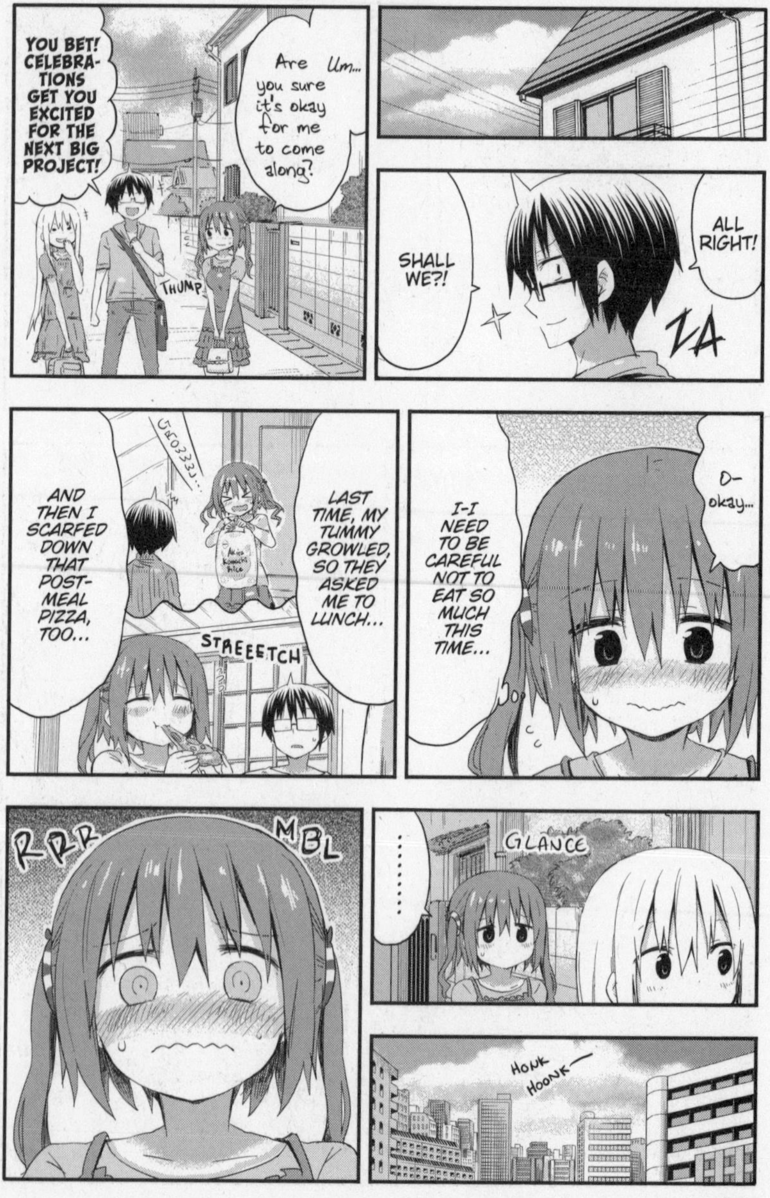
ALL RIGHT!
SHALL WE?!
ZA
Um...
Are you sure it's okay for me to come along?
YOU BET! CELEBRATIONS GET YOU EXCITED FOR THE NEXT BIG PROJECT!
THUMP
O-okay...
I-I NEED TO BE CAREFUL NOT TO EAT SO MUCH THIS TIME...
LAST TIME, MY TUMMY GROWLED, SO THEY ASKED ME TO LUNCH...
AND THEN I SCARFED DOWN THAT POST-MEAL PIZZA, TOO...
STREEETCH
......
GLANCE
HONK HOONK—
RRRMBL

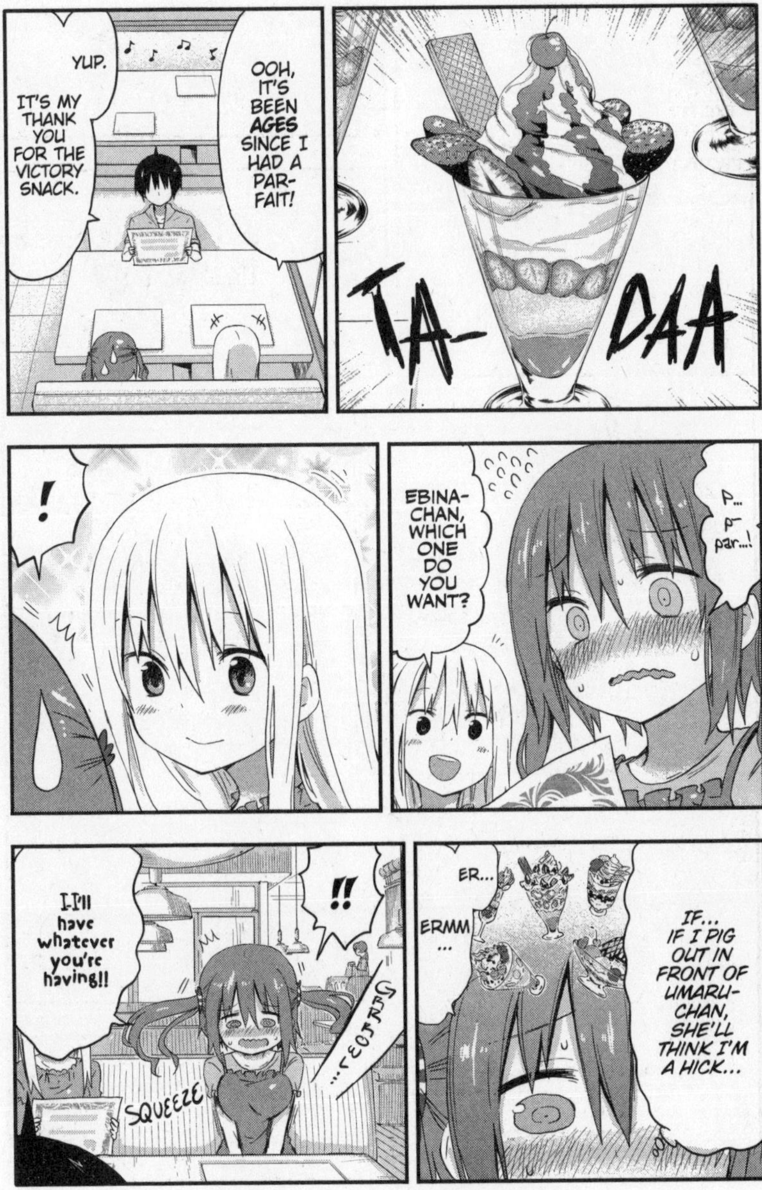
TA-DAA
OOH, IT'S BEEN AGES SINCE I HAD A PAR-FAIT!
YUP.
IT'S MY THANK YOU FOR THE VICTORY SNACK.
P... P- par...!
EBINA-CHAN, WHICH ONE DO YOU WANT?
!
IF... IF I PIG OUT IN FRONT OF UMARU-CHAN, SHE'LL THINK I'M A HICK...
ER...
ERMM...
!!
I-I'll have whatever you're having!!
SQUEEZE

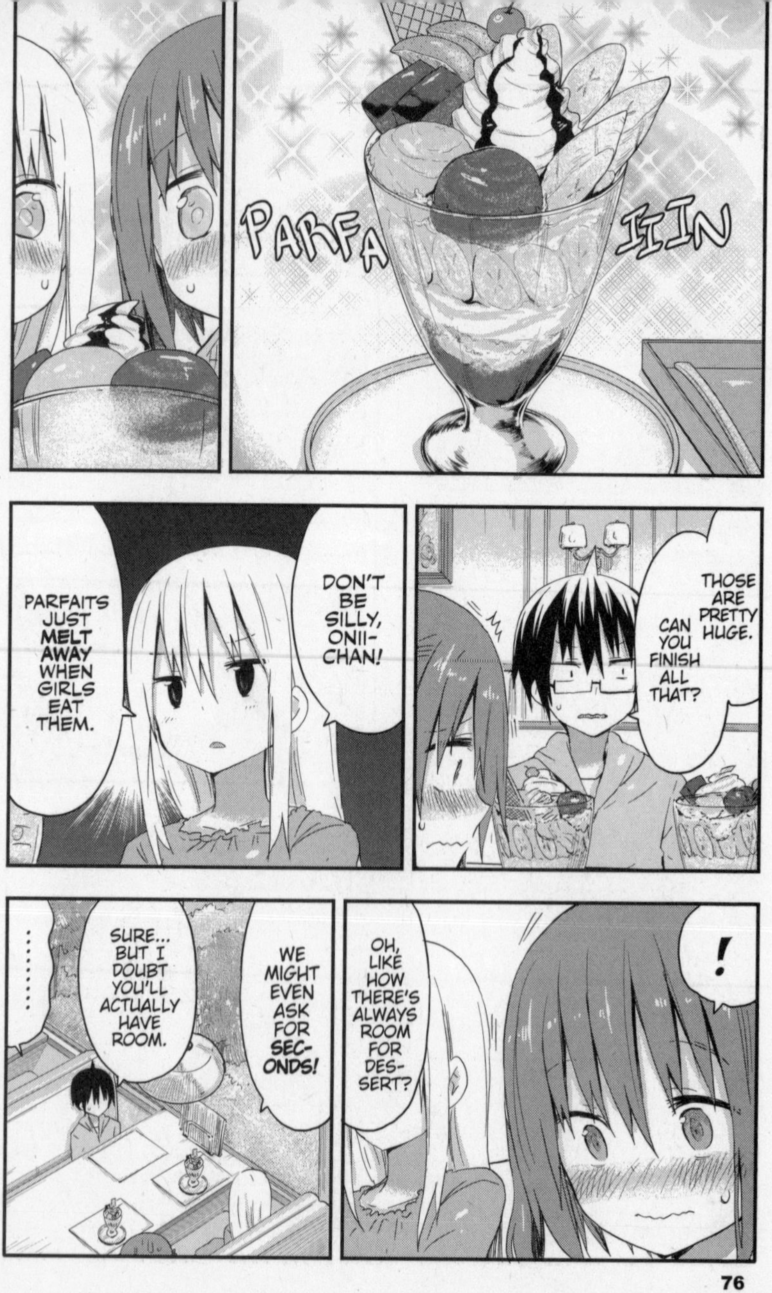
PARFA IIIN
THOSE ARE PRETTY HUGE.
CAN YOU FINISH ALL THAT?
DON'T BE SILLY, ONII-CHAN!
PARFAITS JUST MELT AWAY WHEN GIRLS EAT THEM.
!
OH, LIKE HOW THERE'S ALWAYS ROOM FOR DES-SERT?
WE MIGHT EVEN ASK FOR SEC-ONDS!
SURE... BUT I DOUBT YOU'LL ACTUALLY HAVE ROOM.
....

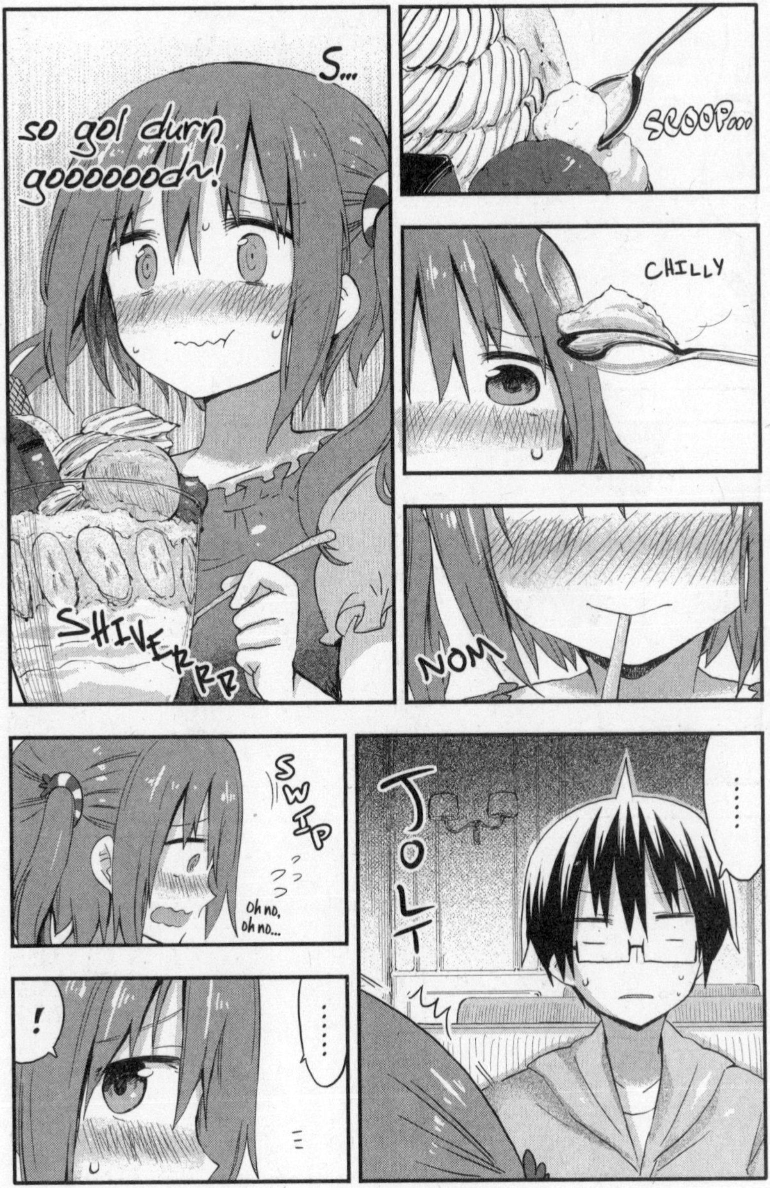
SCOOP...
CHILLY
NOM
S...
so gol durn gooooood~!
SHIVERRR
......
JOLT
SWIP
oh no, oh no...
......
!

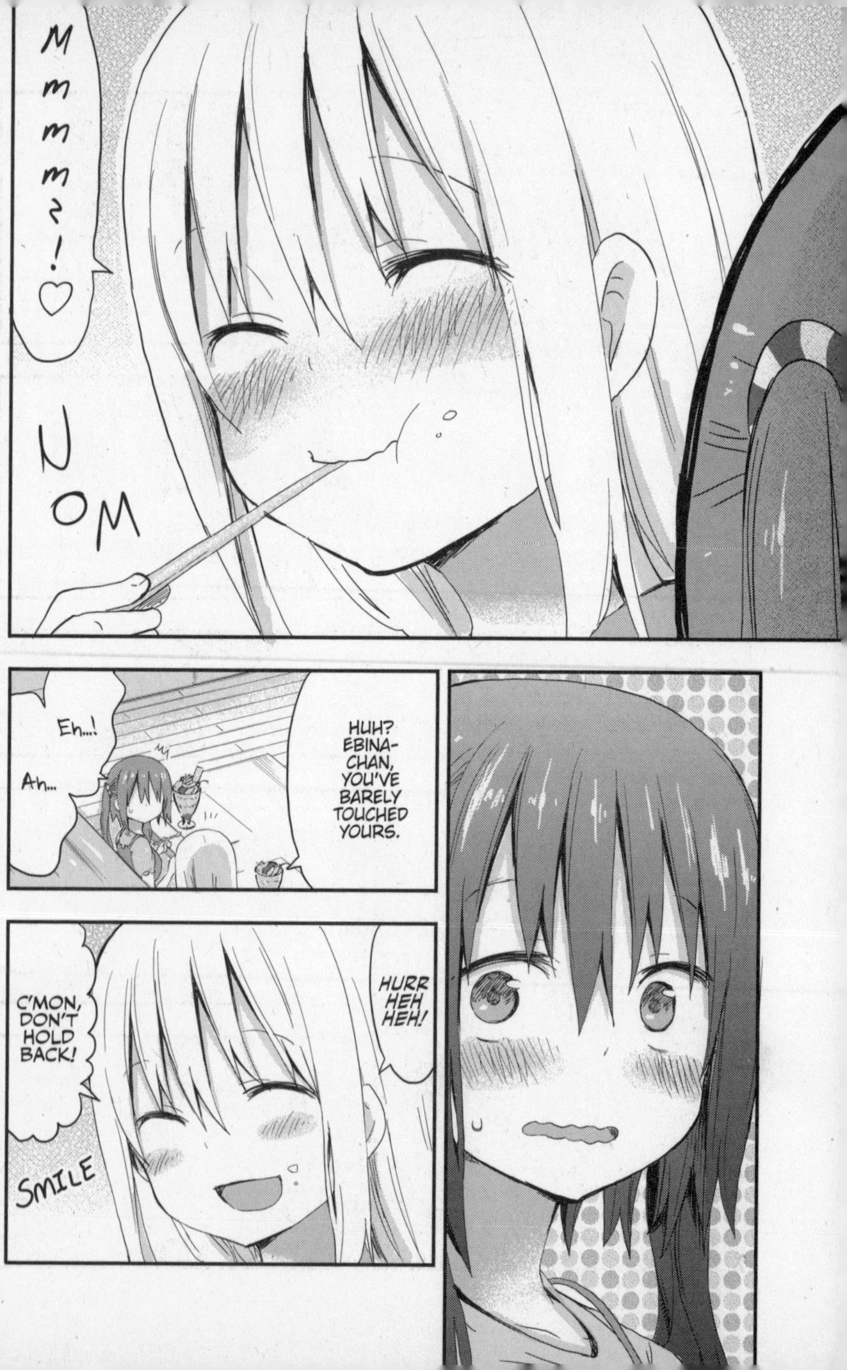
Mmmm~!♡
NOM
HUH? EBINA-CHAN, YOU'VE BARELY TOUCHED YOURS.
Eh...!
Ah...
HURR HEH HEH!
C'MON, DON'T HOLD BACK!
SMILE

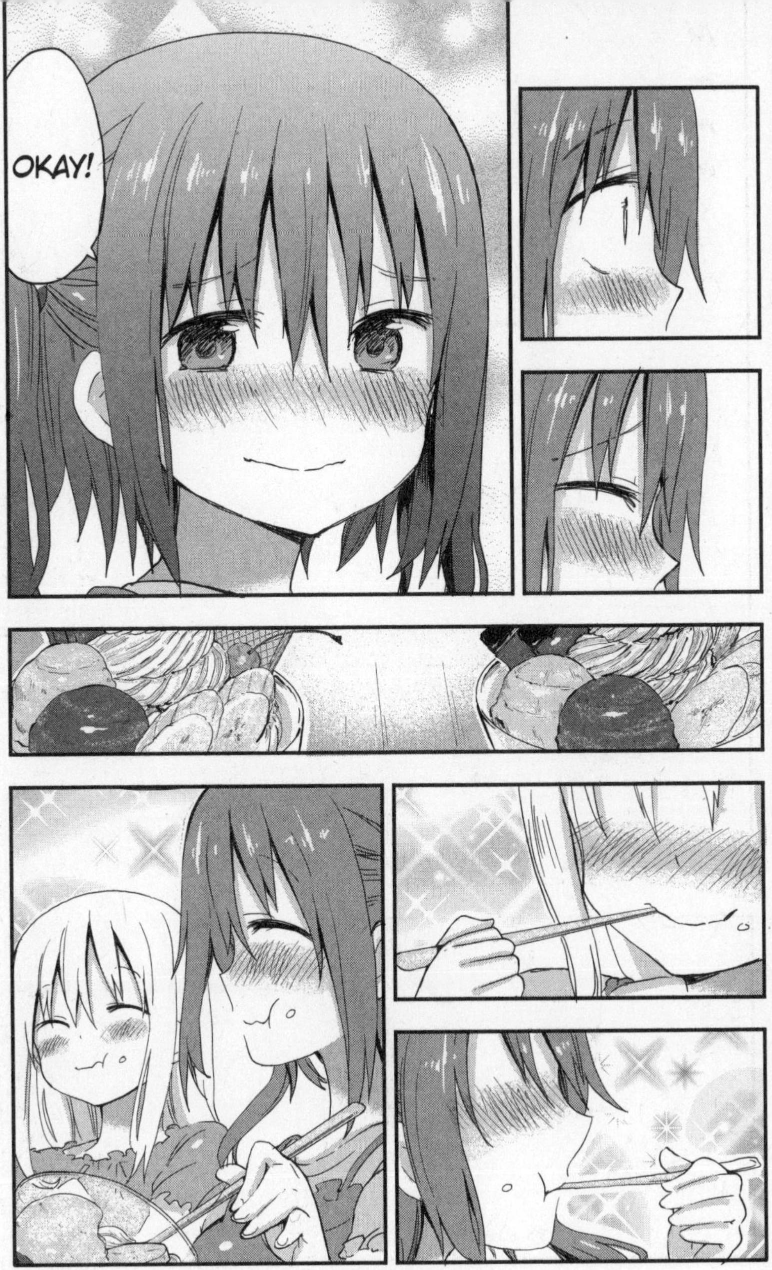
OKAY!

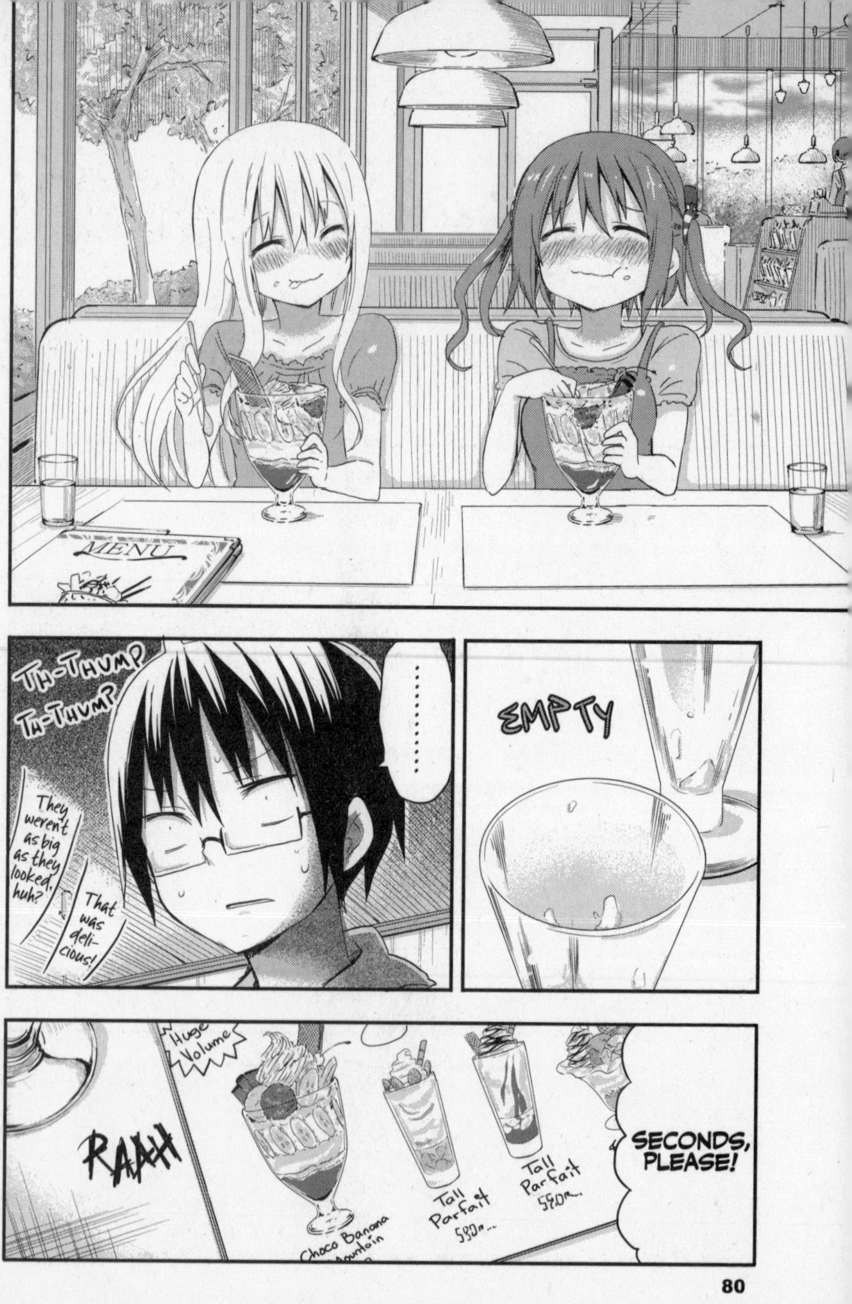
MENU
EMPTY
......
TH-THUMP
TH-THUMP
They weren't as big as they looked, huh?
That was delicious!
SECONDS, PLEASE!
Tall Parfait 580...
Tall Parfait 580...
Huge Volume
Choco Banana Mountain
RAAH

No. 62 Umaru & the Rainy Season

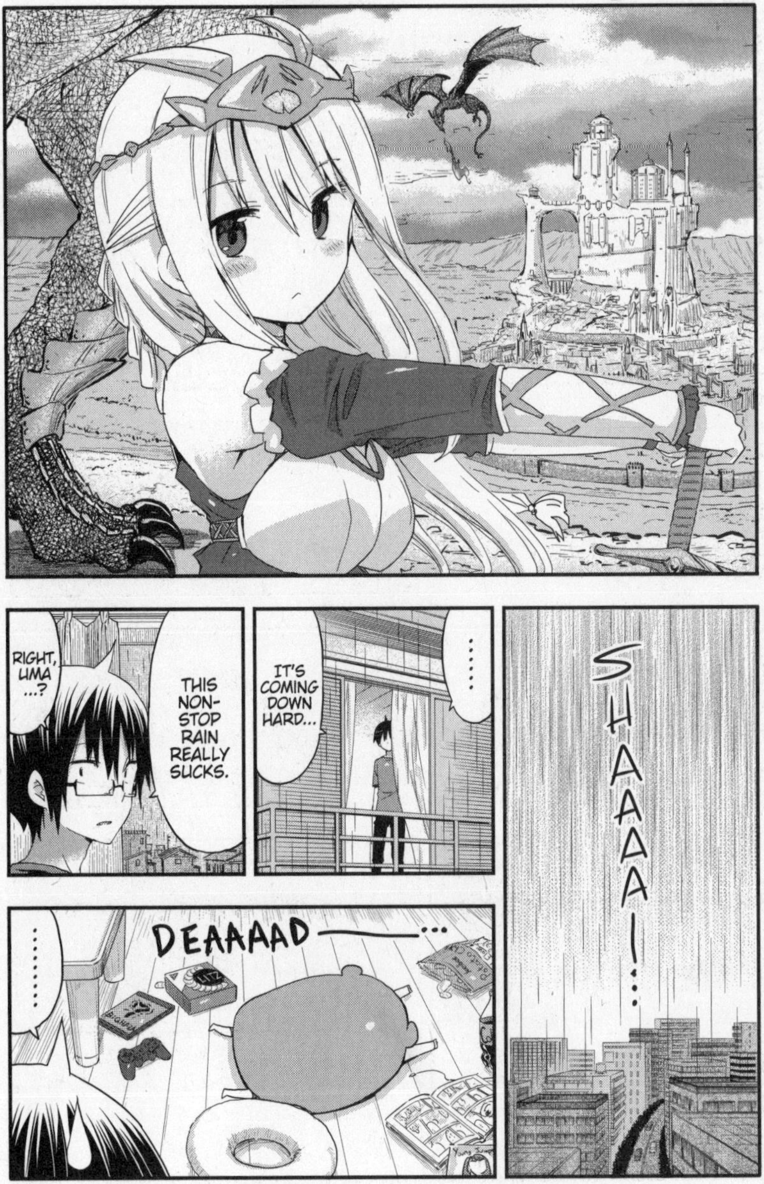
SHAAAAI...
......
IT'S COMING DOWN HARD...
THIS NON-STOP RAIN REALLY SUCKS.
RIGHT, UMA...?
....
DEAAAAD——...

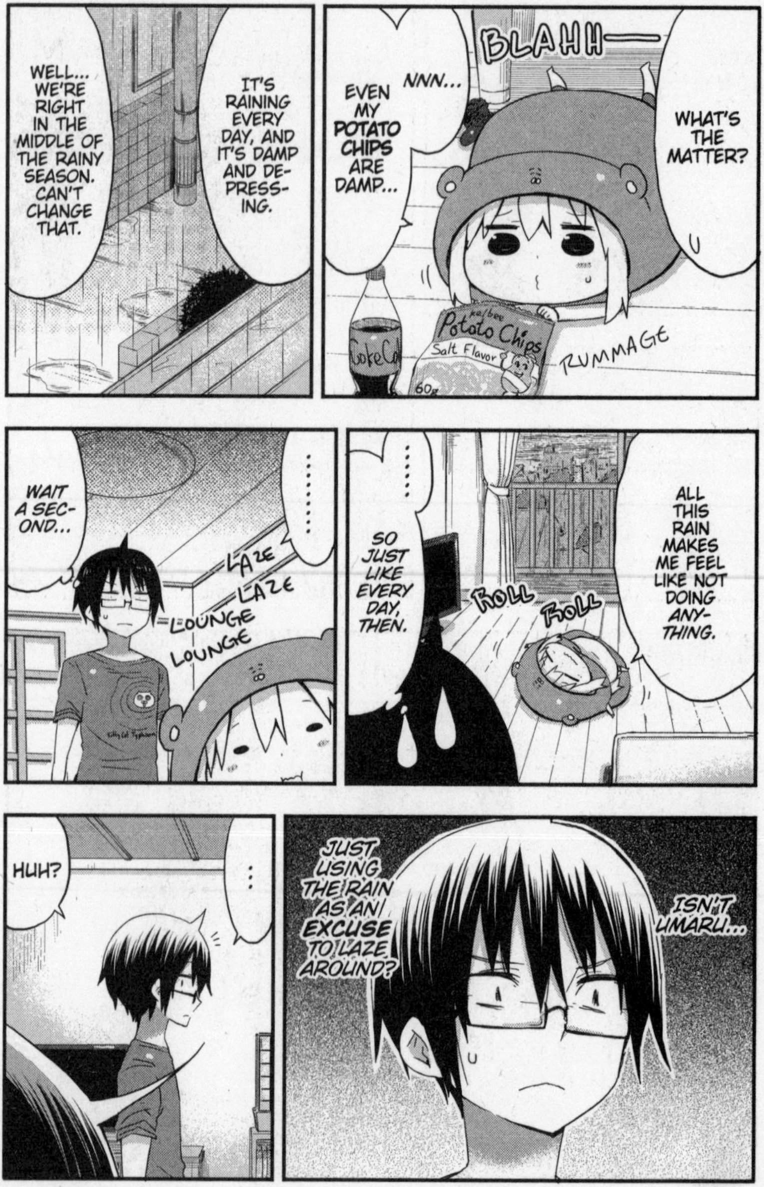
BLAHH—
WHAT'S THE MATTER?
NNN...
EVEN MY POTATO CHIPS ARE DAMP...
Potato Chips
Salt Flavor
60g
RUMMAGE
IT'S RAINING EVERY DAY, AND IT'S DAMP AND DE-PRESSING.
WELL... WE'RE RIGHT IN THE MIDDLE OF THE RAINY SEASON. CAN'T CHANGE THAT.
ALL THIS RAIN MAKES ME FEEL LIKE NOT DOING ANYTHING.
ROLL
ROLL
......
SO JUST LIKE EVERY DAY, THEN.
......
LAZE
LAZE
LOUNGE
LOUNGE
WAIT A SECOND...
ISN'T UMARU...
JUST USING THE RAIN AS AN EXCUSE TO LAZE AROUND?
...
HUH?

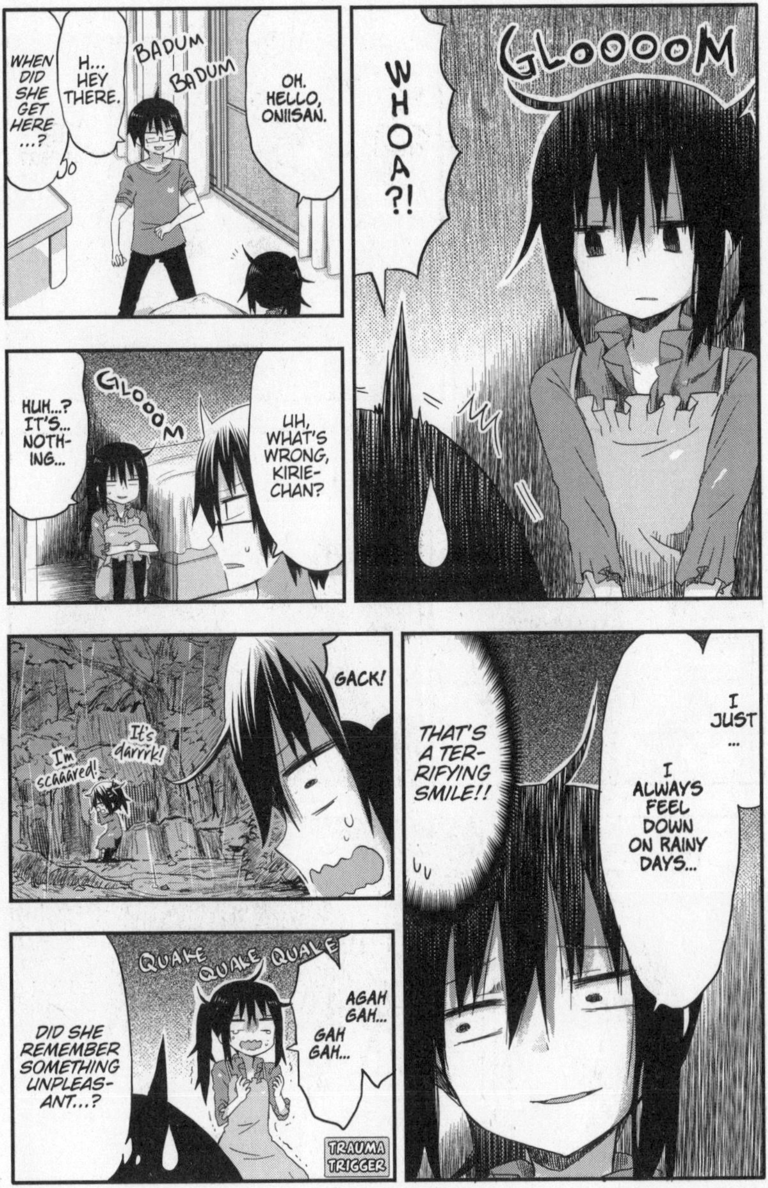
GLOOOOM
WHOA?!
OH. HELLO, ONIISAN.
BADUM BADUM
H... HEY THERE.
WHEN DID SHE GET HERE...?
UH, WHAT'S WRONG, KIRIE-CHAN?
GLOOOM
HUH...? IT'S... NOTHING...
I JUST... I ALWAYS FEEL DOWN ON RAINY DAYS...
THAT'S A TERRIFYING SMILE!!
GACK!
It's darrrk!
I'm scaaared!
QUAKE QUAKE QUAKE
AGAH GAH... GAH GAH...
DID SHE REMEMBER SOMETHING UNPLEASANT...?
TRAUMA TRIGGER

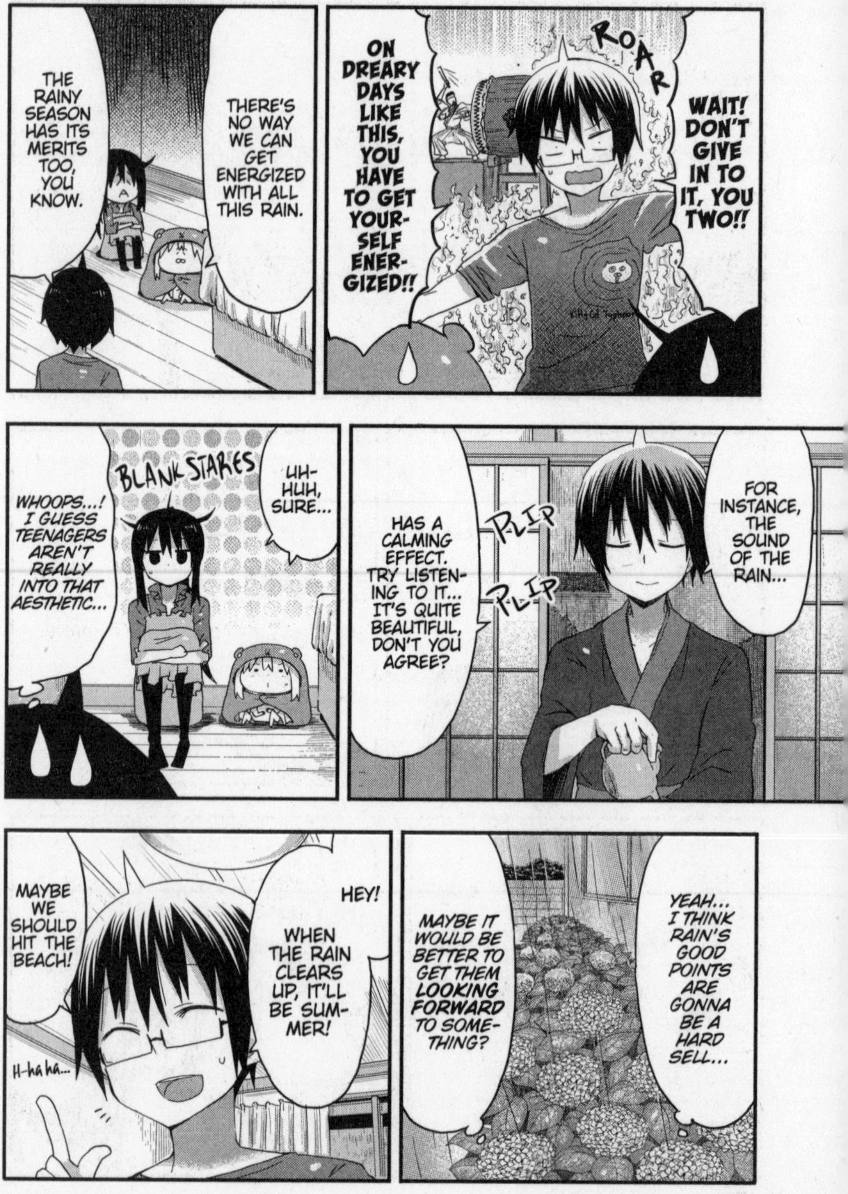
ROAR
WAIT! DON'T GIVE IN TO IT, YOU TWO!!
ON DREARY DAYS LIKE THIS, YOU HAVE TO GET YOURSELF ENERGIZED!!
THERE'S NO WAY WE CAN GET ENERGIZED WITH ALL THIS RAIN.
THE RAINY SEASON HAS ITS MERITS TOO, YOU KNOW.
FOR INSTANCE, THE SOUND OF THE RAIN...
PLIP
PLIP
HAS A CALMING EFFECT. TRY LISTENING TO IT... IT'S QUITE BEAUTIFUL, DON'T YOU AGREE?
UH-HUH, SURE...
BLANK STARES
WHOOPS...! I GUESS TEENAGERS AREN'T REALLY INTO THAT AESTHETIC...
YEAH... I THINK RAIN'S GOOD POINTS ARE GONNA BE A HARD SELL...
MAYBE IT WOULD BE BETTER TO GET THEM LOOKING FORWARD TO SOMETHING?
HEY!
WHEN THE RAIN CLEARS UP, IT'LL BE SUMMER!
MAYBE WE SHOULD HIT THE BEACH!
H-ha ha...

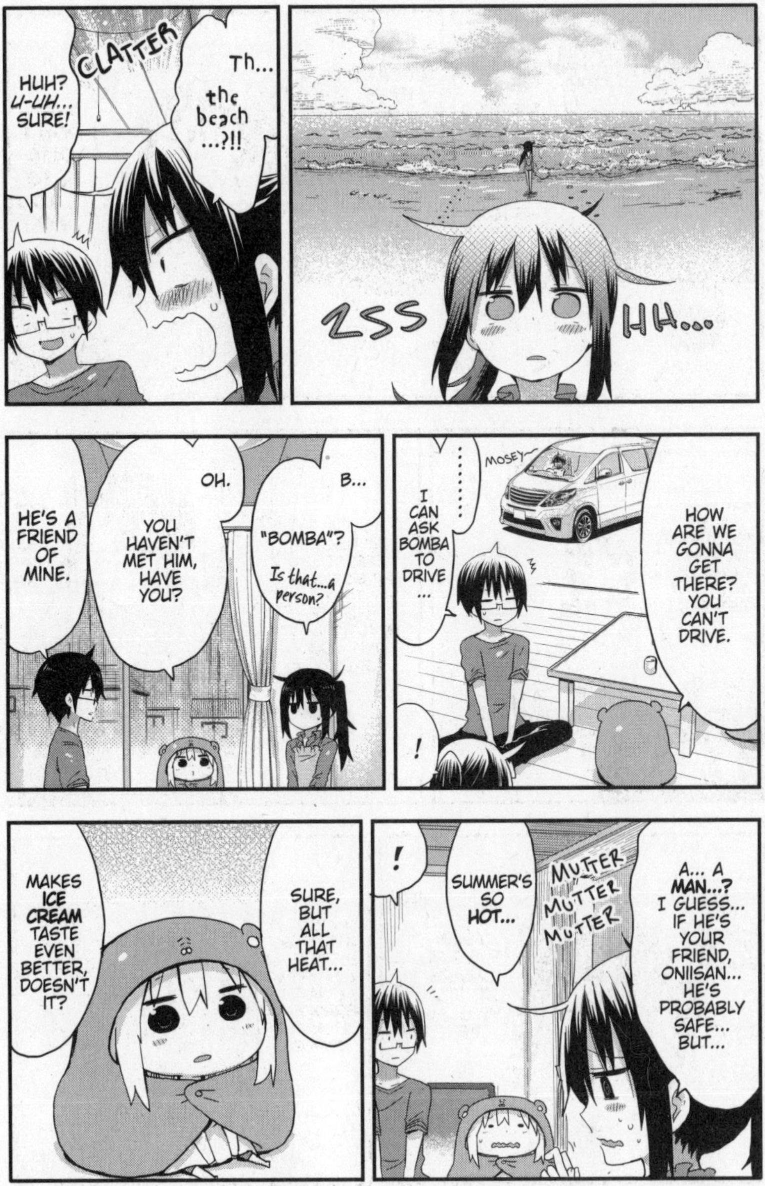
ZSS
HH...
Th... the beach ...?!!
CLATTER
HUH? U-UH... SURE!
HOW ARE WE GONNA GET THERE? YOU CAN'T DRIVE.
!
...... I CAN ASK BOMBA TO DRIVE ...
MOSEY~
B... "BOMBA"? Is that...a person?
OH. YOU HAVEN'T MET HIM, HAVE YOU?
HE'S A FRIEND OF MINE.
A... A MAN...? I GUESS... IF HE'S YOUR FRIEND, ONIISAN... HE'S PROBABLY SAFE... BUT...
MUTTER MUTTER MUTTER
SUMMER'S SO HOT...
!
SURE, BUT ALL THAT HEAT...
MAKES ICE CREAM TASTE EVEN BETTER, DOESN'T IT?

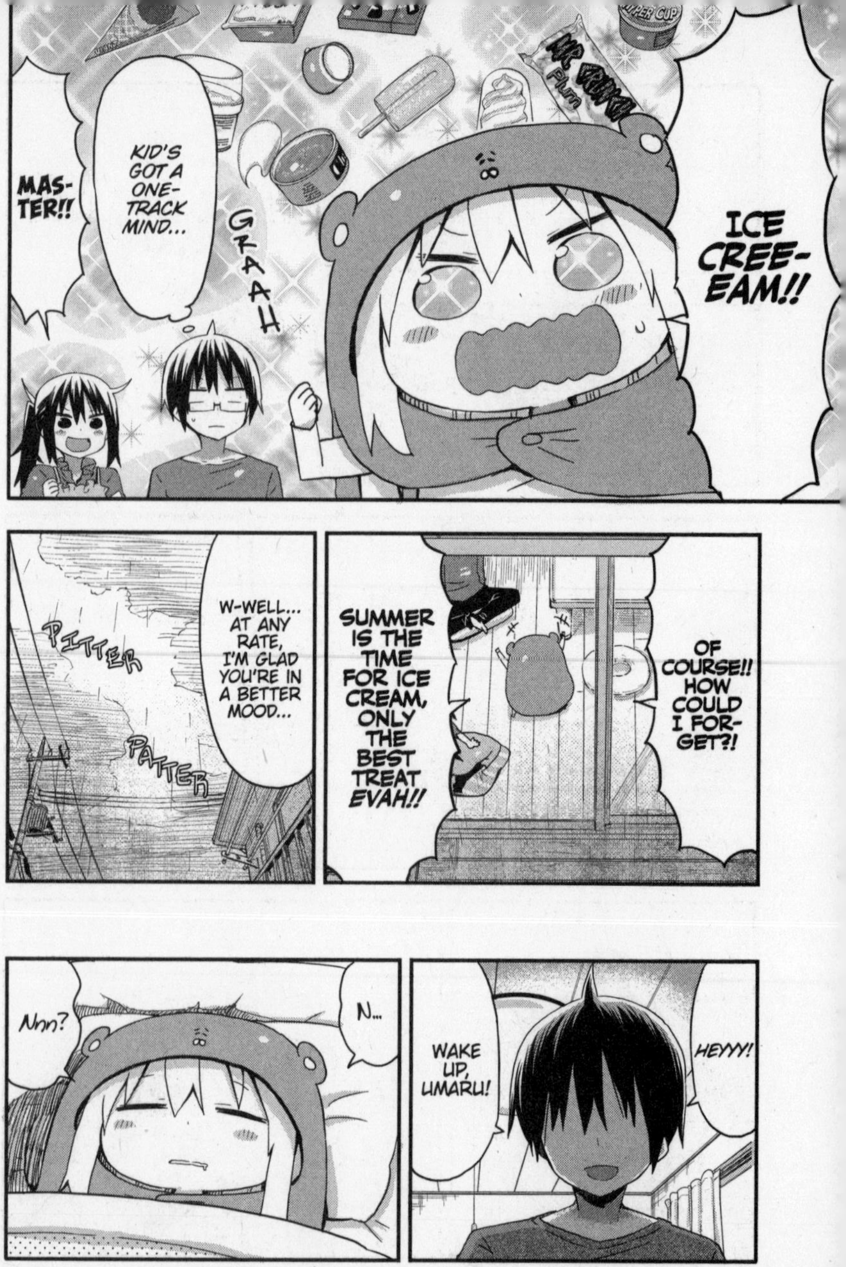
ICE CREEE-EAM!!
GRAAH
KID'S GOT A ONE-TRACK MIND...
MAS-TER!!
OF COURSE!! HOW COULD I FOR-GET?!
SUMMER IS THE TIME FOR ICE CREAM, ONLY THE BEST TREAT EVAH!!
W-WELL... AT ANY RATE, I'M GLAD YOU'RE IN A BETTER MOOD...
PITTER
PATTER
HEYYY!
WAKE UP, UMARU!
N...
Nnn?

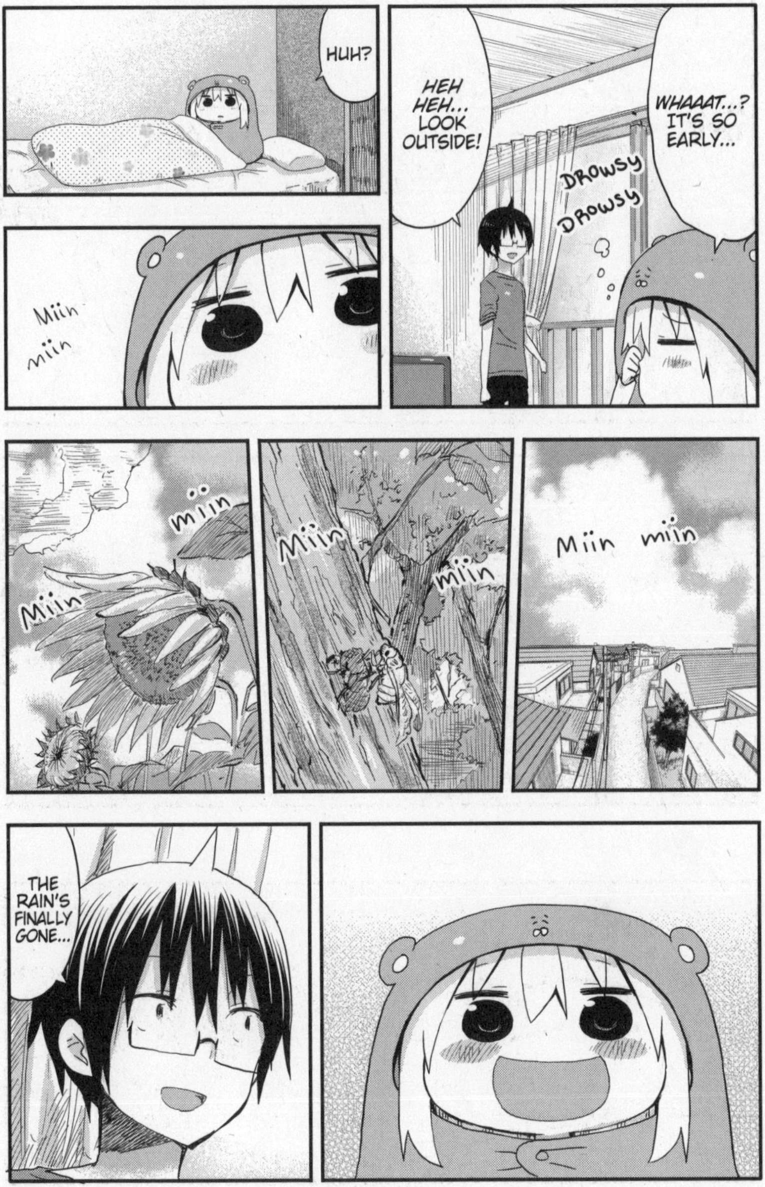
WHAAAT...? IT'S SO EARLY...
HEH HEH... LOOK OUTSIDE!
DROWSY DROWSY
HUH?
Miin miin
Miin miin
Miin miin
miin Miin
THE RAIN'S FINALLY GONE...

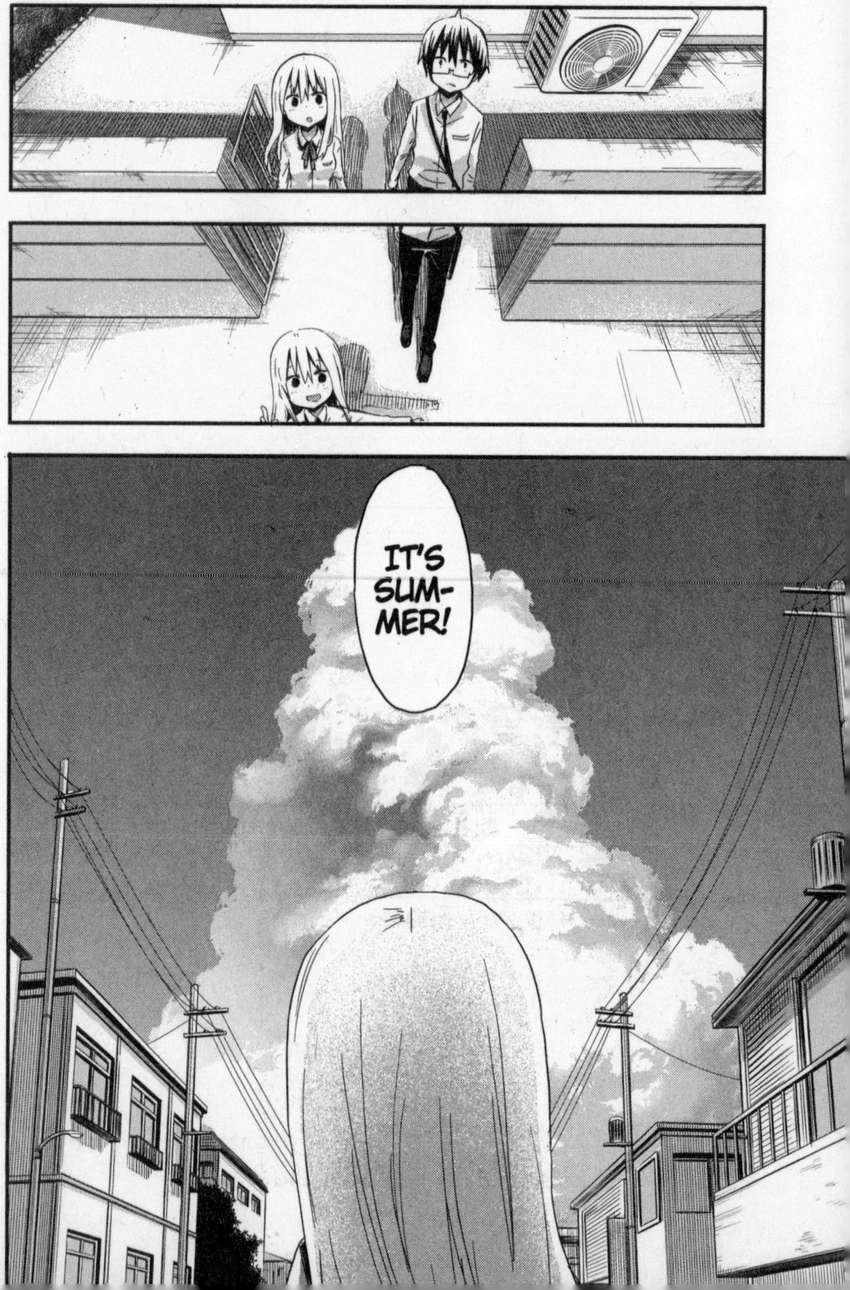
IT'S SUM-MER!

No. 63 Umaru & Ice Cream

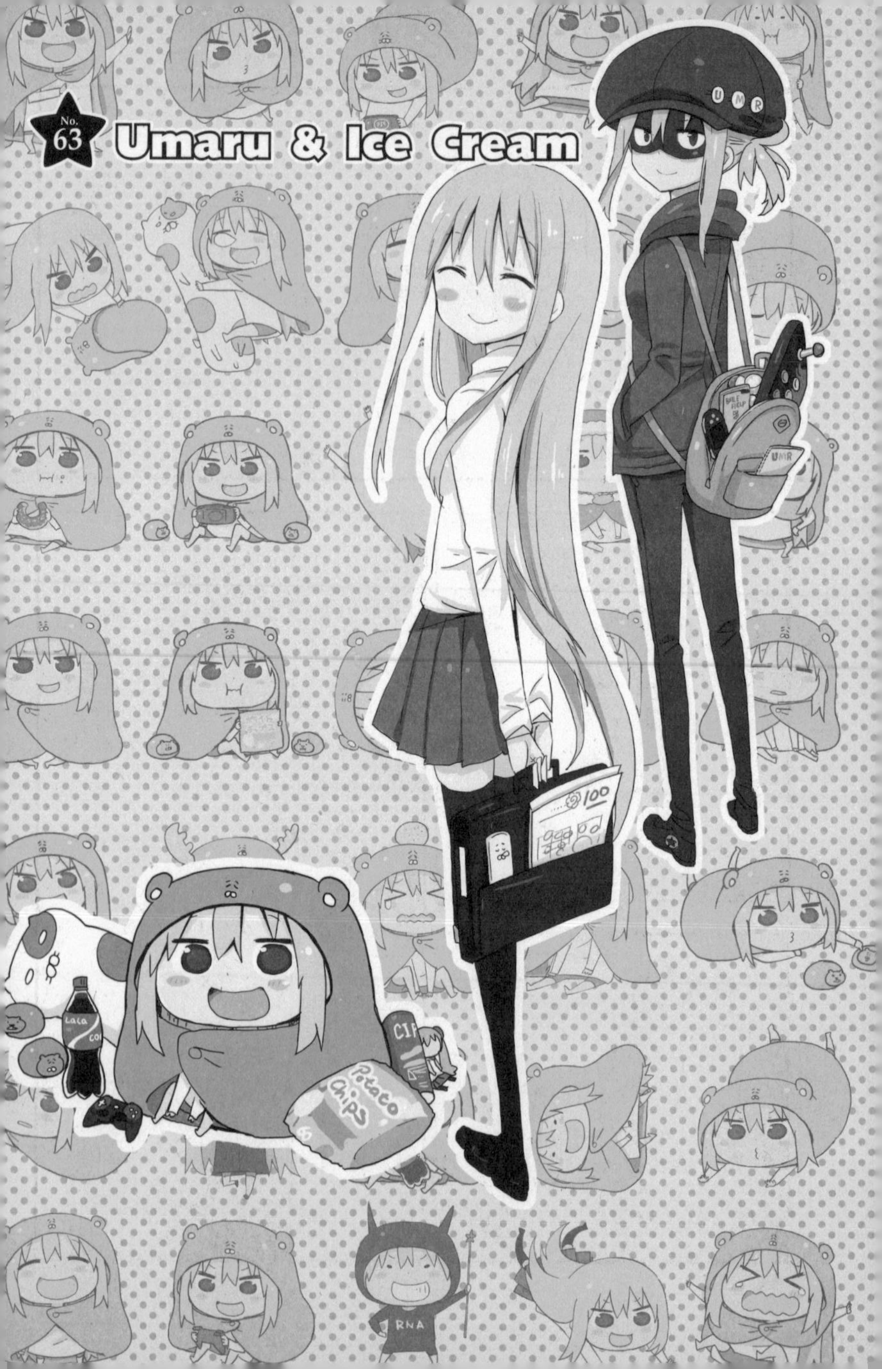
UMR
UMR
100
Potato Chips
RNA

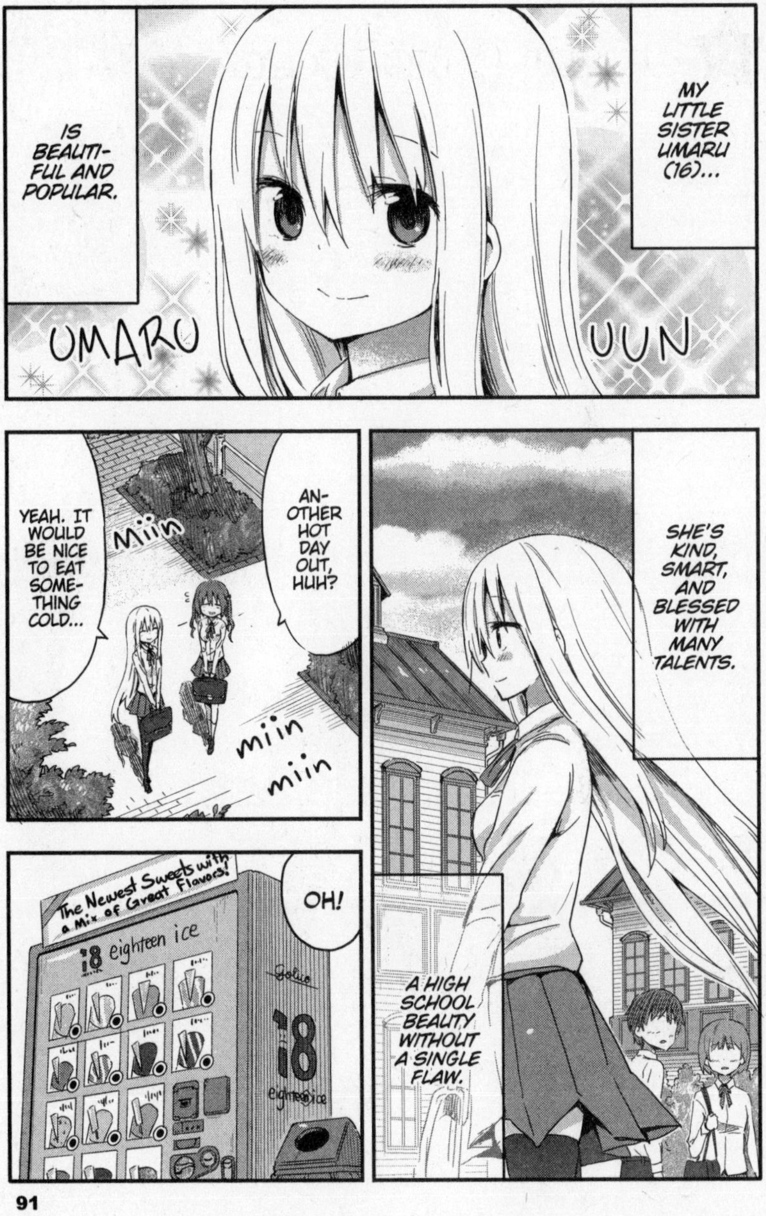
MY LITTLE SISTER UMARU (16)...
IS BEAUTI-FUL AND POPULAR.
UMARU
UUN
SHE'S KIND, SMART, AND BLESSED WITH MANY TALENTS.
A HIGH SCHOOL BEAUTY WITHOUT A SINGLE FLAW.
AN-OTHER HOT DAY OUT, HUH?
YEAH. IT WOULD BE NICE TO EAT SOME-THING COLD...
miin
miin
miin
OH!
The Newest Sweets with a Mix of Great Flavors!
eighteen ice
i8
i8
eighteen ice

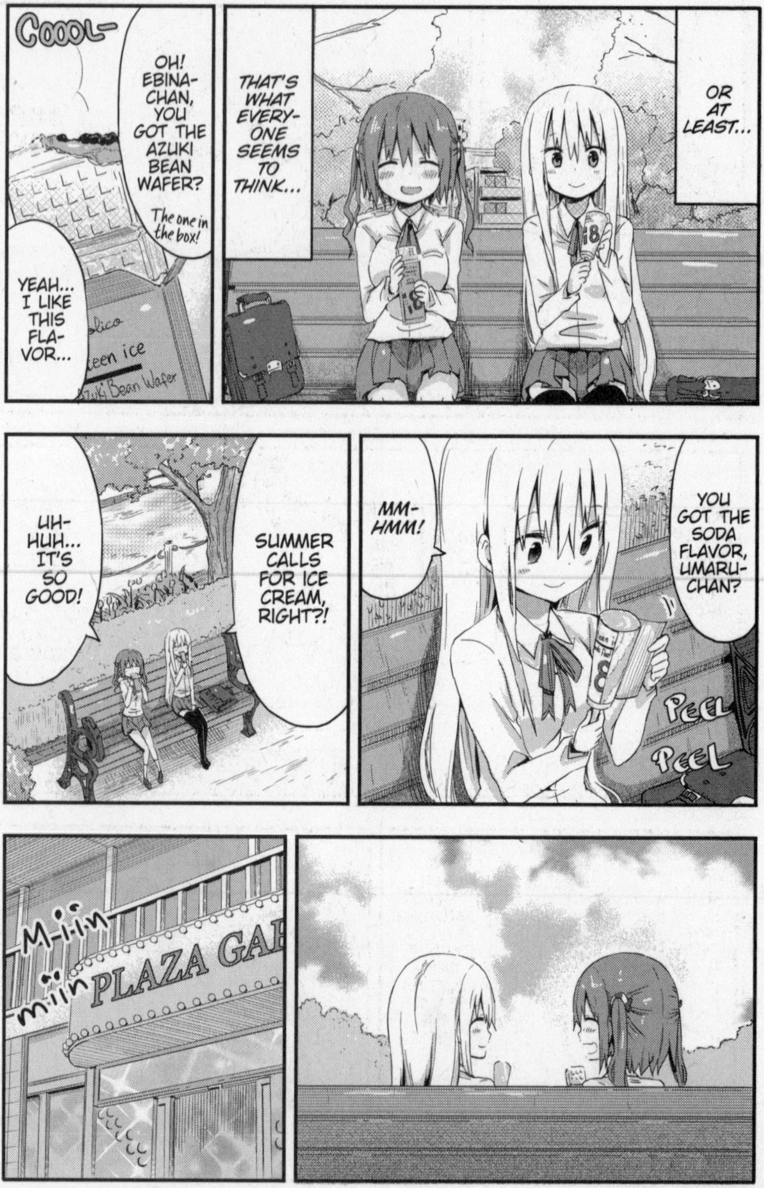
OR AT LEAST...
THAT'S WHAT EVERY-ONE SEEMS TO THINK...
OH! EBINA-CHAN, YOU GOT THE AZUKI BEAN WAFER?
The one in the box!
COOOL-
YEAH... I LIKE THIS FLA-VOR...
Azuki Bean Wafer
YOU GOT THE SODA FLAVOR, UMARU-CHAN?
MM-HMM!
PEEL
PEEL
SUMMER CALLS FOR ICE CREAM, RIGHT?!
UH-HUH... IT'S SO GOOD!
M-i-in
mi-in

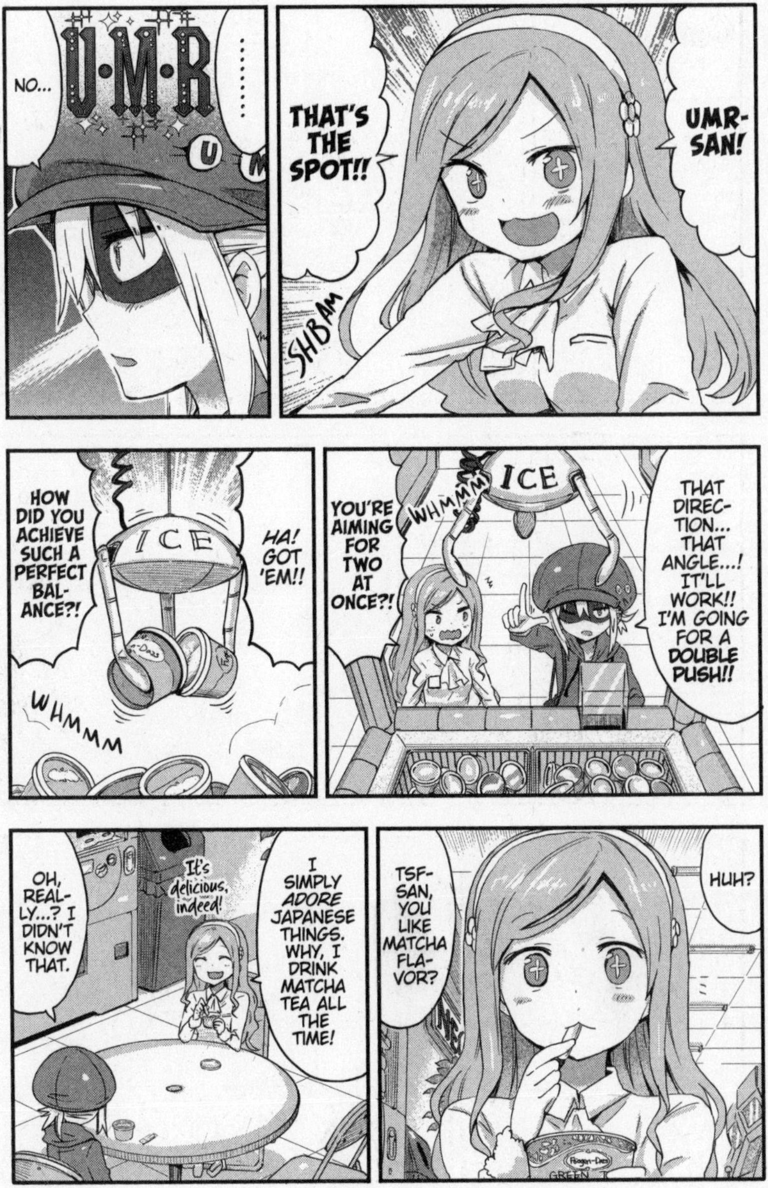
UMR-SAN!
THAT'S THE SPOT!!
SHBAM
U·M·R
......
NO...
U M
THAT DIRECTION... THAT ANGLE...! IT'LL WORK!! I'M GOING FOR A DOUBLE PUSH!!
YOU'RE AIMING FOR TWO AT ONCE?!
WHMMMM
ICE
HOW DID YOU ACHIEVE SUCH A PERFECT BALANCE?!
HA! GOT 'EM!!
ICE
WHMMMM
HUH?
TSF-SAN, YOU LIKE MATCHA FLAVOR?
I SIMPLY ADORE JAPANESE THINGS. WHY, I DRINK MATCHA TEA ALL THE TIME!
It's delicious, indeed!
OH, REALLY...? I DIDN'T KNOW THAT.

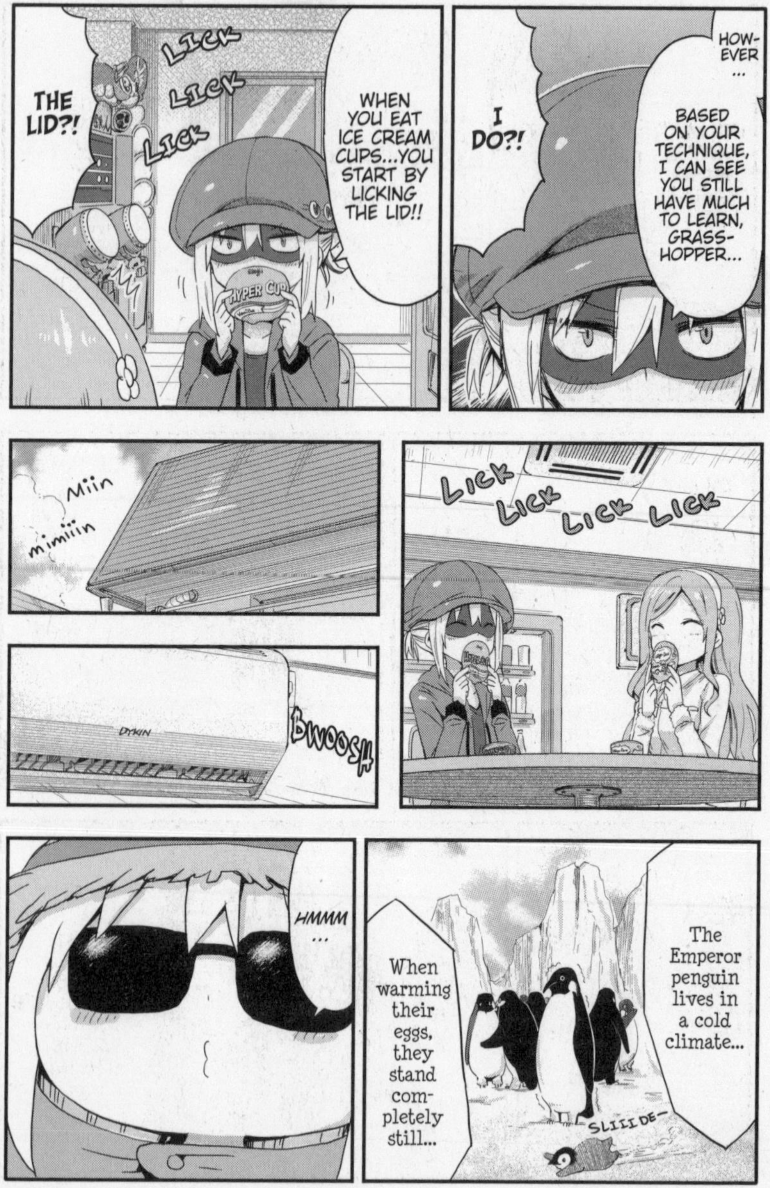
HOW-EVER...
BASED ON YOUR TECHNIQUE, I CAN SEE YOU STILL HAVE MUCH TO LEARN, GRASS-HOPPER...
I DO?!
WHEN YOU EAT ICE CREAM CUPS...YOU START BY LICKING THE LID!!
LICK
LICK
LICK
THE LID?!
HYPER CUP
LICK
LICK
LICK
LICK
Miin
mimiiin
DYKIN
BWOOSH
The Emperor penguin lives in a cold climate...
When warming their eggs, they stand com-pletely still...
SLIIIDE—
HMMM...

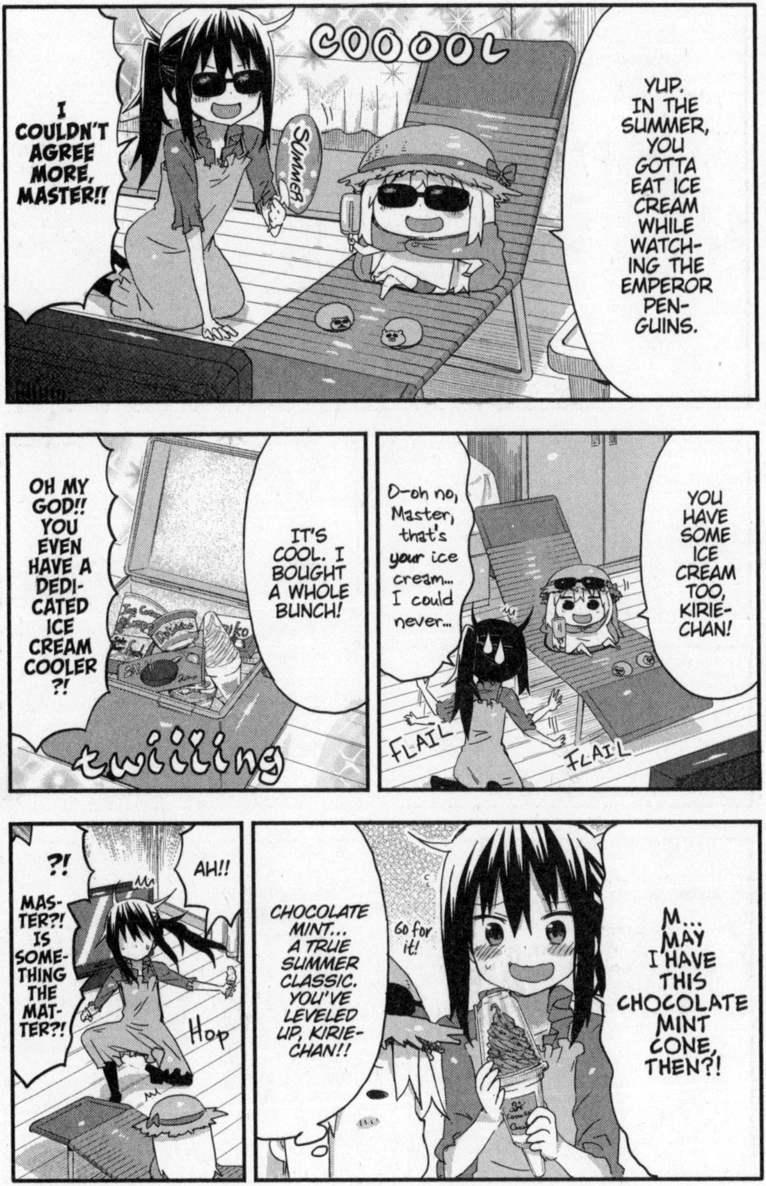
YUP. IN THE SUMMER, YOU GOTTA EAT ICE CREAM WHILE WATCHING THE EMPEROR PENGUINS.
COOOOL
SUMMER
I COULDN'T AGREE MORE, MASTER!!
YOU HAVE SOME ICE CREAM TOO, KIRIE-CHAN!
O-oh no, Master, that's your ice cream... I could never...
FLAIL
FLAIL
IT'S COOL. I BOUGHT A WHOLE BUNCH!
OH MY GOD!! YOU EVEN HAVE A DEDICATED ICE CREAM COOLER?!
twiiiing
M... MAY I HAVE THIS CHOCOLATE MINT CONE, THEN?!
Go for it!
CHOCOLATE MINT... A TRUE SUMMER CLASSIC. YOU'VE LEVELED UP, KIRIE-CHAN!!
AH!!
?!
MASTER?! IS SOMETHING THE MATTER?!
Hop

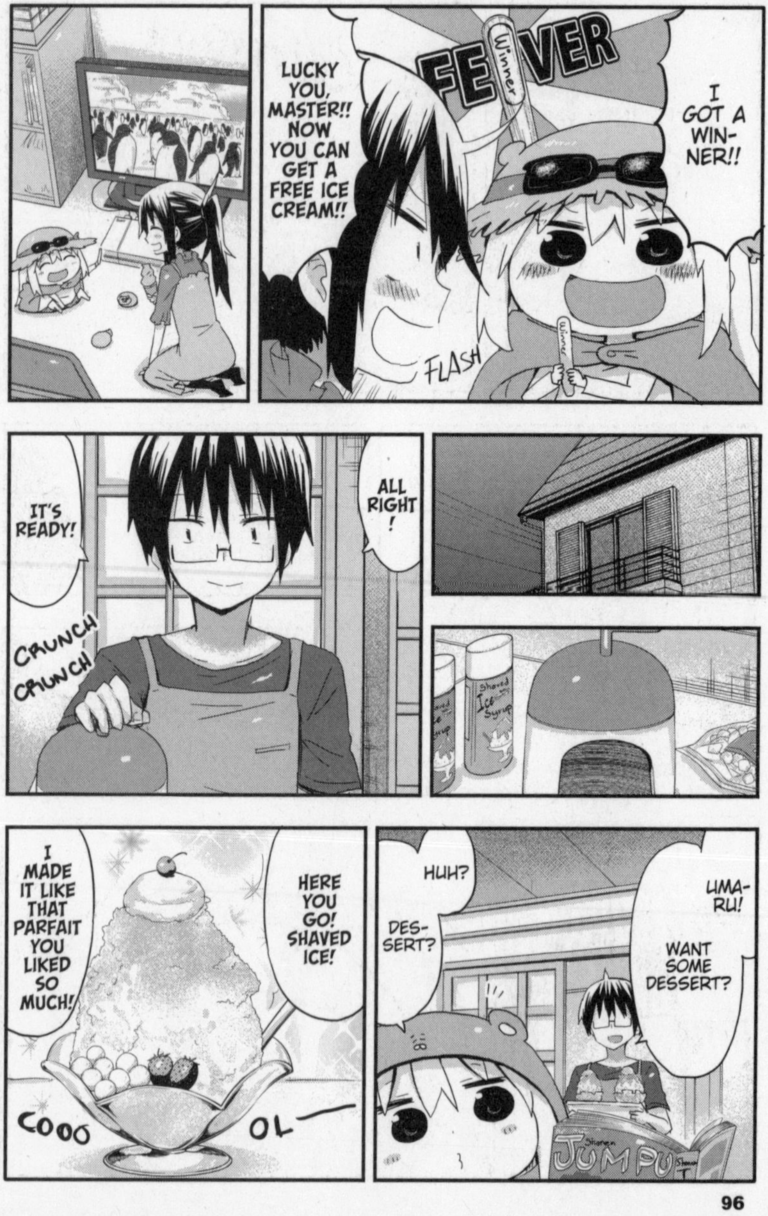

FEVER
Winner
I GOT A WINNER!!
LUCKY YOU, MASTER!! NOW YOU CAN GET A FREE ICE CREAM!!
Winner
FLASH
Shaved Ice Syrup
ALL RIGHT!
IT'S READY!
CRUNCH CRUNCH
UMA-RU!
WANT SOME DESSERT?
HUH?
DES-SERT?
JUMP
HERE YOU GO! SHAVED ICE!
I MADE IT LIKE THAT PARFAIT YOU LIKED SO MUCH!
COOO OL—

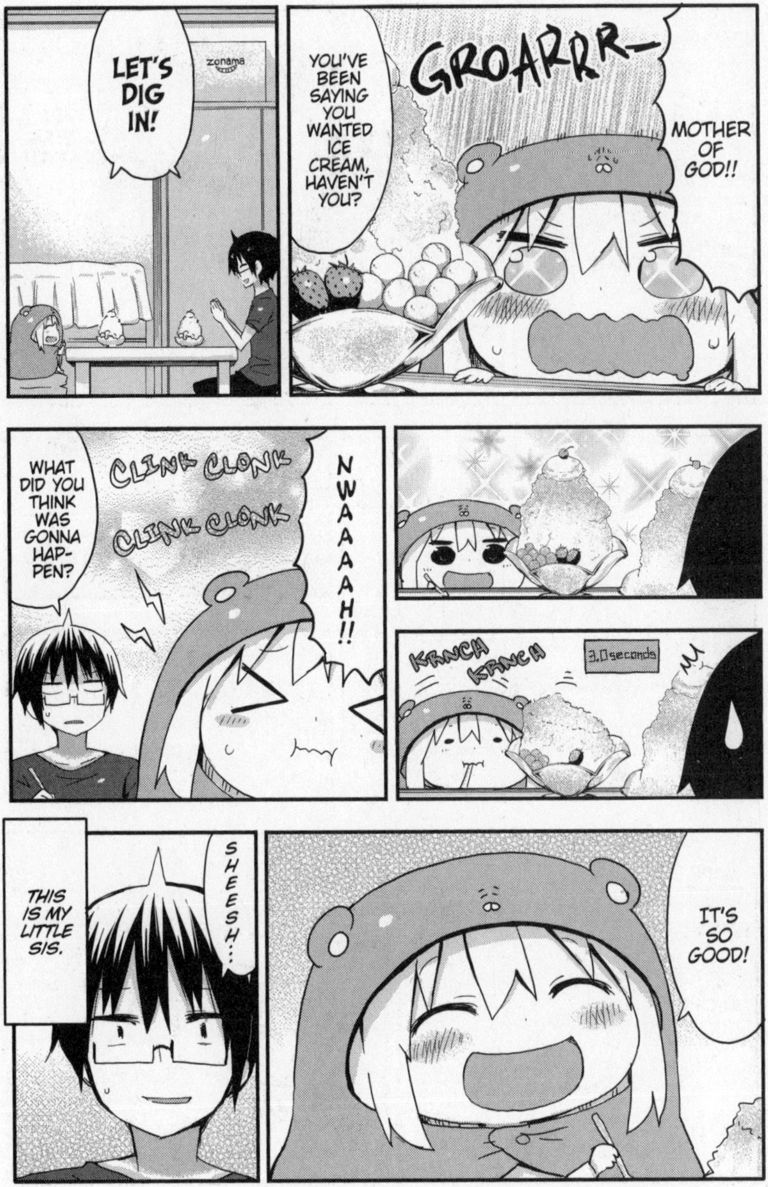
GROARRR—
MOTHER OF GOD!!
YOU'VE BEEN SAYING YOU WANTED ICE CREAM, HAVEN'T YOU?
LET'S DIG IN!
zonama
KRNCH KRNCH
3.0seconds
NWAAAAAH!!
CLINK CLONK
CLINK CLONK
WHAT DID YOU THINK WAS GONNA HAP-PEN?
IT'S SO GOOD!
SHEESH...
THIS IS MY LITTLE SIS.

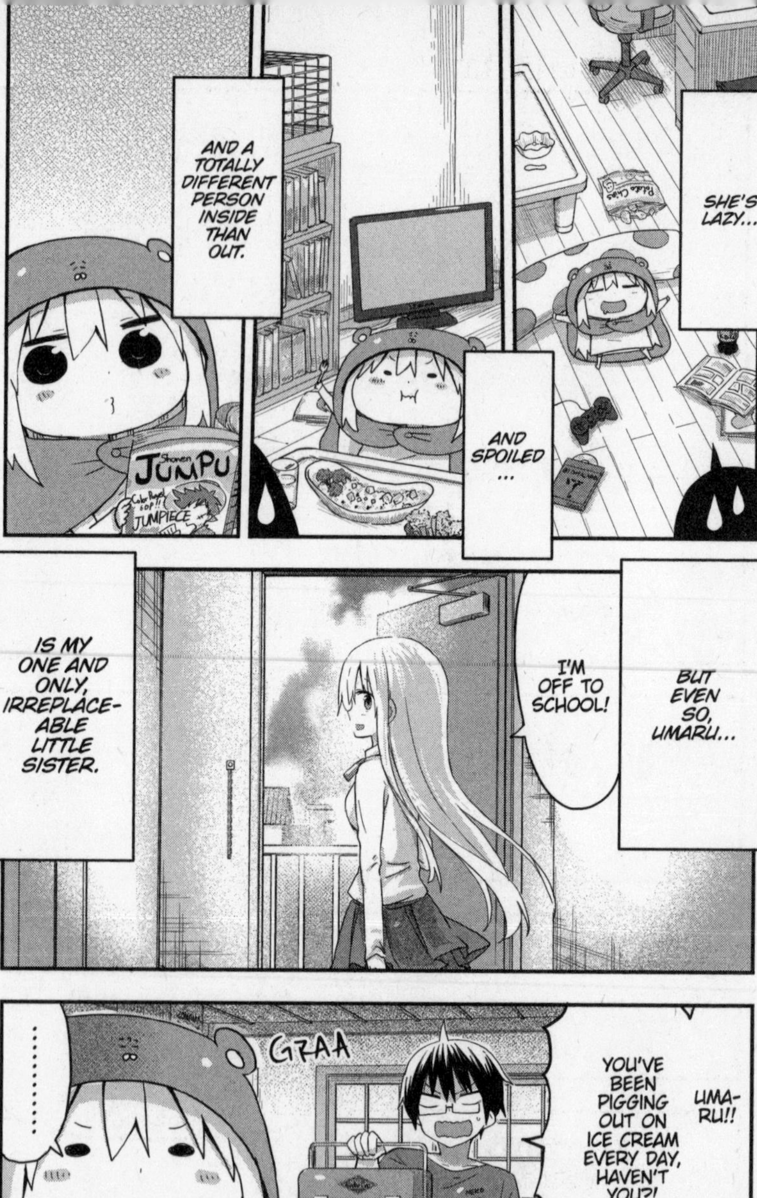
SHE'S LAZY...
AND SPOILED ...
AND A TOTALLY DIFFERENT PERSON INSIDE THAN OUT.
Shonen JUMPU
JUMPIECE
BUT EVEN SO, UMARU...
I'M OFF TO SCHOOL!
IS MY ONE AND ONLY, IRREPLACE-ABLE LITTLE SISTER.
UMA-RU!!
YOU'VE BEEN PIGGING OUT ON ICE CREAM EVERY DAY, HAVEN'T YOU?!
You even have a cooler full of it!!
GRAA
......

No. 64 Umaru & Baths

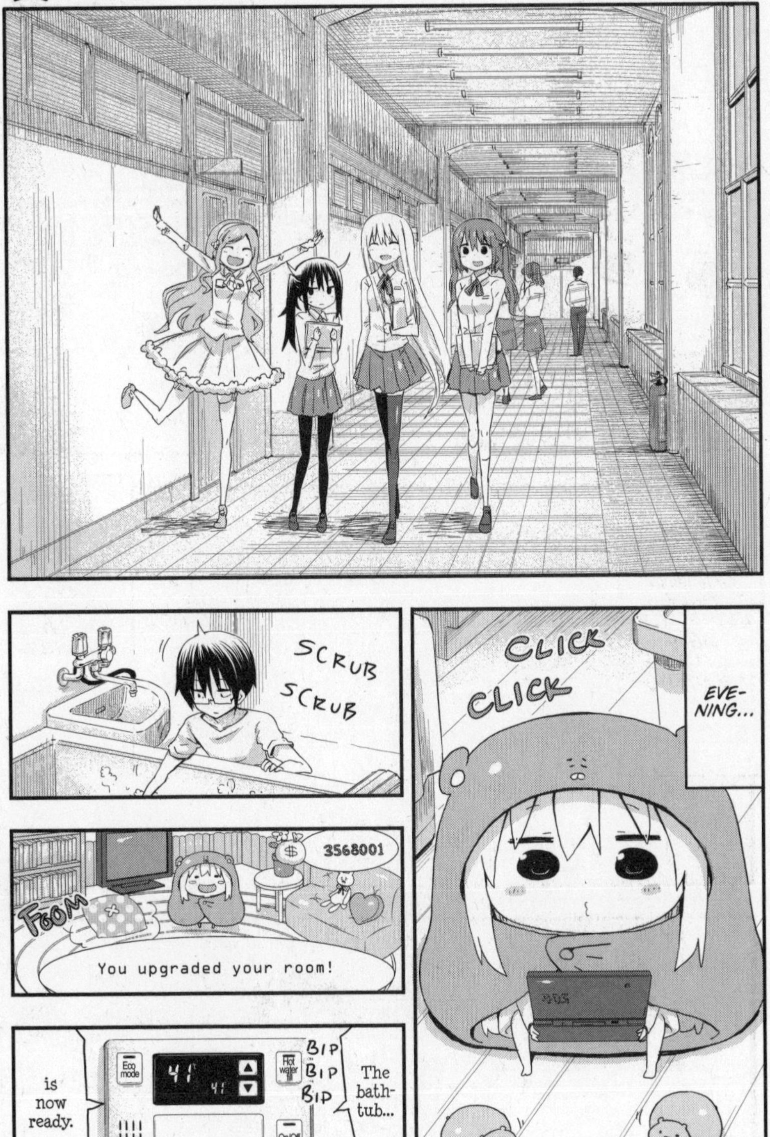
EVE-NING...
CLICK CLICK
SCRUB SCRUB
3568001
FOOM
You upgraded your room!
The bath-tub...
BIP BIP BIP
Eco mode
Hot water fill
On/Off
Ronnai
is now ready.

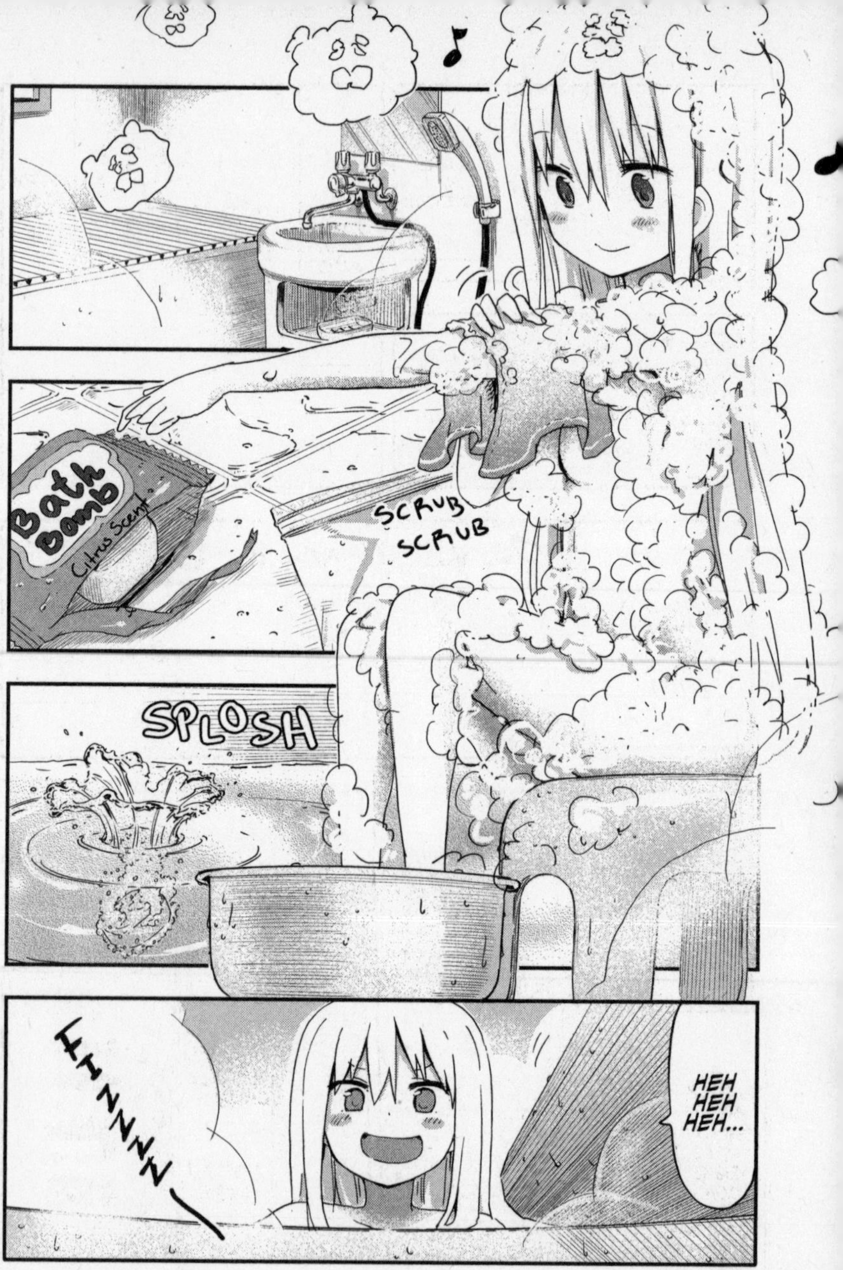
Bath Bomb
Citrus Scent
SCRUB SCRUB
SPLOSH
HEH HEH HEH...
IINNNN—

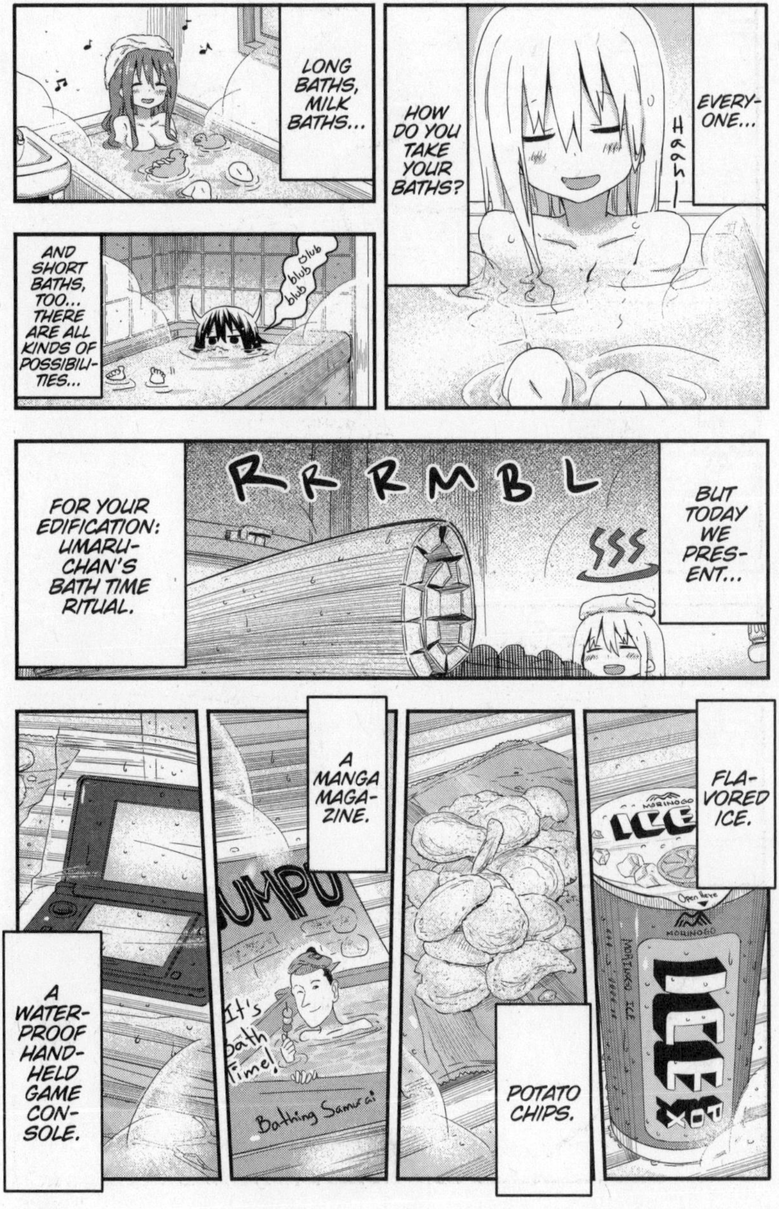
EVERY-ONE...
Haah
HOW DO YOU TAKE YOUR BATHS?
LONG BATHS, MILK BATHS...
AND SHORT BATHS, TOO... THERE ARE ALL KINDS OF POSSIBILITIES...
blub blub blub
BUT TODAY WE PRESENT...
RRRMBL
FOR YOUR EDIFICATION: UMARU-CHAN'S BATH TIME RITUAL.
FLAVORED ICE.
MORINOGO
ICE
Open Here
MORINOGO
ICE
POTATO CHIPS.
A MANGA MAGAZINE.
It's Bath Time!
Bathing Samurai
A WATERPROOF HANDHELD GAME CONSOLE.

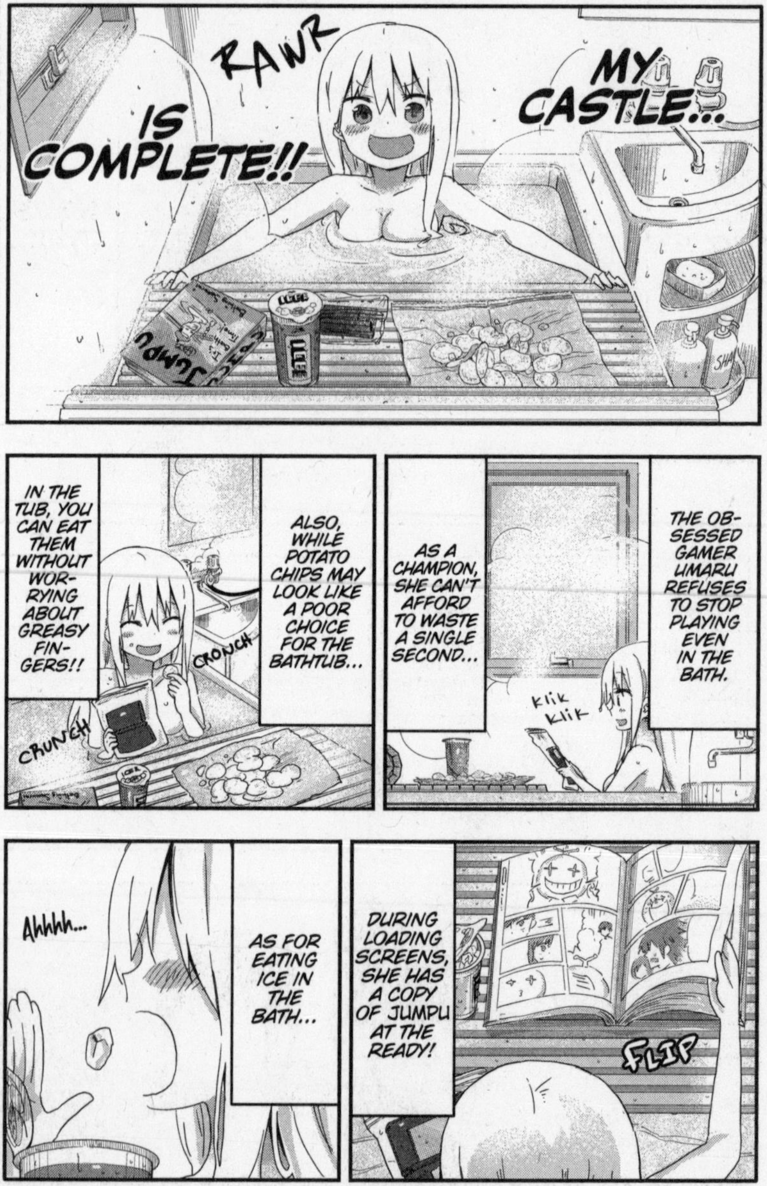
MY CASTLE...
RAWR
IS COMPLETE!!
THE OB-SESSED GAMER UMARU REFUSES TO STOP PLAYING EVEN IN THE BATH.
AS A CHAMPION, SHE CAN'T AFFORD TO WASTE A SINGLE SECOND...
klik klik
ALSO, WHILE POTATO CHIPS MAY LOOK LIKE A POOR CHOICE FOR THE BATHTUB...
IN THE TUB, YOU CAN EAT THEM WITHOUT WOR-RYING ABOUT GREASY FIN-GERS!!
CRUNCH
CRUNCH
DURING LOADING SCREENS, SHE HAS A COPY OF JUMPU AT THE READY!
FLIP
AS FOR EATING ICE IN THE BATH...
Ahhhh...

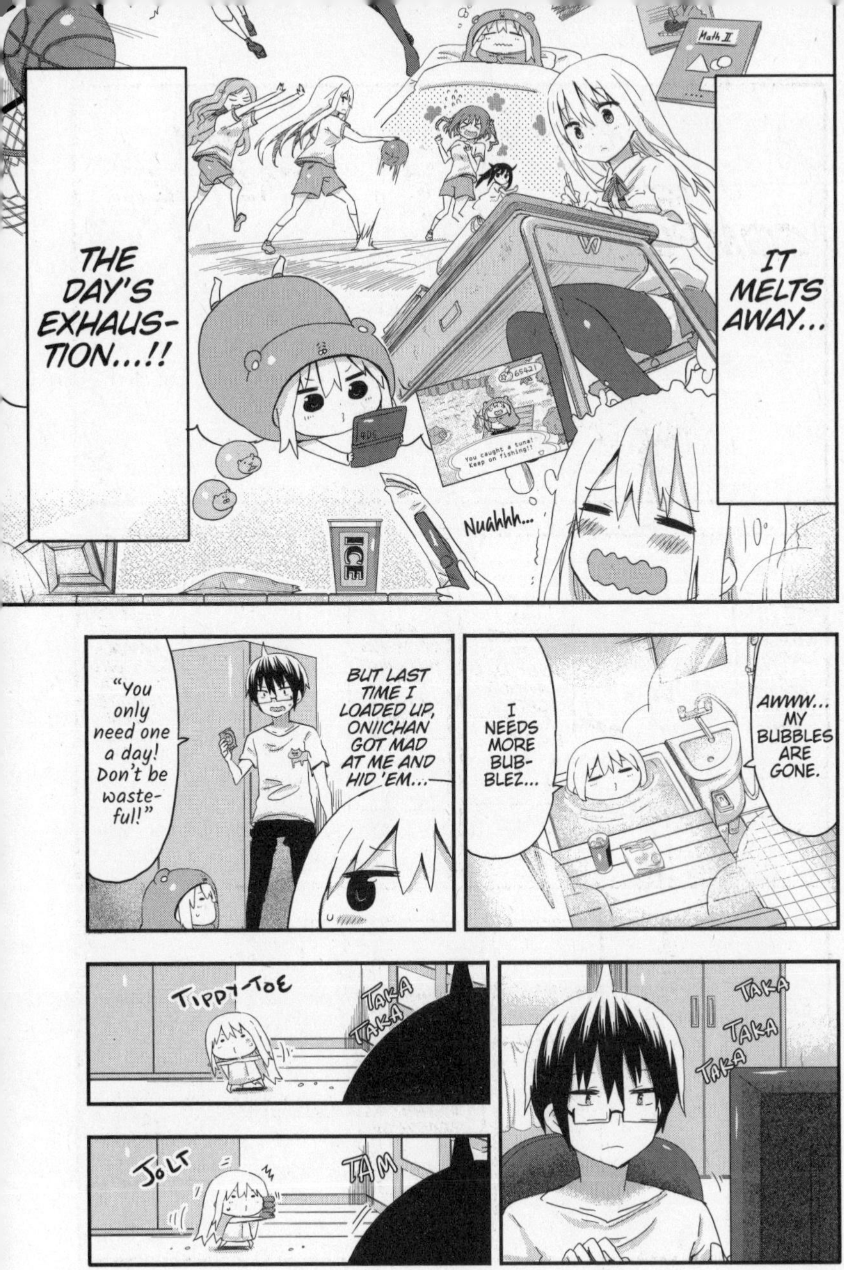
IT MELTS AWAY...
THE DAY'S EXHAUS-TION...!!
Math II
6542
You caught a tuna! Keep on fishing!!
Nuahhh...
ICE
AWWW... MY BUBBLES ARE GONE.
I NEEDS MORE BUB-BLEZ...
BUT LAST TIME I LOADED UP, ONIICHAN GOT MAD AT ME AND HID 'EM...
"You only need one a day! Don't be waste-ful!"
TAKA TAKA TAKA
TAKA TAKA
TIPPY-TOE
TAM
JOLT

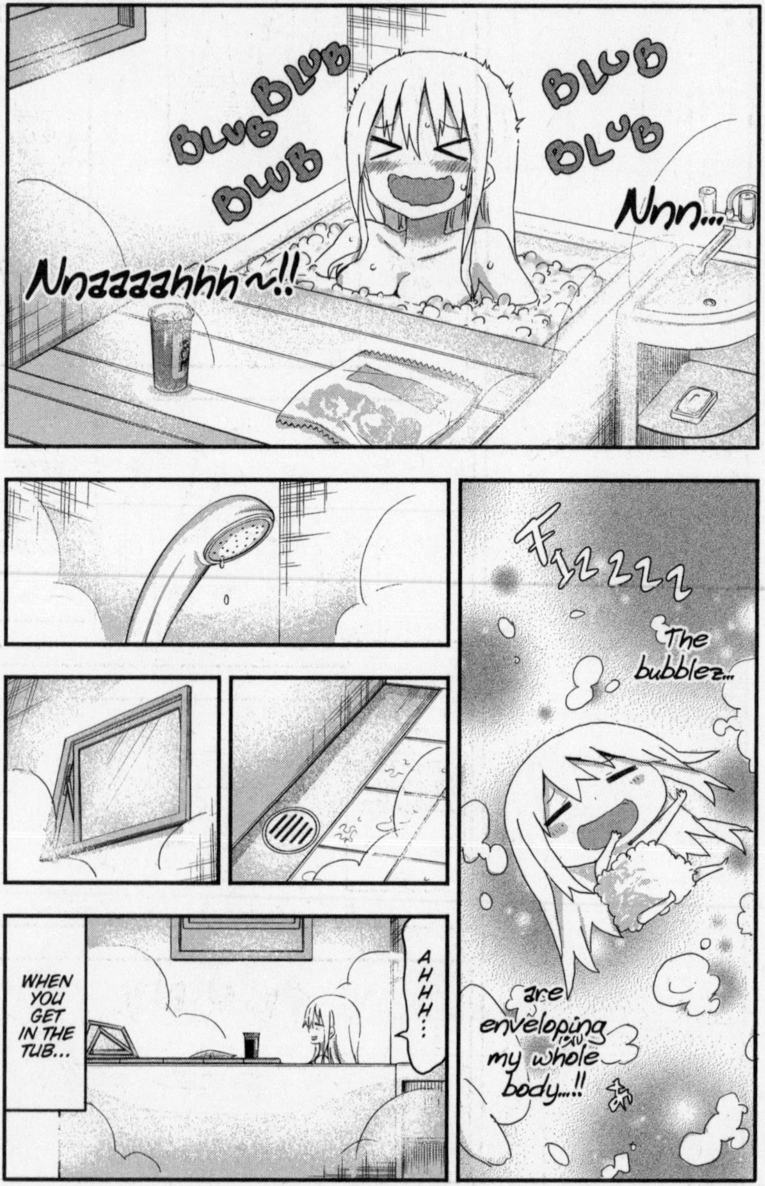
BLUB
BLUB
Nnn...
BLUB
BLUB
BLUB
Nnaaaaahhh~!!
FIZZZZZ
The bubblez...
are enveloping my whole body...!!
AHHH...
WHEN YOU GET IN THE TUB...

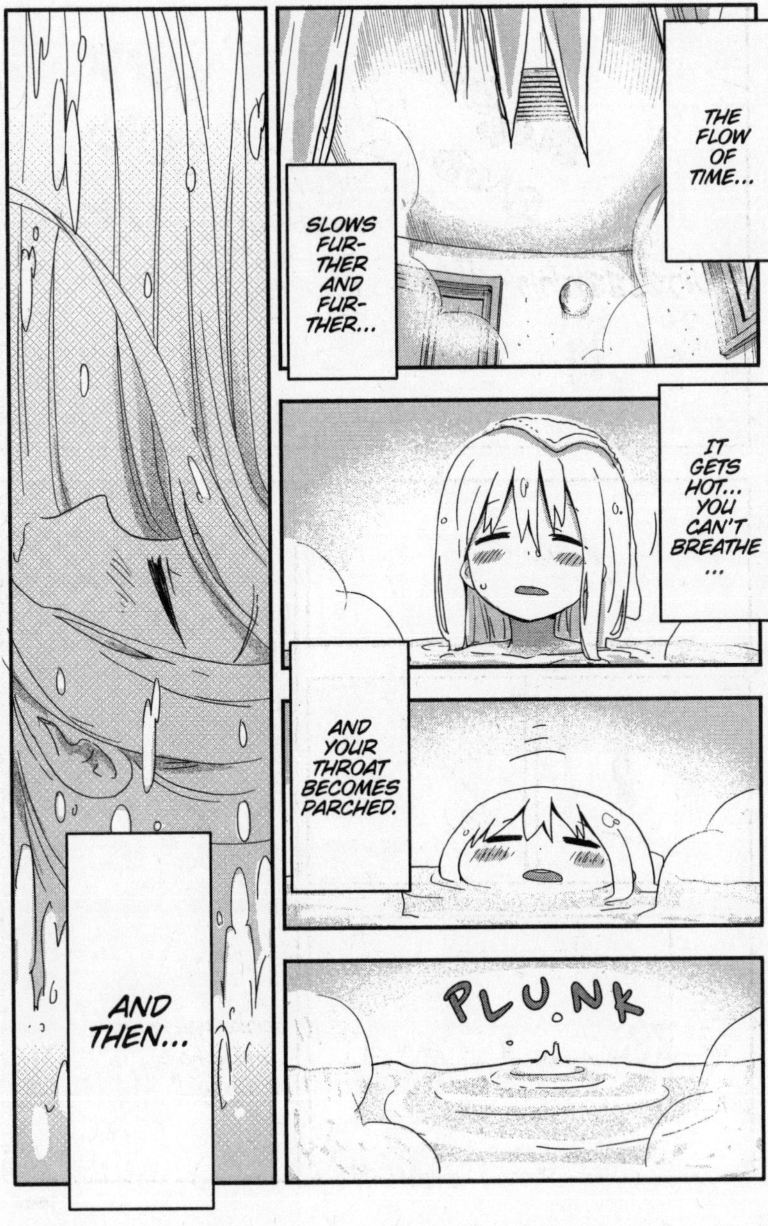
THE FLOW OF TIME...
SLOWS FURTHER AND FURTHER...
IT GETS HOT... YOU CAN'T BREATHE...
AND YOUR THROAT BECOMES PARCHED.
PLUNK
AND THEN...

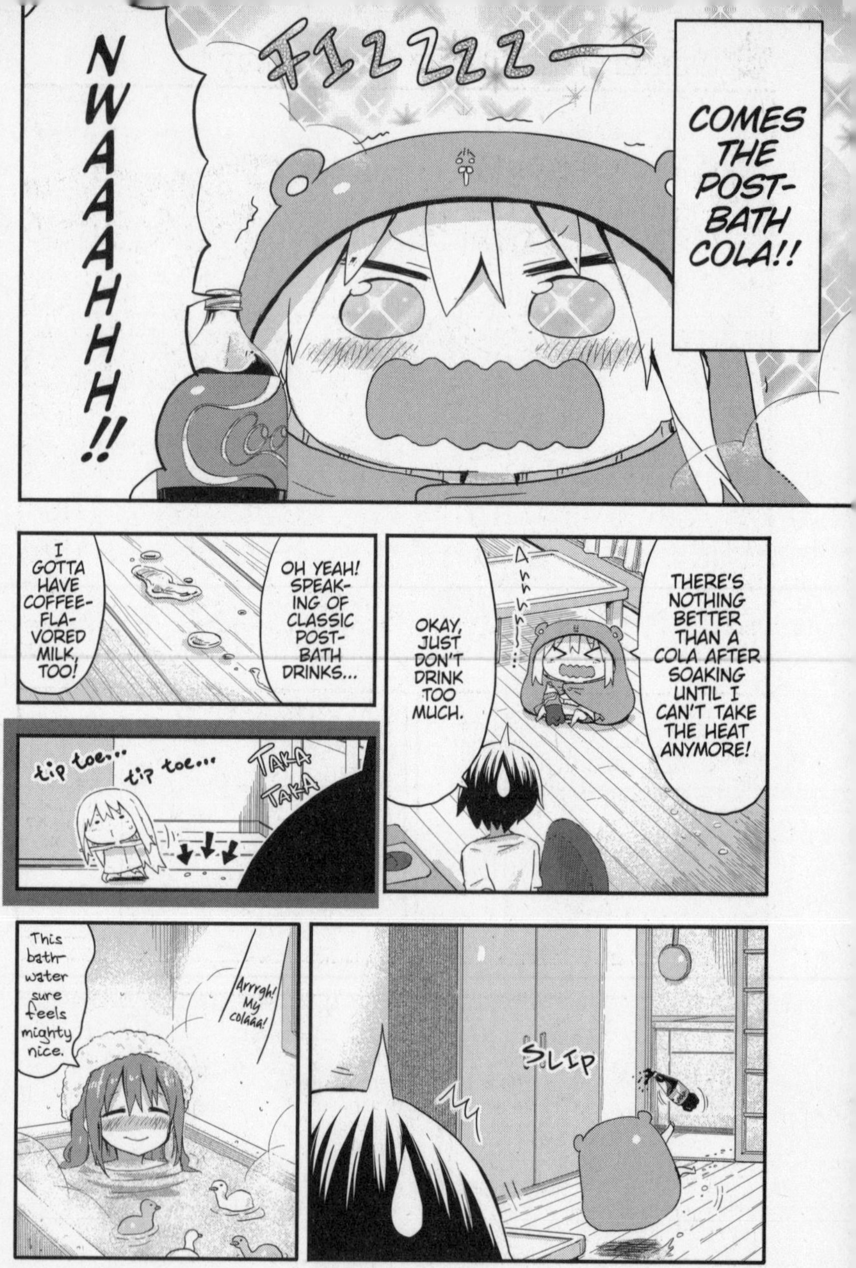
COMES THE POST-BATH COLA!!
FIZZZZZ—
NWAAAAHHHH!!
THERE'S NOTHING BETTER THAN A COLA AFTER SOAKING UNTIL I CAN'T TAKE THE HEAT ANYMORE!
Ahhh—...
OKAY, JUST DON'T DRINK TOO MUCH.
OH YEAH! SPEAKING OF CLASSIC POST-BATH DRINKS...
I GOTTA HAVE COFFEE-FLAVORED MILK, TOO!
TAKA TAKA
tip toe... tip toe...
SLIP
Arrrgh! My colaaa!
This bath water sure feels mighty nice.

No. 65 Umaru & the Penny Candy Shop

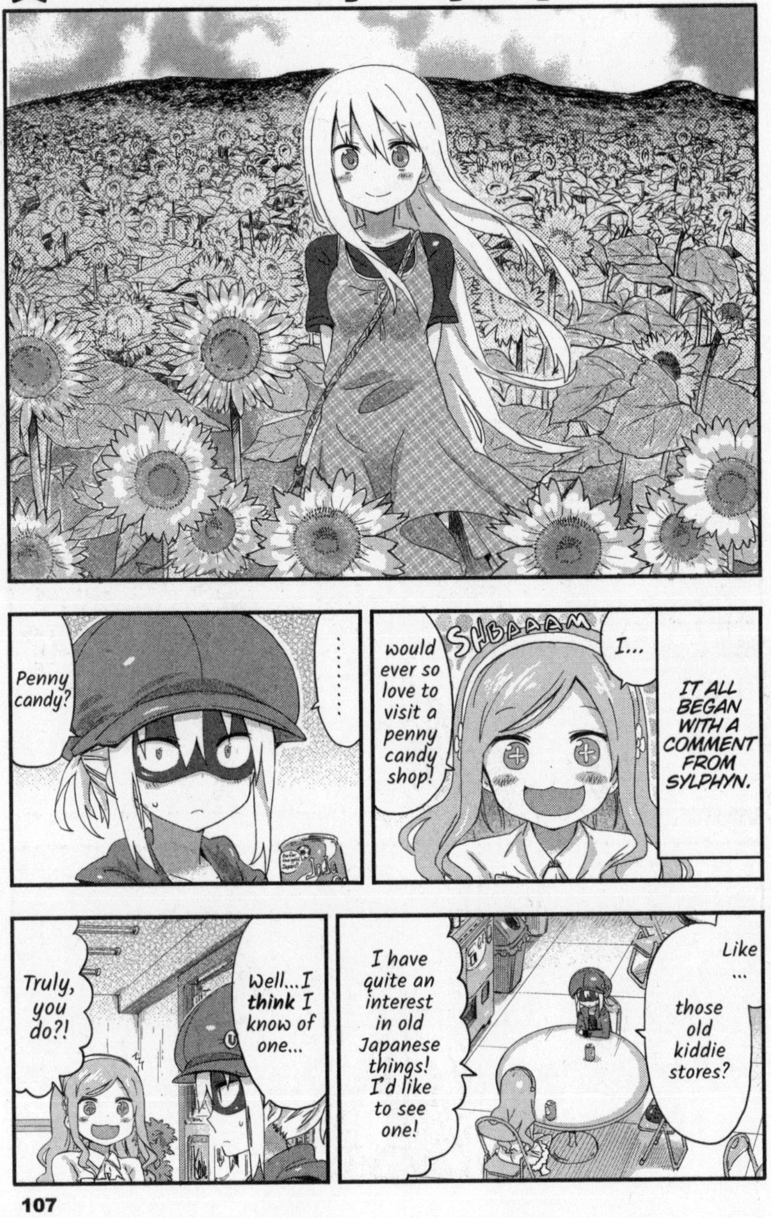

IT ALL BEGAN WITH A COMMENT FROM SYLPHYN.
I...
SHBAAAM
would ever so love to visit a penny candy shop!
......
Penny candy?
Like ... those old kiddie stores?
I have quite an interest in old Japanese things! I'd like to see one!
Well...I **think** I know of one...
Truly, you do?!

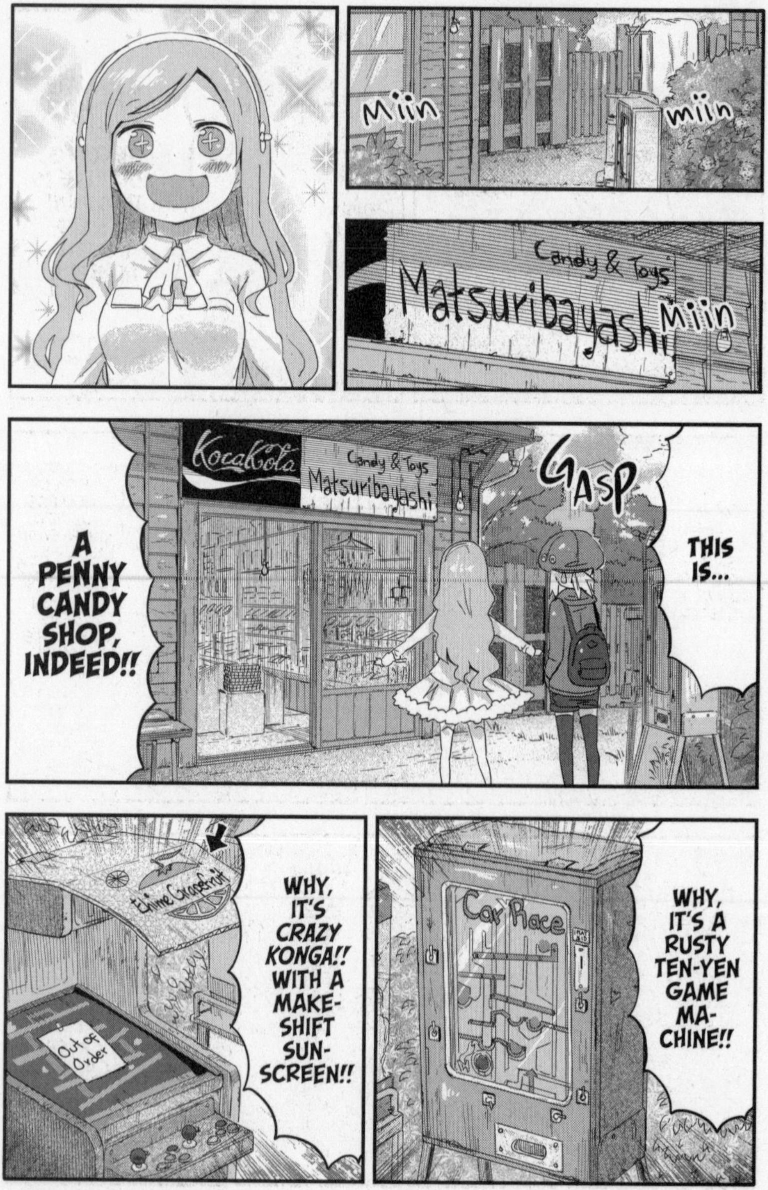
miin
Miin
Candy & Toys
Matsuribayashi
Miin
KocaKola
Candy & Toys
Matsuribayashi
GASP
THIS IS...
A PENNY CANDY SHOP, INDEED!!
Car Race
WHY, IT'S A RUSTY TEN-YEN GAME MA-CHINE!!
Ehime Grapefruit
Out of Order
WHY, IT'S CRAZY KONGA!! WITH A MAKE-SHIFT SUN-SCREEN!!

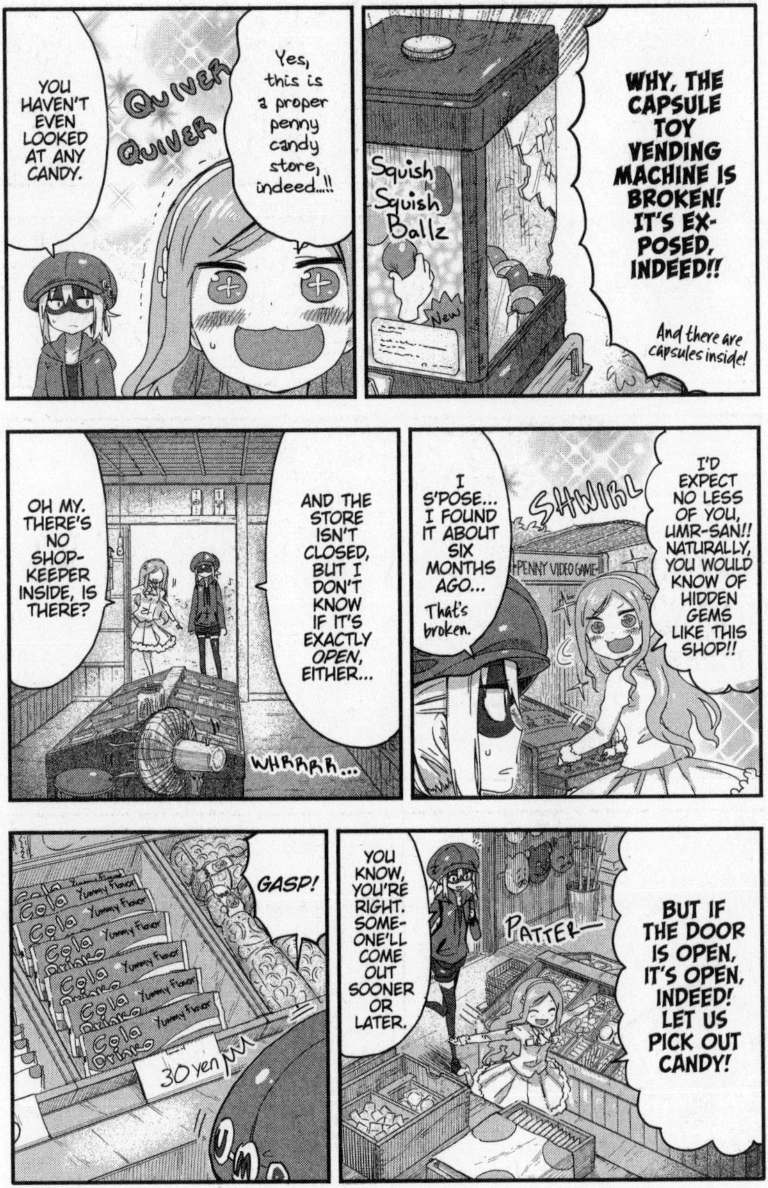
WHY, THE CAPSULE TOY VENDING MACHINE IS BROKEN! IT'S EXPOSED, INDEED!!
Squish Squish Ballz
And there are capsules inside!
New
Yes, this is a proper penny candy store, indeed...!!
QUIVER QUIVER
YOU HAVEN'T EVEN LOOKED AT ANY CANDY.
I'D EXPECT NO LESS OF YOU, UMR-SAN!! NATURALLY, YOU WOULD KNOW OF HIDDEN GEMS LIKE THIS SHOP!!
SHWIRL
I S'POSE... I FOUND IT ABOUT SIX MONTHS AGO...
PENNY VIDEO GAME
That's broken.
AND THE STORE ISN'T CLOSED, BUT I DON'T KNOW IF IT'S EXACTLY OPEN, EITHER...
OH MY. THERE'S NO SHOPKEEPER INSIDE, IS THERE?
WHRRRR...
BUT IF THE DOOR IS OPEN, IT'S OPEN, INDEED! LET US PICK OUT CANDY!
PATTER—
YOU KNOW, YOU'RE RIGHT. SOMEONE'LL COME OUT SOONER OR LATER.
GASP!
Cola Drinko Yummy Flavor
30 yen

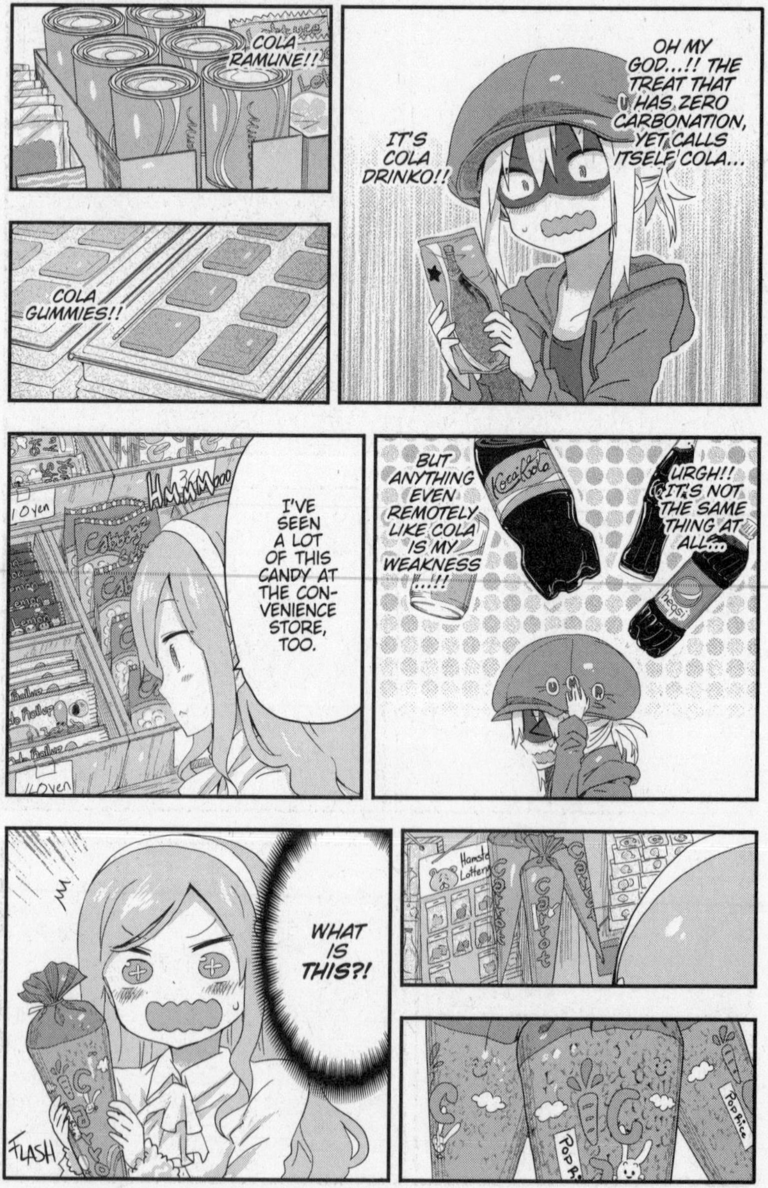
OH MY GOD...!! THE TREAT THAT HAS ZERO CARBONATION, YET CALLS ITSELF COLA...
IT'S COLA DRINKO!!
COLA RAMUNE!!
COLA GUMMIES!!
URGH!! IT'S NOT THE SAME THING AT ALL...
BUT ANYTHING EVEN REMOTELY LIKE COLA IS MY WEAKNESS...!!
Koca Kola
I'VE SEEN A LOT OF THIS CANDY AT THE CON-VENIENCE STORE, TOO.
HMMMMooo
10yen
10yen
Hamster Lottery
Carrot
Pop Rice
WHAT IS THIS?!
FLASH

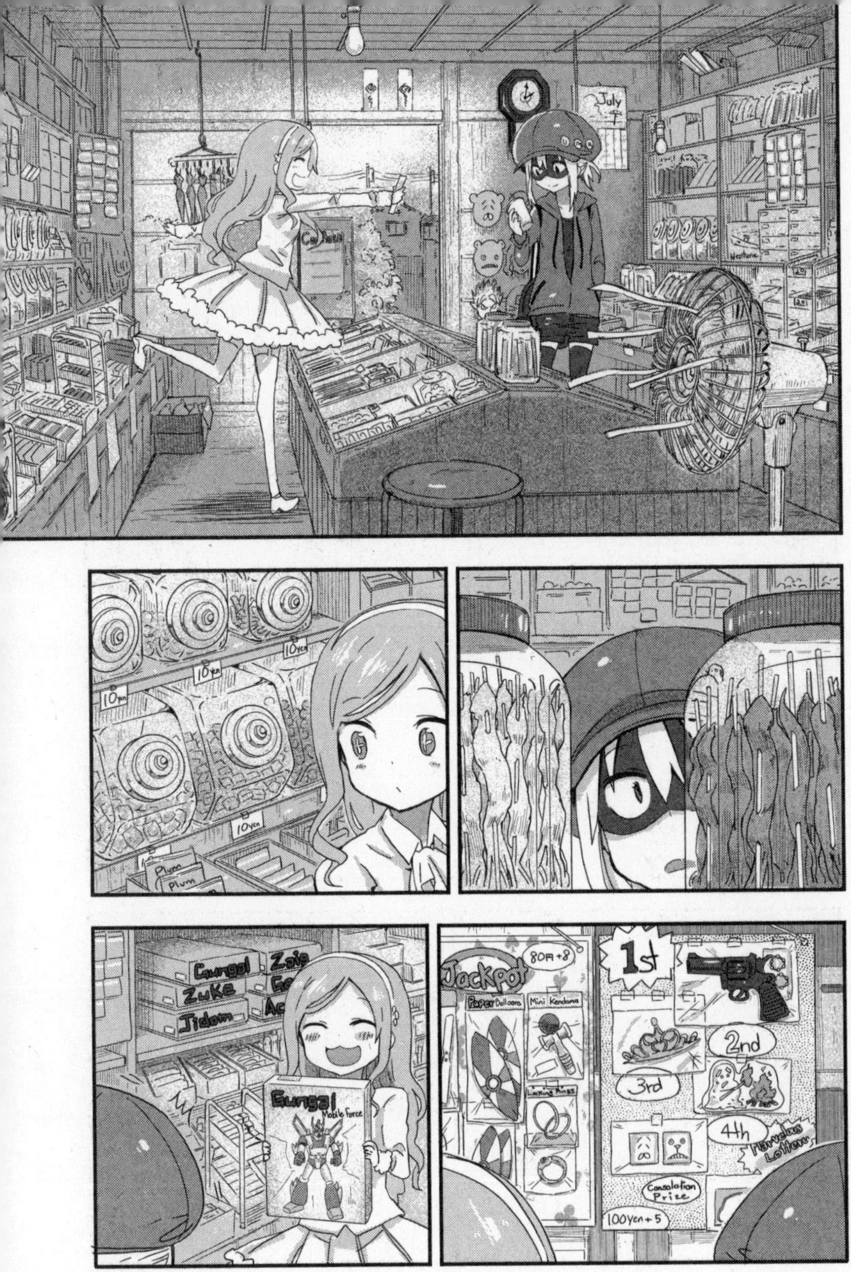
July
10yen
10yen
10yen
10yen
Plum
Plum
Jackpot
80円+8
Paper Balloons
Mini Kendama
Linking Rings
1st
2nd
3rd
4h
Marvelous Lottery
Consolation Prize
100yen+5
Gungal
Zaig
Zuke
Jidom
Gungal
Mobile Force

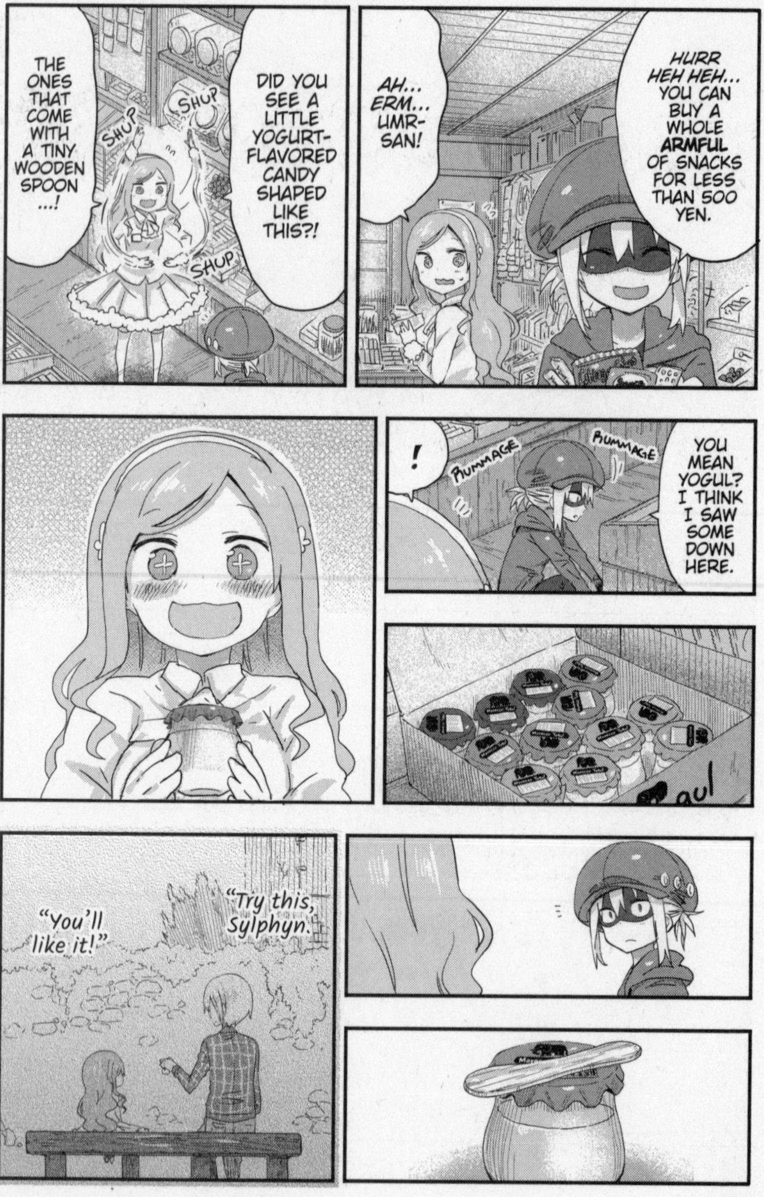
HURR HEH HEH... YOU CAN BUY A WHOLE **ARMFUL** OF SNACKS FOR LESS THAN 500 YEN.
AH... ERM... UMR-SAN!
DID YOU SEE A LITTLE YOGURT-FLAVORED CANDY SHAPED LIKE THIS?!
SHUP
THE ONES THAT COME WITH A TINY WOODEN SPOON ...!
SHUP
SHUP
YOU MEAN YOGUL? I THINK I SAW SOME DOWN HERE.
RUMMAGE
RUMMAGE
!
"Try this, Sylphyn."
"You'll like it!"

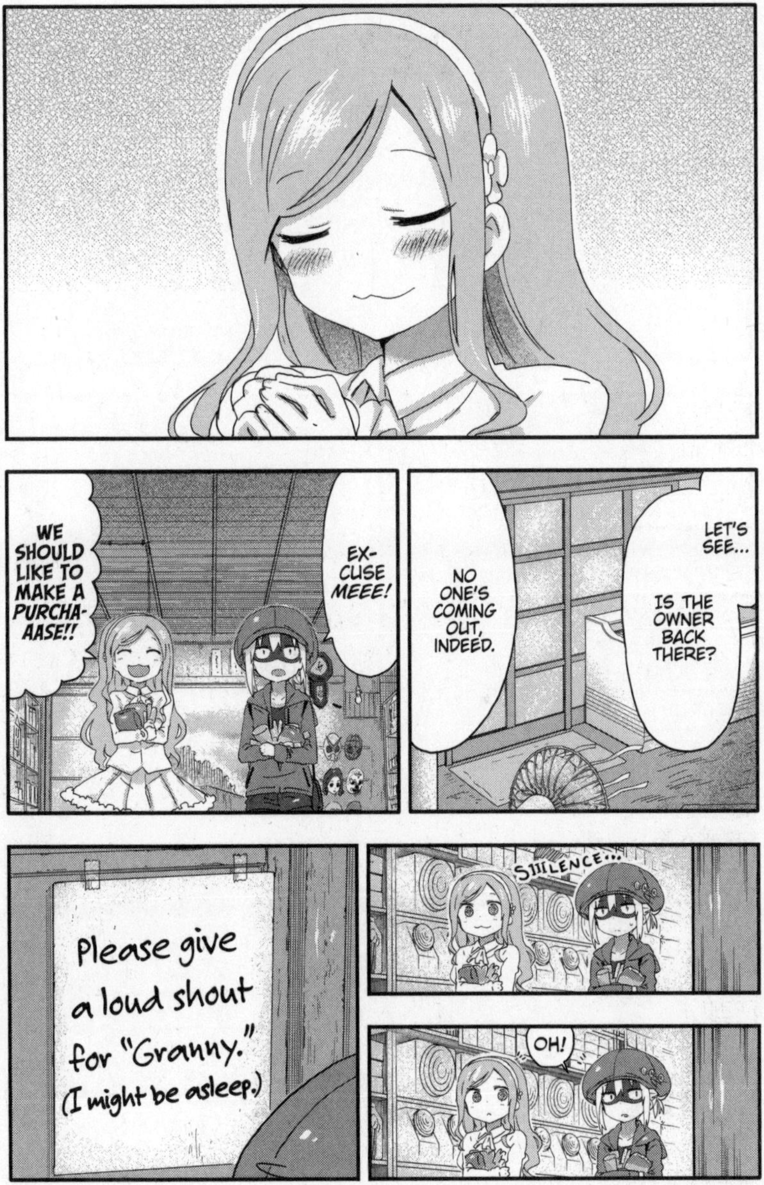
LET'S SEE...
IS THE OWNER BACK THERE?
NO ONE'S COMING OUT, INDEED.
EX-CUSE MEEE!
WE SHOULD LIKE TO MAKE A PURCHA-AASE!!
SIIILENCE...
OH!
Please give a loud shout for "Granny."
(I might be asleep.)

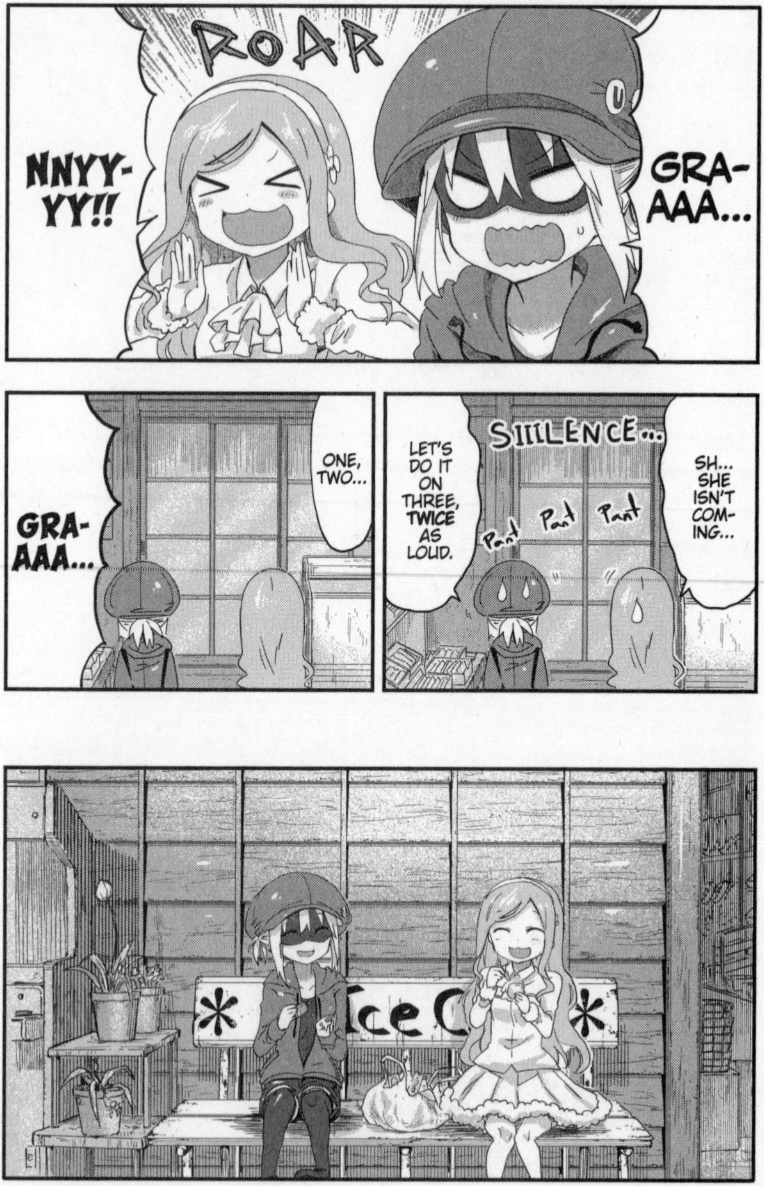
ROAR
GRA-AAA...
NNYY-YY!!
SH... SHE ISN'T COMING...
SIIILENCE...
Pant Pant Pant Pant
LET'S DO IT ON THREE, TWICE AS LOUD.
ONE, TWO...
GRA-AAA...
Ice C

Granny

HIMOUTO! UMARU-CHAN

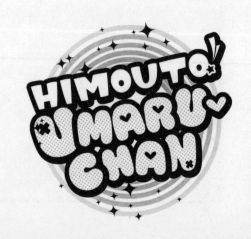

No. 66 Umaru & Packing

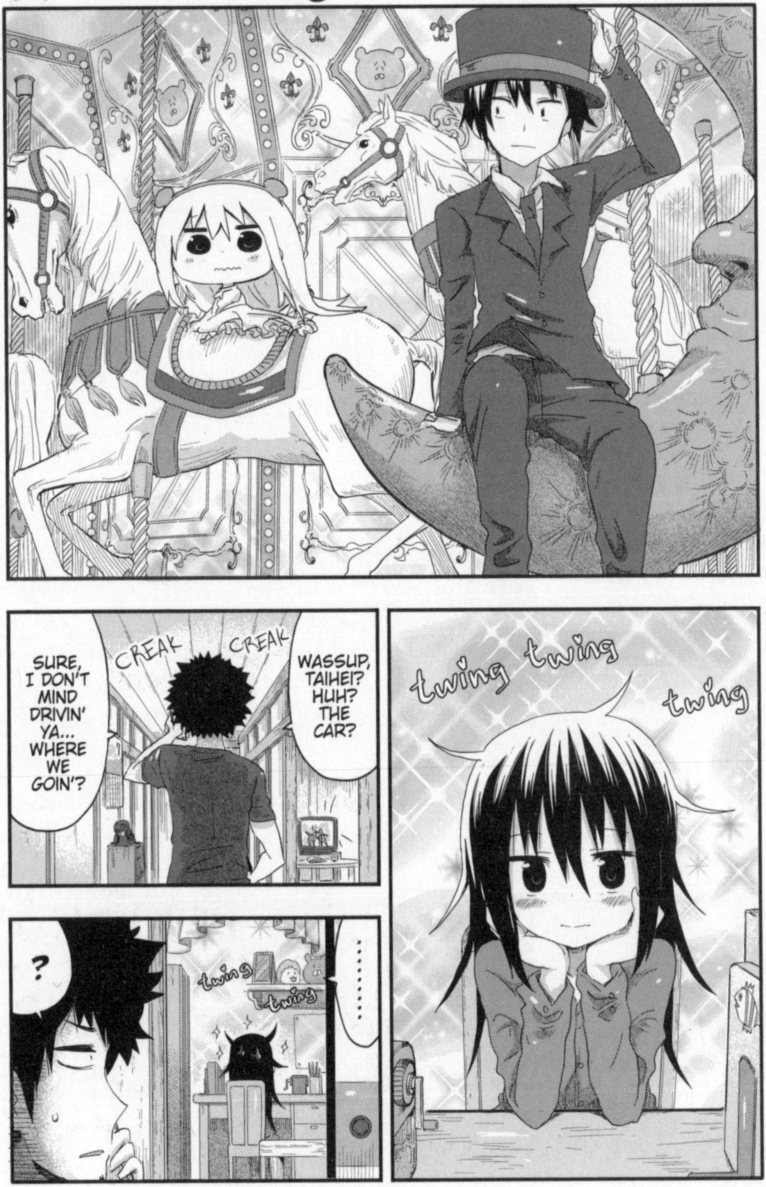
twing twing
twing
WASSUP, TAIHEI? HUH? THE CAR?
CREAK CREAK
SURE, I DON'T MIND DRIVIN' YA... WHERE WE GOIN'?
....
twing twing
?

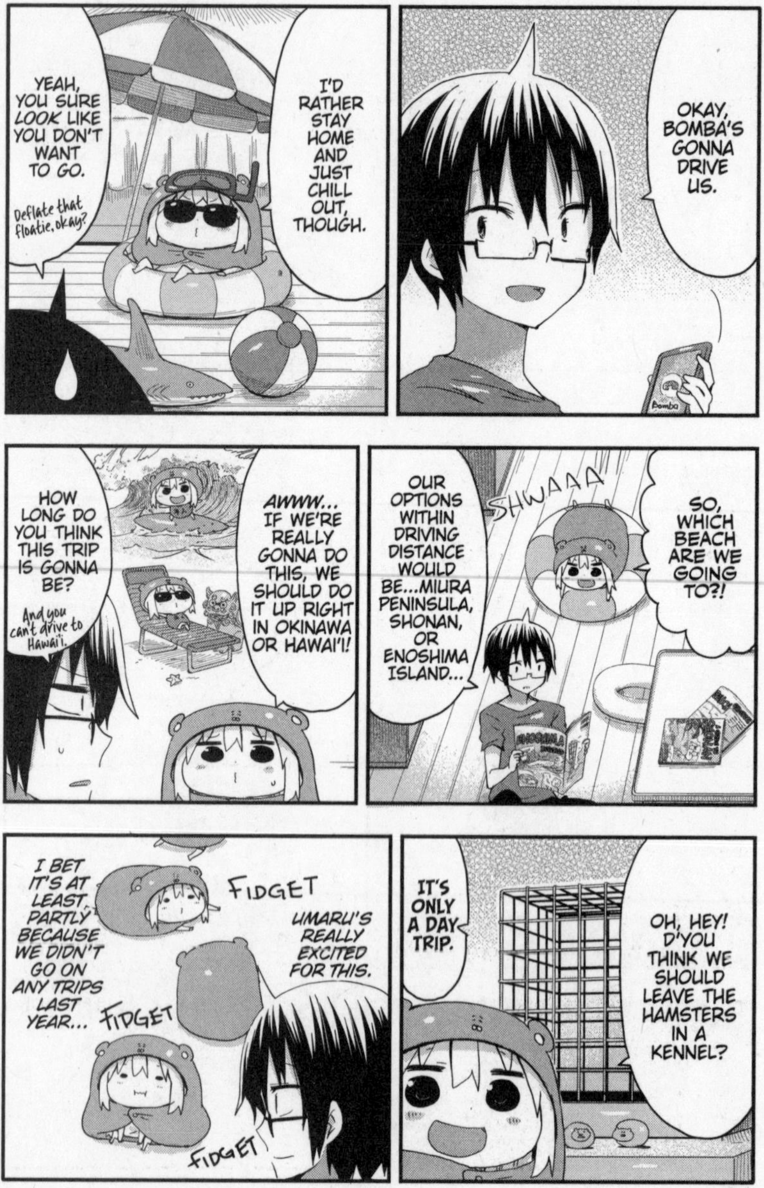
OKAY, BOMBA'S GONNA DRIVE US.
Bomba
I'D RATHER STAY HOME AND JUST CHILL OUT, THOUGH.
YEAH, YOU SURE *LOOK* LIKE YOU DON'T WANT TO GO.
Deflate that floatie, okay?
SO, WHICH BEACH ARE WE GOING TO?!
SHWAAA
OUR OPTIONS WITHIN DRIVING DISTANCE WOULD BE...MIURA PENINSULA, SHONAN, OR ENOSHIMA ISLAND...
AWWW... IF WE'RE REALLY GONNA DO THIS, WE SHOULD DO IT UP RIGHT IN OKINAWA OR HAWAI'I!
HOW LONG DO YOU THINK THIS TRIP IS GONNA BE?
And you can't drive to Hawaii.
OH, HEY! D'YOU THINK WE SHOULD LEAVE THE HAMSTERS IN A KENNEL?
IT'S ONLY A DAY TRIP.
FIDGET
UMARU'S REALLY EXCITED FOR THIS.
I BET IT'S AT LEAST PARTLY BECAUSE WE DIDN'T GO ON ANY TRIPS LAST YEAR...
FIDGET
FIDGET

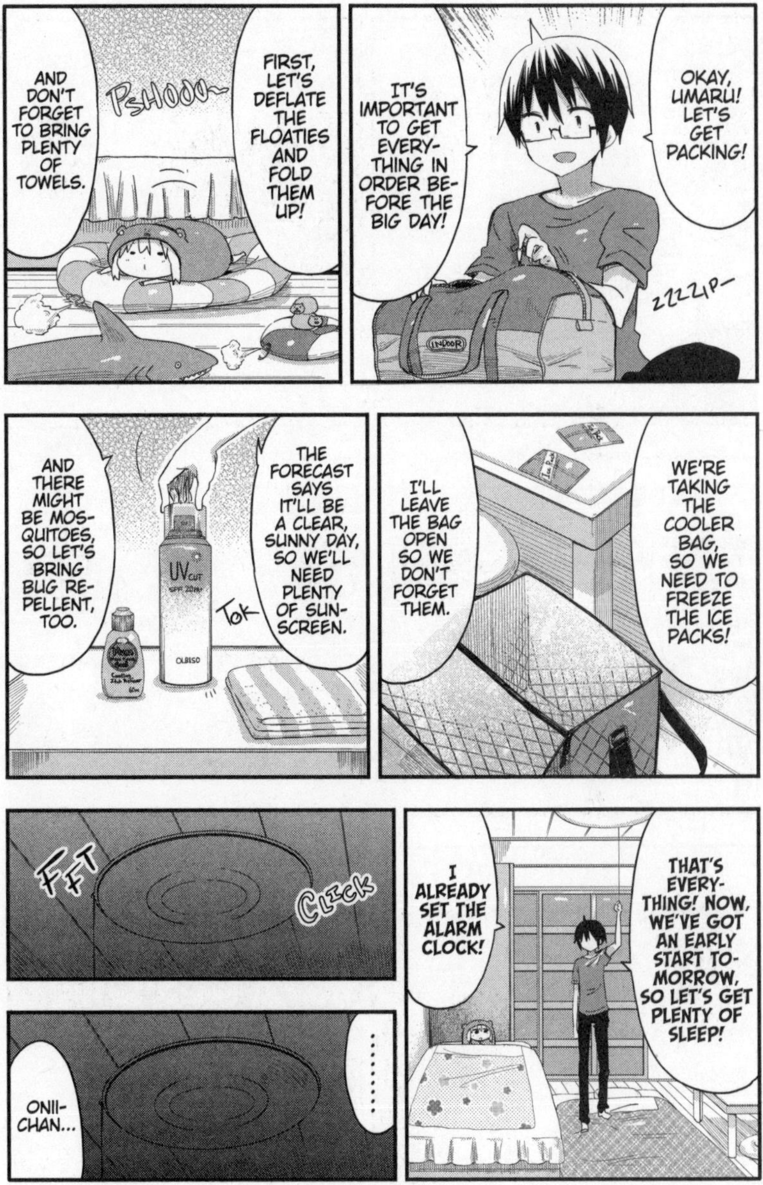
OKAY, UMARU! LET'S GET PACKING!
IT'S IMPORTANT TO GET EVERYTHING IN ORDER BEFORE THE BIG DAY!
ZZZZIP—
INDOOR
FIRST, LET'S DEFLATE THE FLOATIES AND FOLD THEM UP!
PSHOOO~
AND DON'T FORGET TO BRING PLENTY OF TOWELS.
WE'RE TAKING THE COOLER BAG, SO WE NEED TO FREEZE THE ICE PACKS!
I'LL LEAVE THE BAG OPEN SO WE DON'T FORGET THEM.
THE FORECAST SAYS IT'LL BE A CLEAR, SUNNY DAY, SO WE'LL NEED PLENTY OF SUNSCREEN.
TOK
UV CUT
OLBISO
AND THERE MIGHT BE MOSQUITOES, SO LET'S BRING BUG REPELLENT, TOO.
THAT'S EVERYTHING! NOW, WE'VE GOT AN EARLY START TOMORROW, SO LET'S GET PLENTY OF SLEEP!
I ALREADY SET THE ALARM CLOCK!
CLICK
FFT
....
ONII-CHAN...

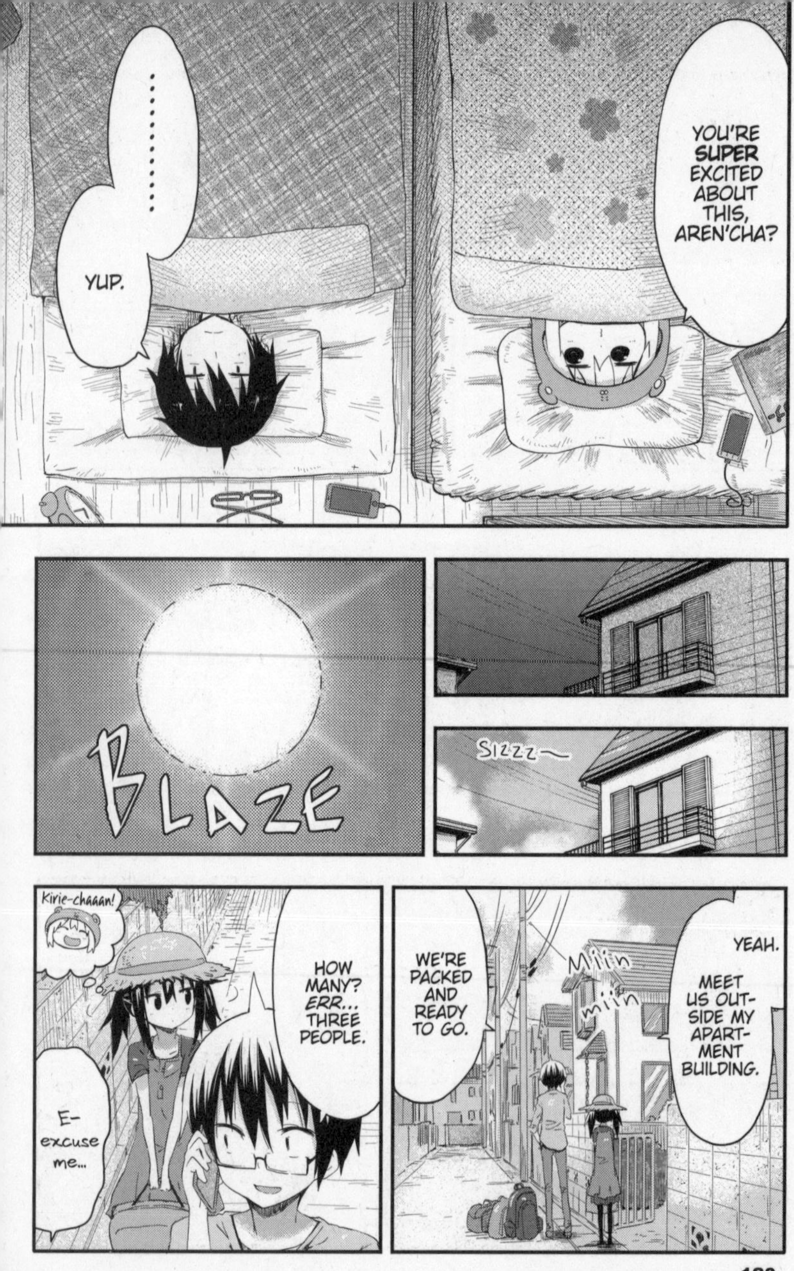
YOU'RE SUPER EXCITED ABOUT THIS, AREN'CHA?
......
YUP.
SIZZZ~
BLAZE
YEAH.
MEET US OUT-SIDE MY APART-MENT BUILDING.
Miin miin
WE'RE PACKED AND READY TO GO.
HOW MANY? ERR... THREE PEOPLE.
Kirie-chaaan!
E-excuse me...

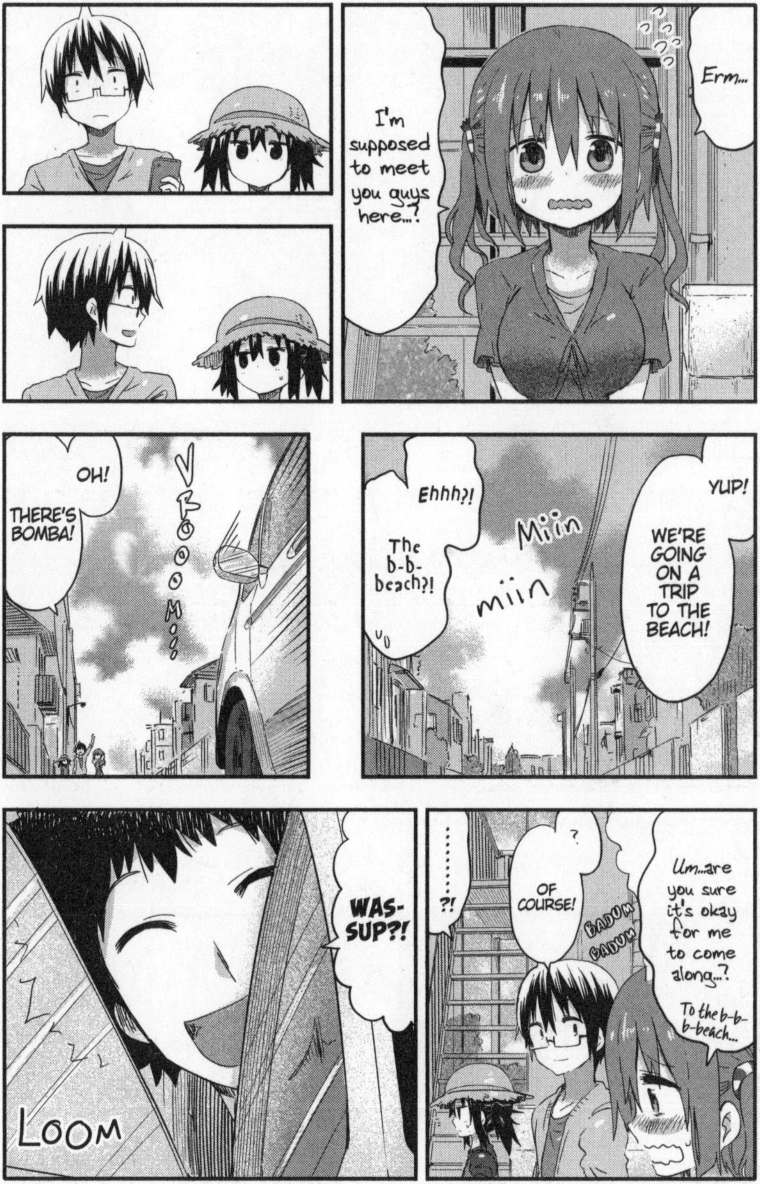
Erm...
I'm supposed to meet you guys here...?
YUP!
WE'RE GOING ON A TRIP TO THE BEACH!
Miin
miin
Ehhh?!
The b-b-beach?!
OH!
THERE'S BOMBA!
VROOOOM...
Um...are you sure it's okay for me to come along...?
To the b-b-b-beach...
BADUM BADUM
?
OF COURSE!
......?!
WAS-SUP?!
LOOM

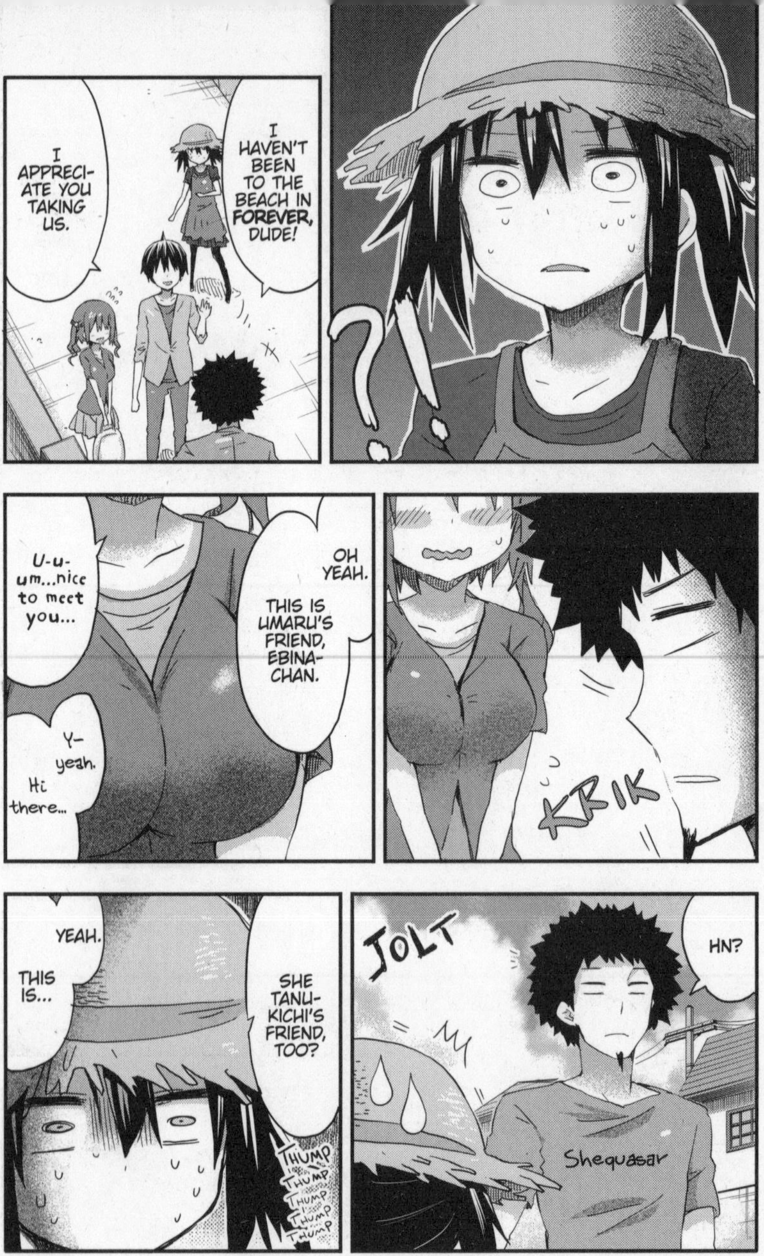
I HAVEN'T BEEN TO THE BEACH IN **FOREVER**, DUDE!
I APPRECIATE YOU TAKING US.
KRIK
OH YEAH.
THIS IS UMARU'S FRIEND, EBINA-CHAN.
U-u-um...nice to meet you...
Y-yeah.
Hi there...
HN?
JOLT
Shequasar
SHE TANUKICHI'S FRIEND, TOO?
YEAH.
THIS IS...
THUMP THUMP THUMP THUMP THUMP

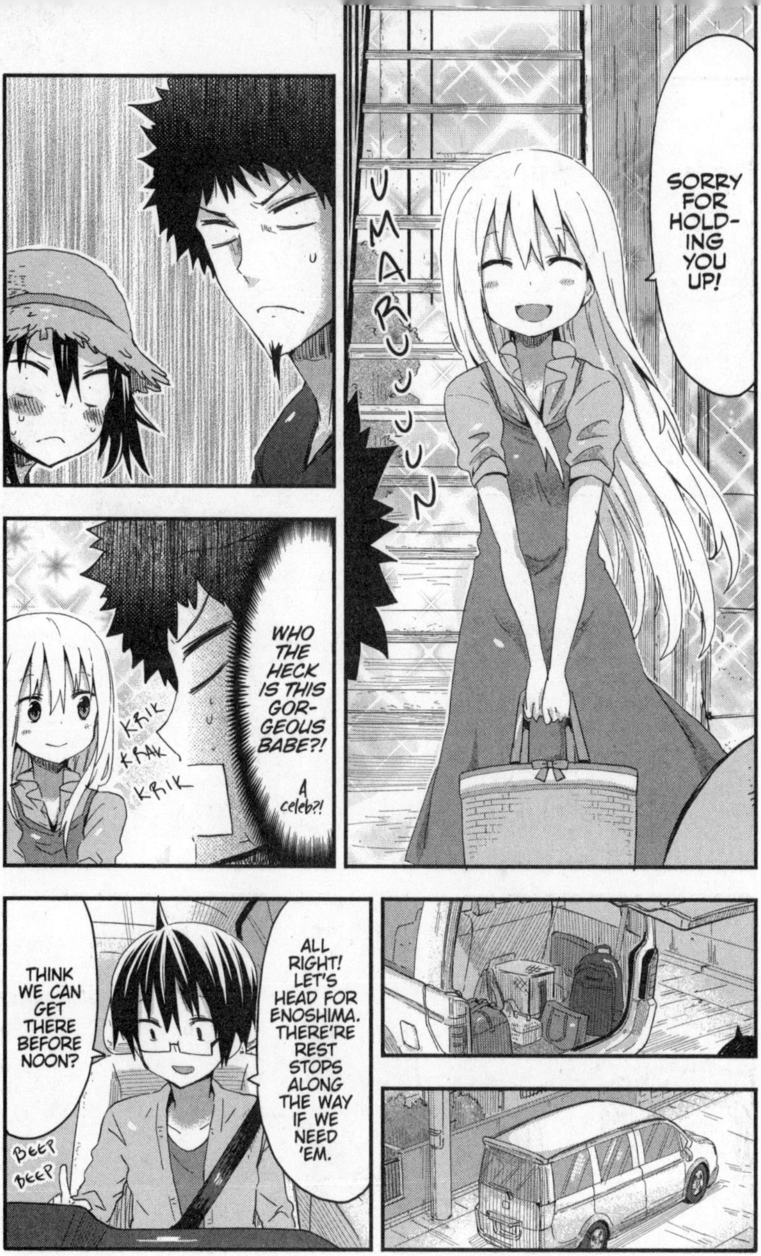

SORRY FOR HOLDING YOU UP!
UMARUUUN
WHO THE HECK IS THIS GORGEOUS BABE?!
A celeb?!
KRIK KRAK KRIK
ALL RIGHT! LET'S HEAD FOR ENOSHIMA. THERE'RE REST STOPS ALONG THE WAY IF WE NEED 'EM.
THINK WE CAN GET THERE BEFORE NOON?
BEEP BEEP

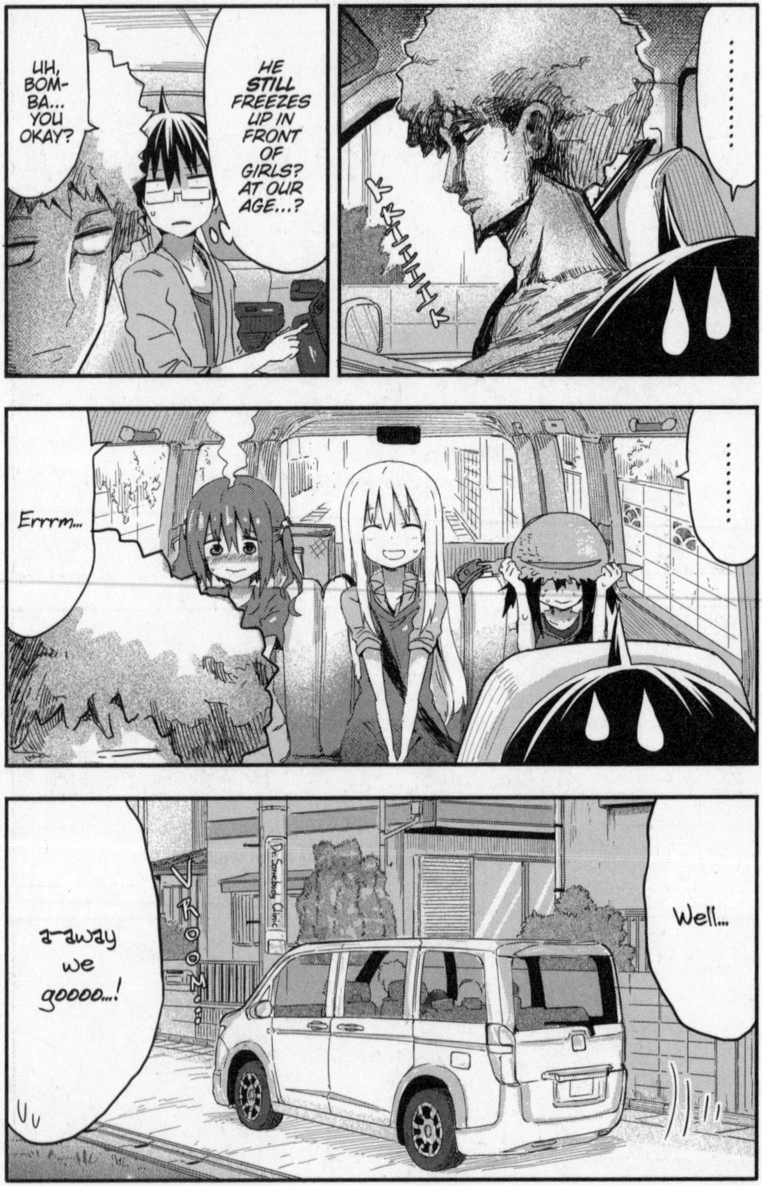
......
KRIIIIIIK
HE STILL FREEZES UP IN FRONT OF GIRLS? AT OUR AGE...?
UH, BOMBA... YOU OKAY?
......
Errrm...
Well...
Dr. Somebody Clinic
VROOM...
a-away we goooo...!

No. 67 Umaru & the Beach Part 1

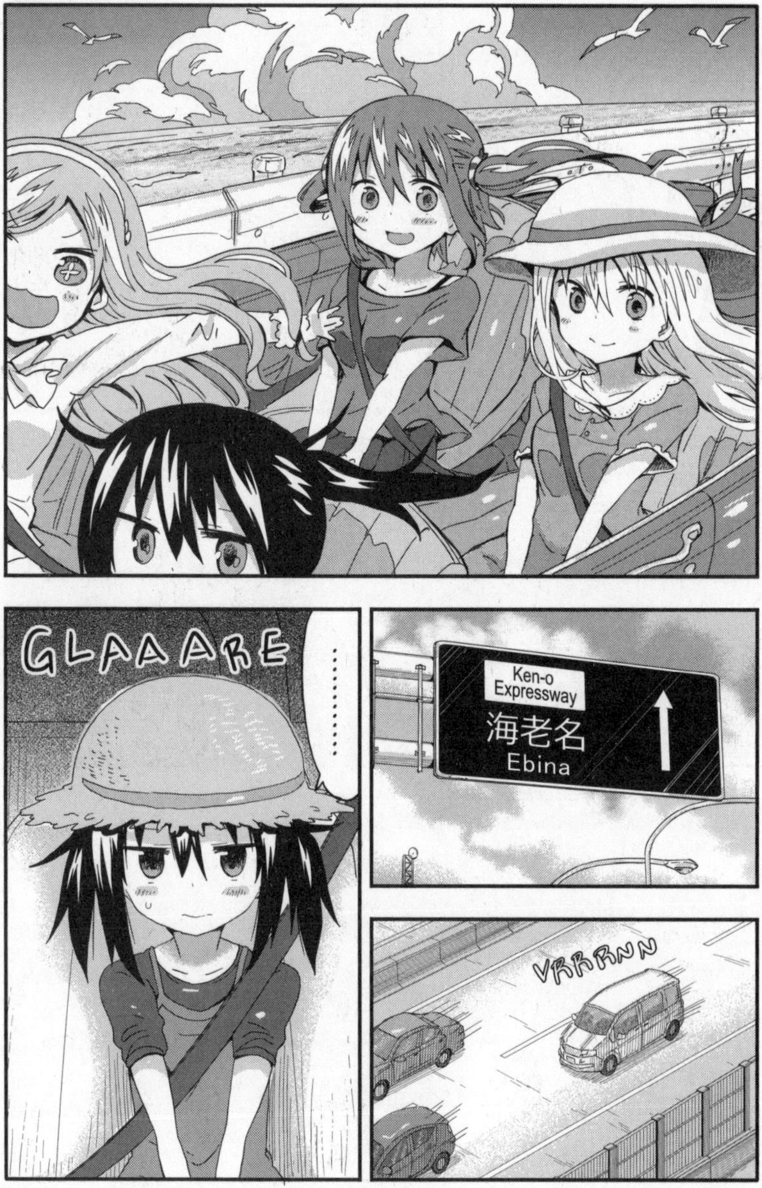
Ken-o Expressway
海老名
Ebina
VRRRNN
GLAAARE
......

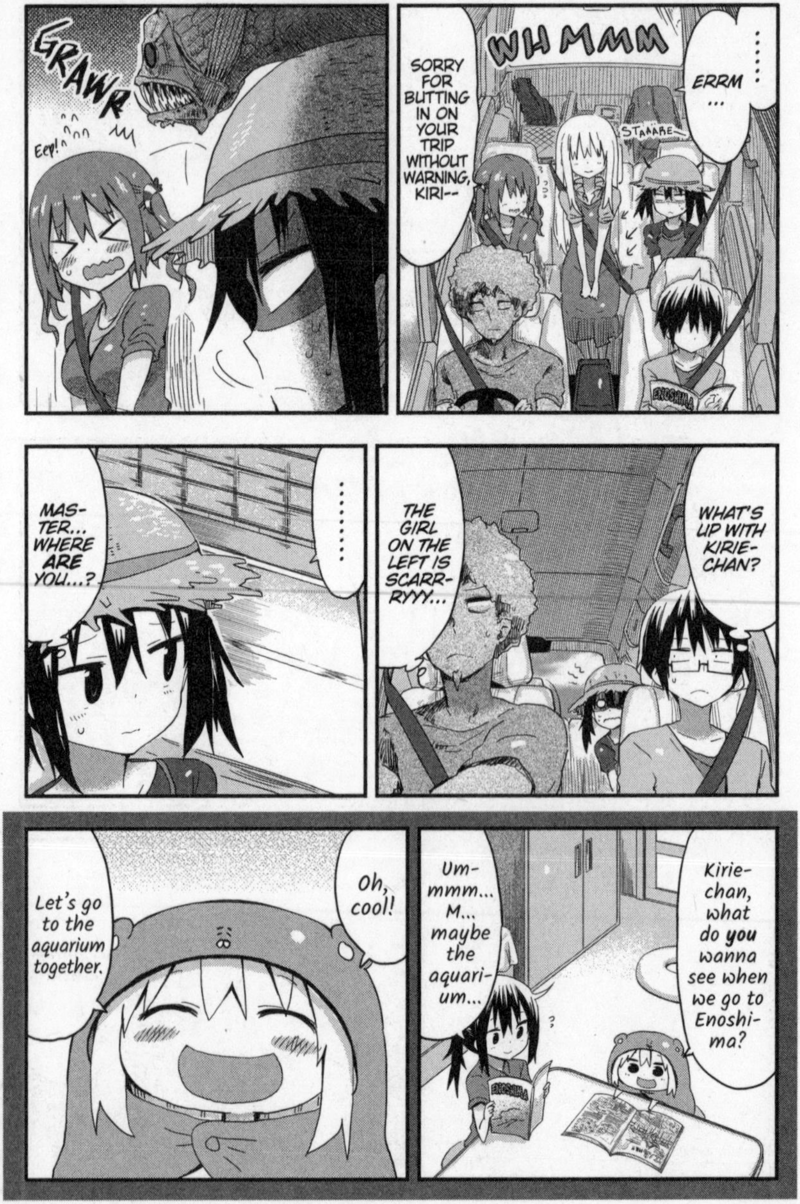
......
ERRM...
STAAARE
WH MMM
SORRY FOR BUTTING IN ON YOUR TRIP WITHOUT WARNING, KIRI--
ENOSHIMA
GRAWR
Eep!
WHAT'S UP WITH KIRIE-CHAN?
THE GIRL ON THE LEFT IS SCARRRYYY...
......
MASTER... WHERE ARE YOU...?
Kirie-chan, what do you wanna see when we go to Enoshima?
Um-mmm... M... maybe the aquarium...
ENOSHIMA
Oh, cool!
Let's go to the aquarium together.

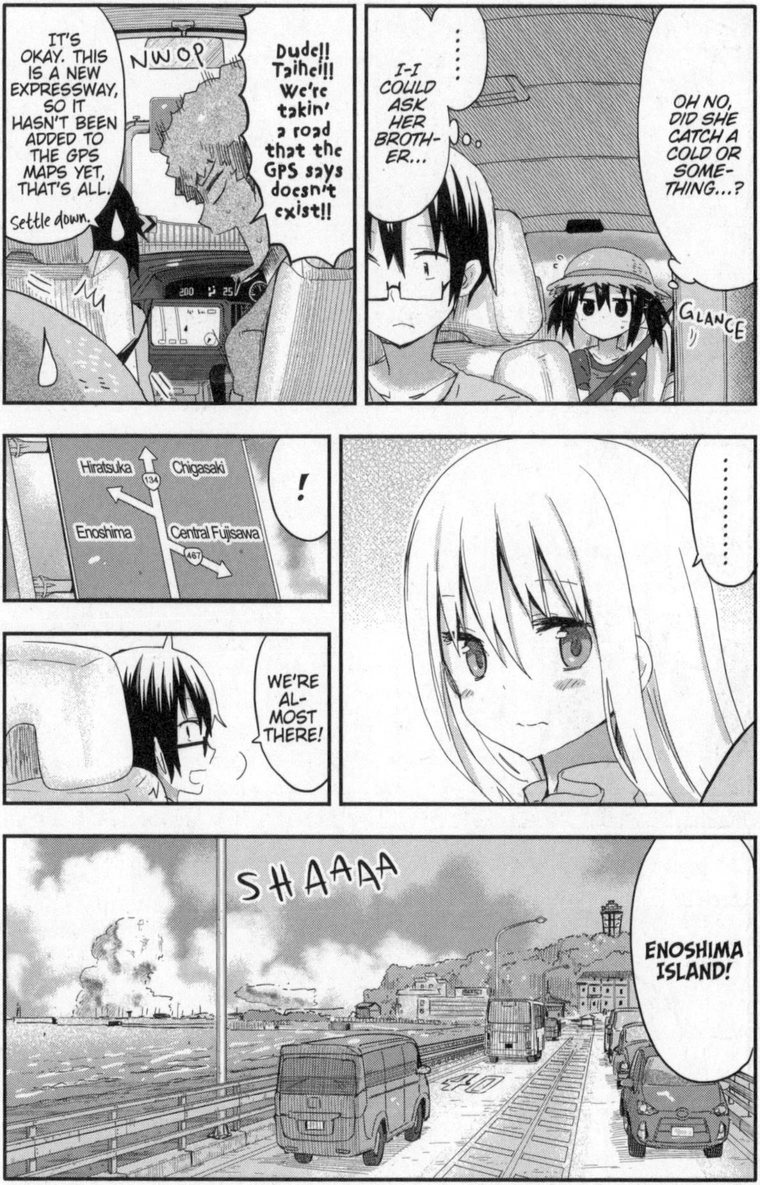
OH NO, DID SHE CATCH A COLD OR SOME-THING...?
......
I-I COULD ASK HER BROTH-ER...
GLANCE
Dude!! Taihei!! We're takin' a road that the GPS says doesn't exist!!
NWOP
IT'S OKAY. THIS IS A NEW EXPRESSWAY, SO IT HASN'T BEEN ADDED TO THE GPS MAPS YET, THAT'S ALL.
Settle down.
....
!
Hiratsuka
Chigasaki
134
Enoshima
Central Fujisawa
467
WE'RE AL-MOST THERE!
ENOSHIMA ISLAND!
SHAAAA

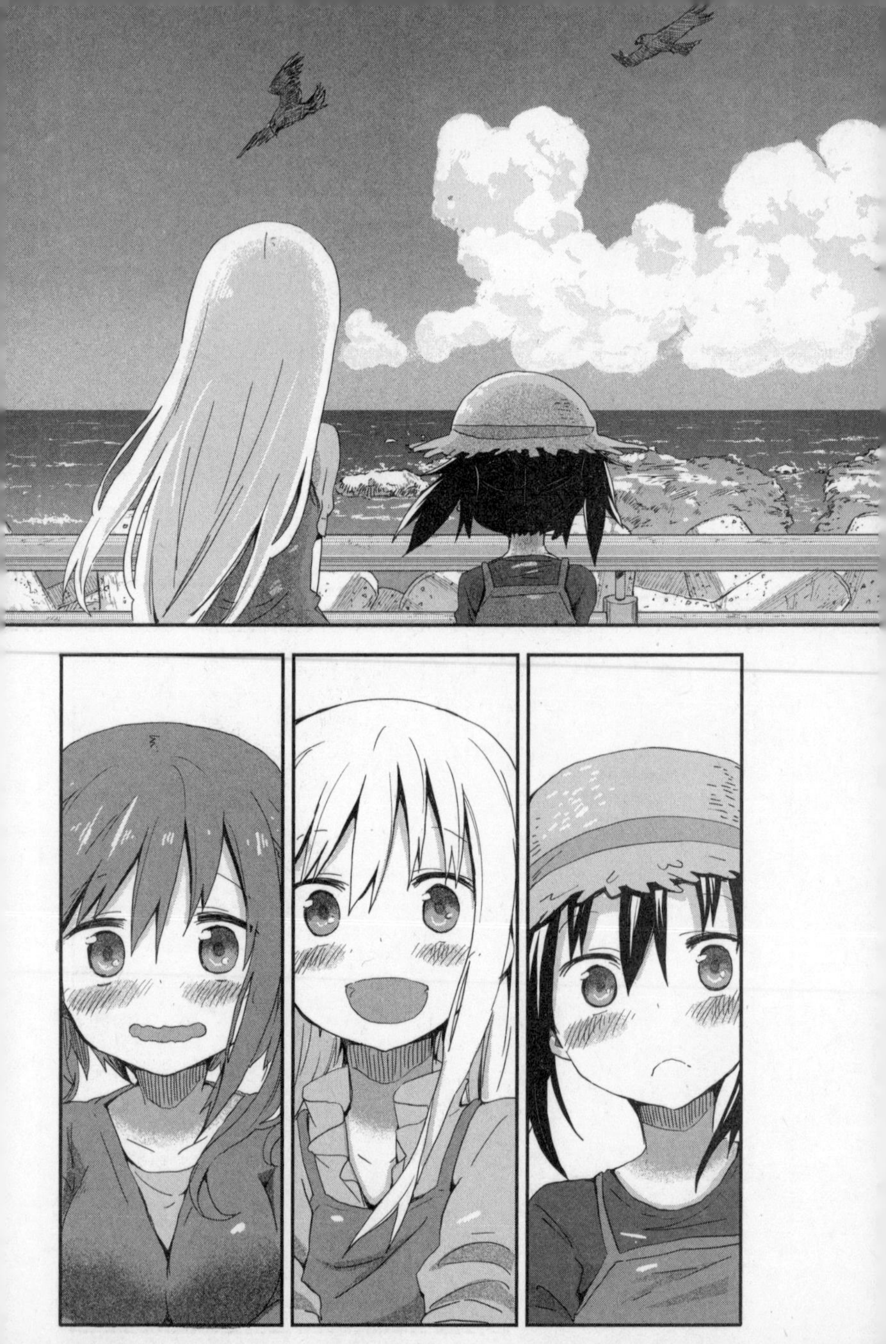

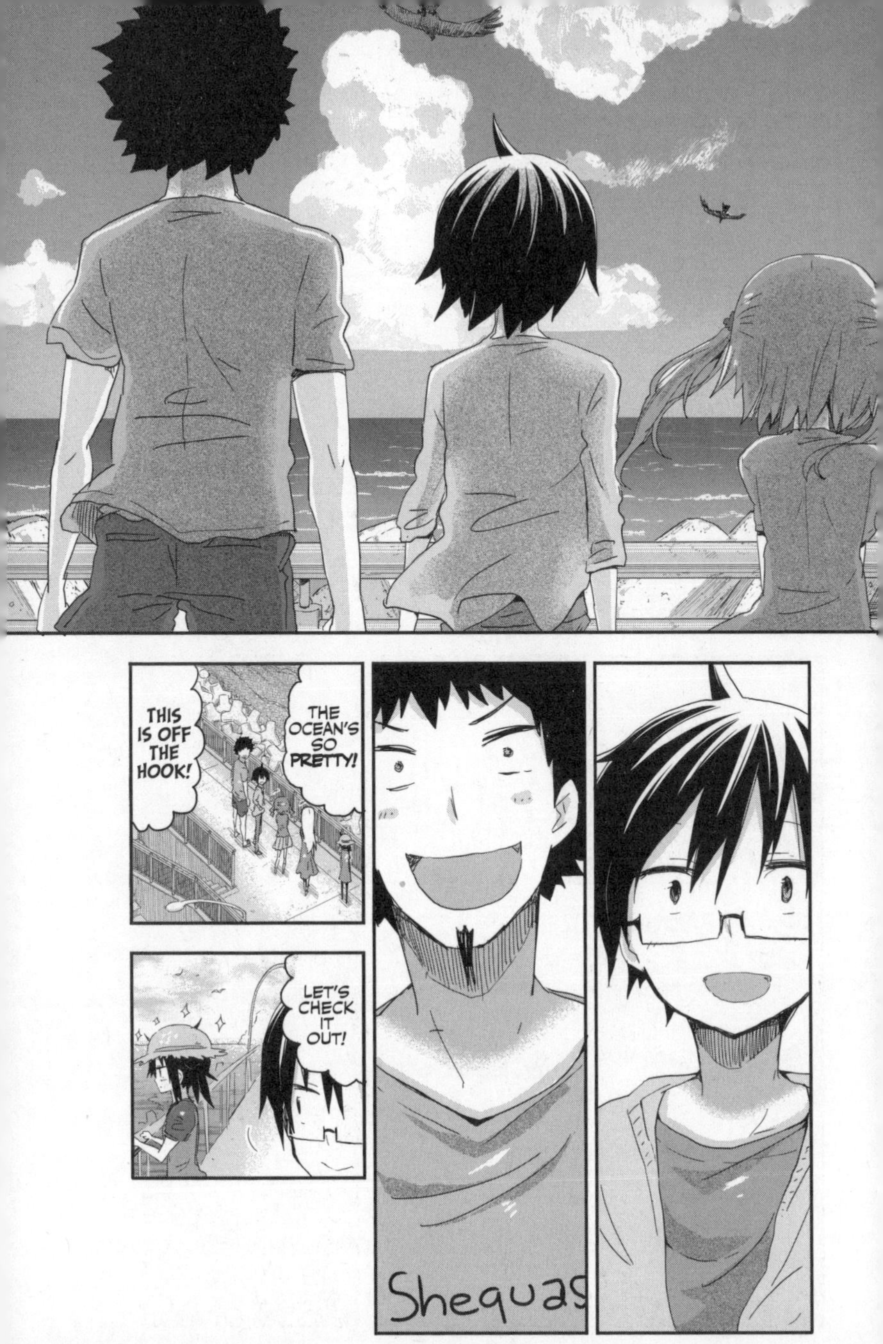
Shequas
THE OCEAN'S SO PRETTY!
THIS IS OFF THE HOOK!
LET'S CHECK IT OUT!

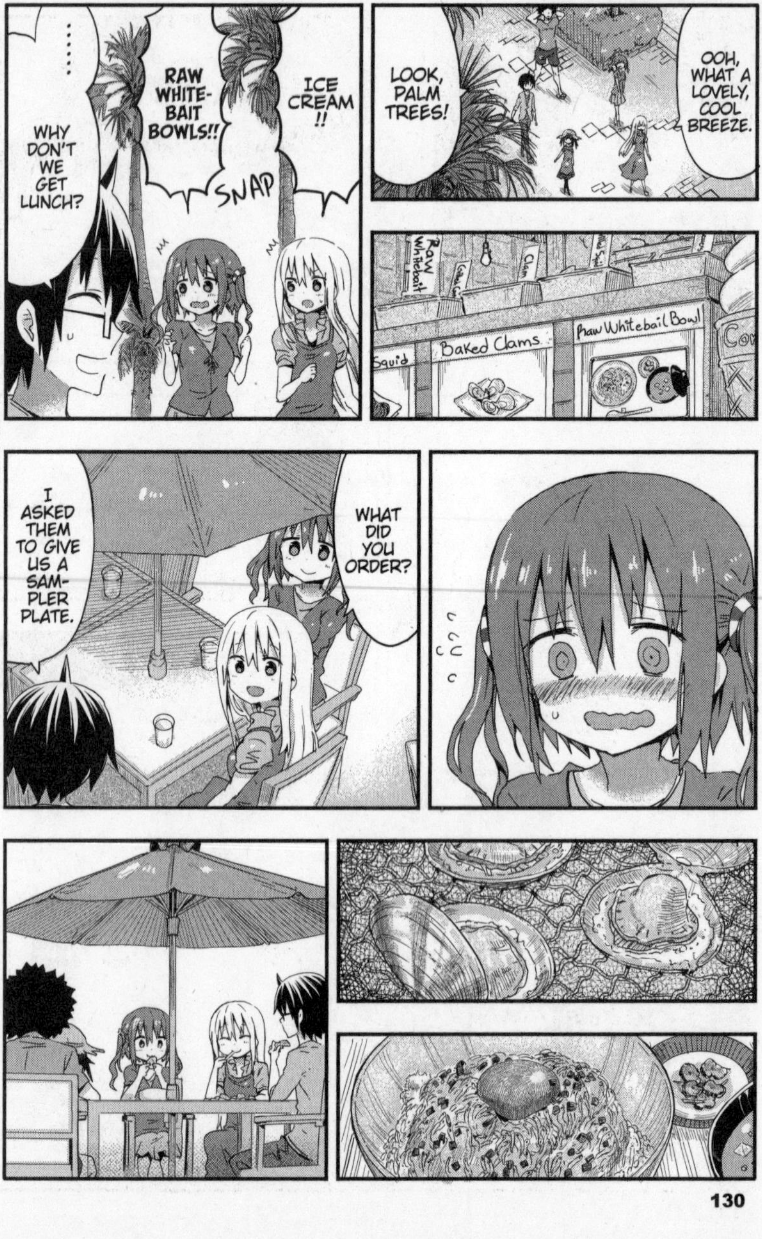
OOH, WHAT A LOVELY, COOL BREEZE.
LOOK, PALM TREES!
Raw Whitebait
Clam
Raw Whitebail Bowl
Baked Clams
Squid
ICE CREAM!!
RAW WHITE-BAIT BOWLS!!
SNAP
......
WHY DON'T WE GET LUNCH?
WHAT DID YOU ORDER?
I ASKED THEM TO GIVE US A SAM-PLER PLATE.

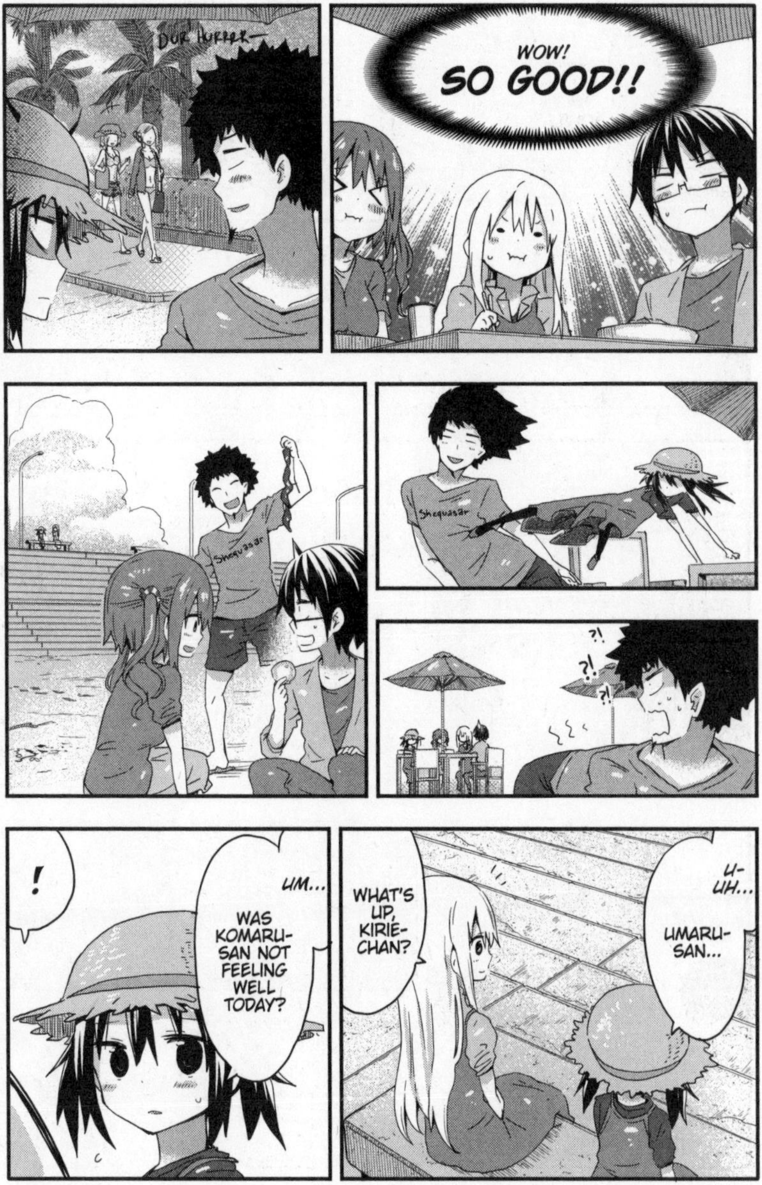
WOW! SO GOOD!!
DUR HURRR—
?!
?!
?!
U-UH...
UMARU-SAN...
WHAT'S UP, KIRIE-CHAN?
UM...
WAS KOMARU-SAN NOT FEELING WELL TODAY?
!

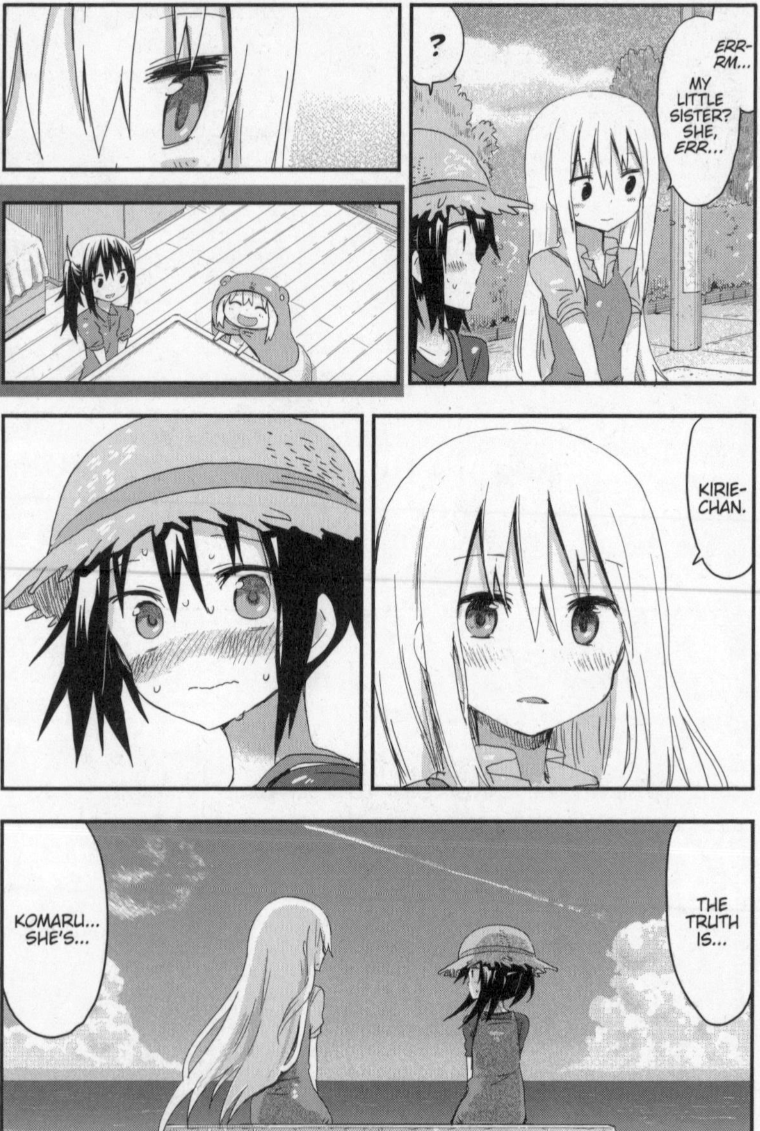
ERR-RM... MY LITTLE SISTER? SHE, ERR...
?
KIRIE-CHAN.
THE TRUTH IS...
KOMARU... SHE'S...

No. 68 Umaru & the Beach Part 2

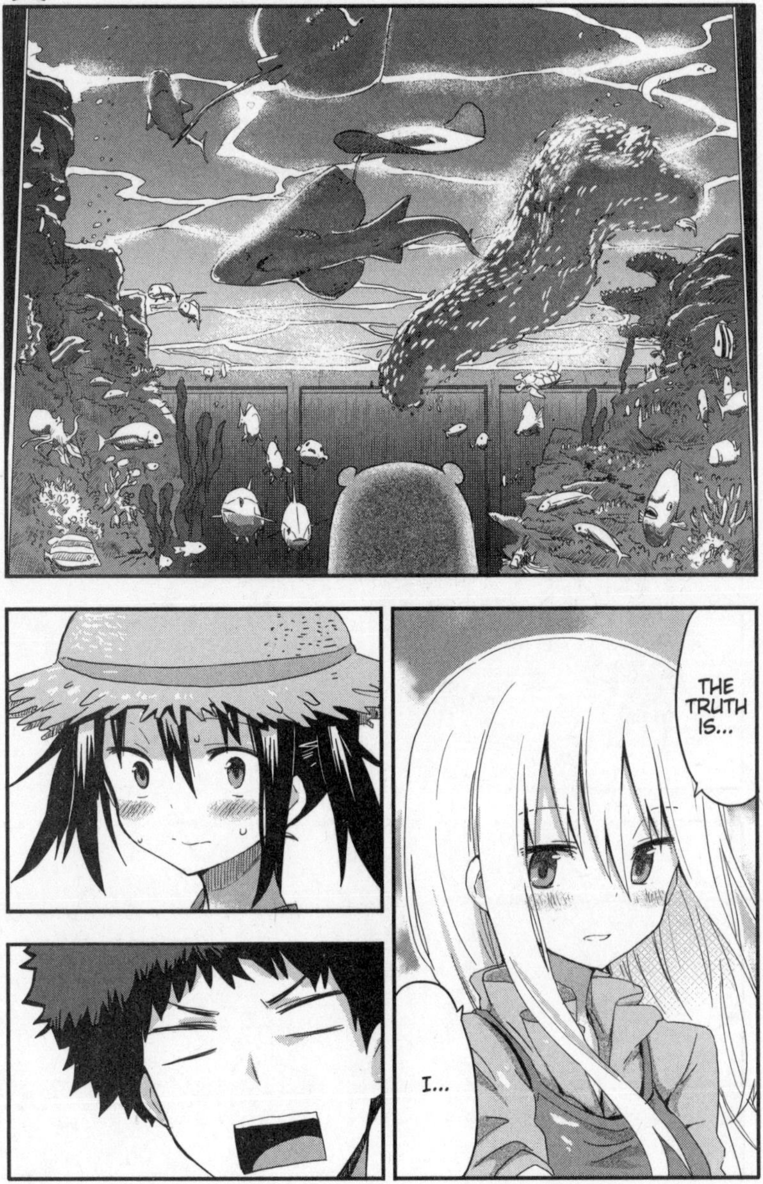
THE TRUTH IS...
I...

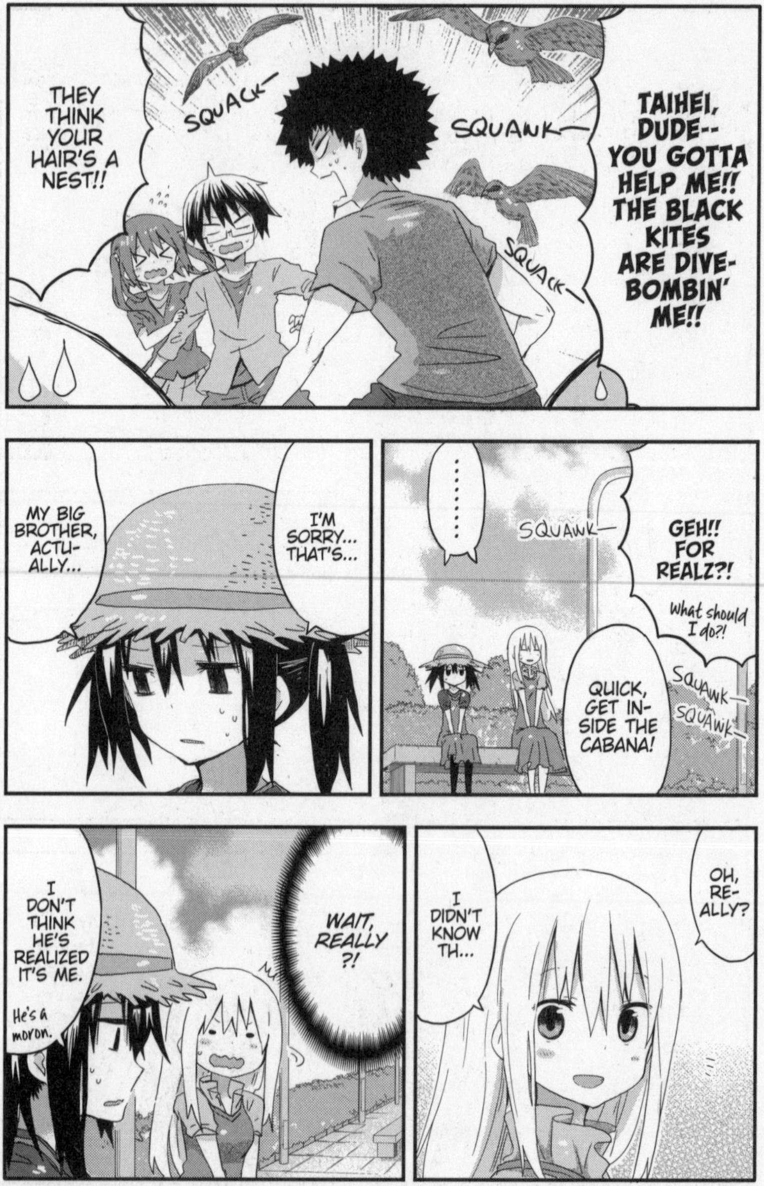
TAIHEI, DUDE-- YOU GOTTA HELP ME!! THE BLACK KITES ARE DIVE-BOMBIN' ME!!
SQUAWK—
SQUACK—
SQUACK—
THEY THINK YOUR HAIR'S A NEST!!
GEH!! FOR REALZ?!
What should I do?!
SQUAWK—
QUICK, GET INSIDE THE CABANA!
SQUAWK—
SQUAWK—
SQUAWK—
......
I'M SORRY... THAT'S...
MY BIG BROTHER, ACTUALLY...
OH, REALLY?
I DIDN'T KNOW TH...
WAIT, REALLY?!
I DON'T THINK HE'S REALIZED IT'S ME.
He's a moron.

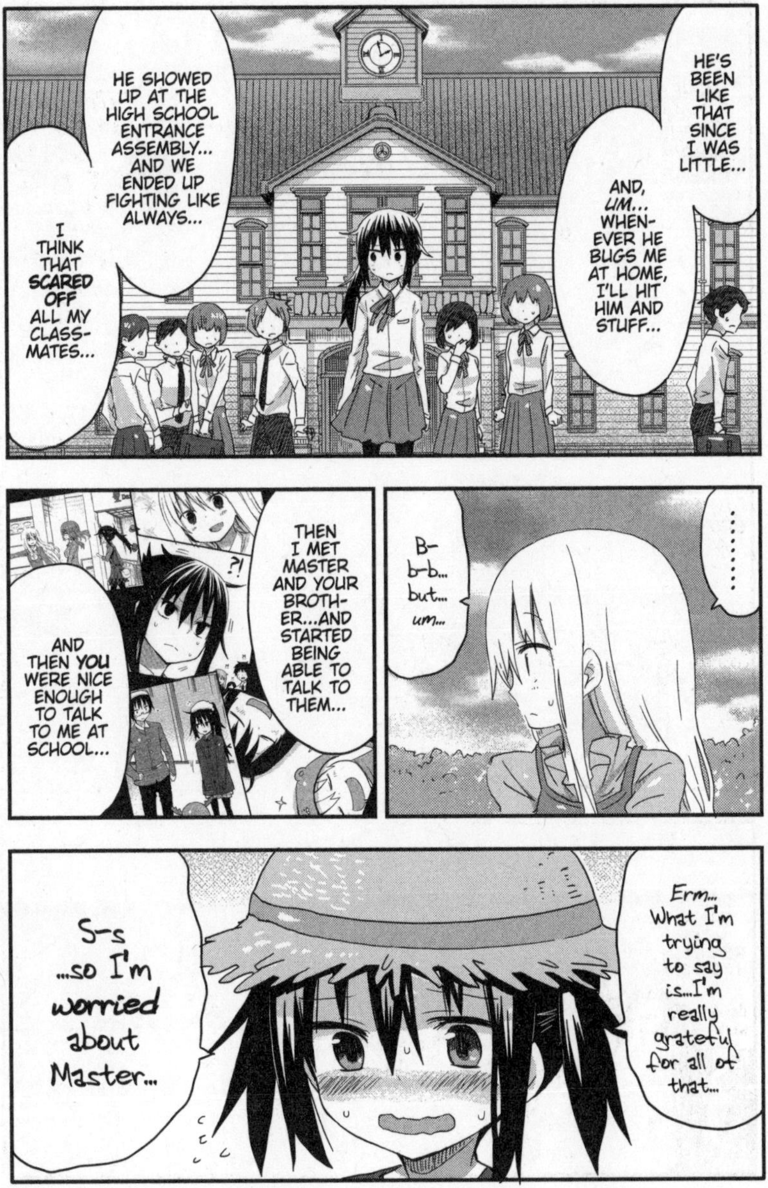
HE'S BEEN LIKE THAT SINCE I WAS LITTLE...
AND, UM... WHEN-EVER HE BUGS ME AT HOME, I'LL HIT HIM AND STUFF...
HE SHOWED UP AT THE HIGH SCHOOL ENTRANCE ASSEMBLY... AND WE ENDED UP FIGHTING LIKE ALWAYS...
I THINK THAT SCARED OFF ALL MY CLASS-MATES...
....
B- b-b... but... um...
THEN I MET MASTER AND YOUR BROTH-ER...AND STARTED BEING ABLE TO TALK TO THEM...
?!
AND THEN YOU WERE NICE ENOUGH TO TALK TO ME AT SCHOOL...
Erm... What I'm trying to say is...I'm really grateful for all of that...
S-s ...so I'm worried about Master...

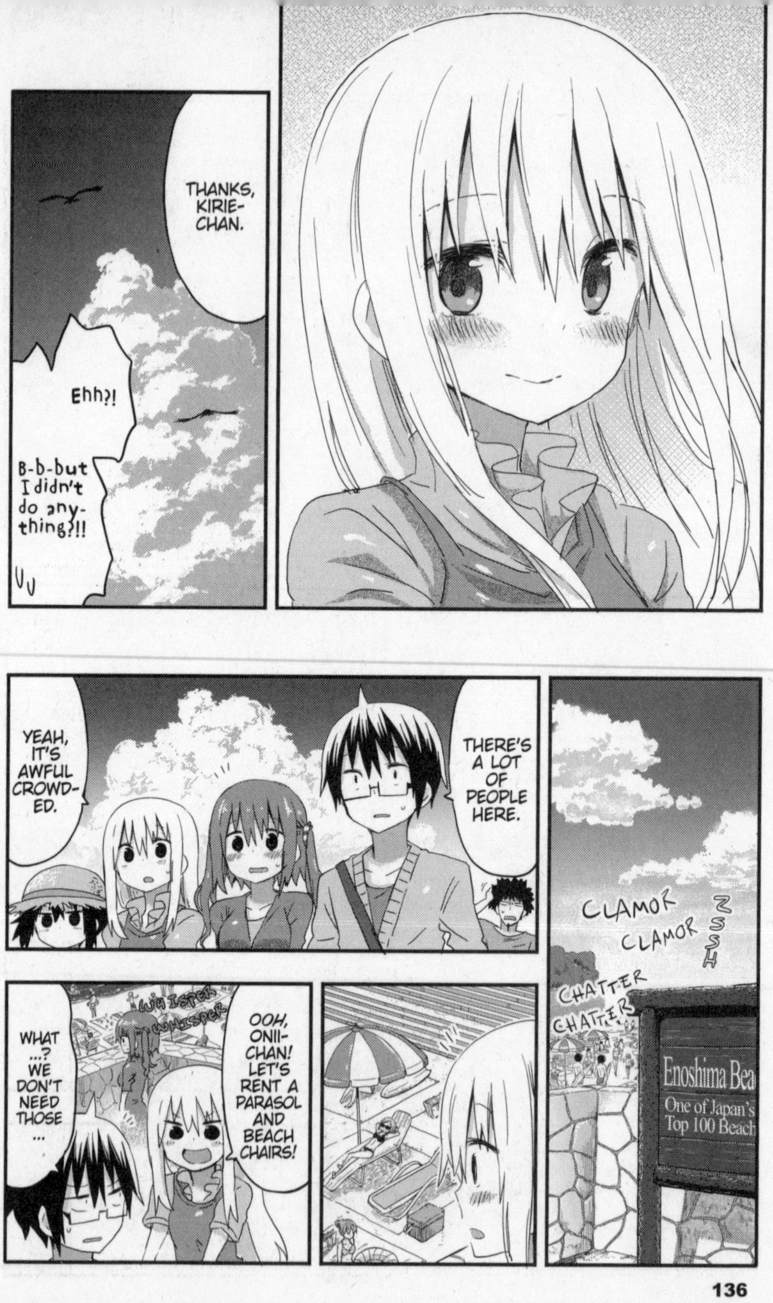
THANKS, KIRIE-CHAN.
Ehh?!
B-b-but I didn't do any-thing?!!
Enoshima Bea
One of Japan's
Top 100 Beach
CLAMOR CLAMOR
ZSSH
CHATTER CHATTER
THERE'S A LOT OF PEOPLE HERE.
YEAH, IT'S AWFUL CROWD-ED.
OOH, ONII-CHAN! LET'S RENT A PARASOL AND BEACH CHAIRS!
WHISPER WHISPER
WHAT ...? WE DON'T NEED THOSE ...

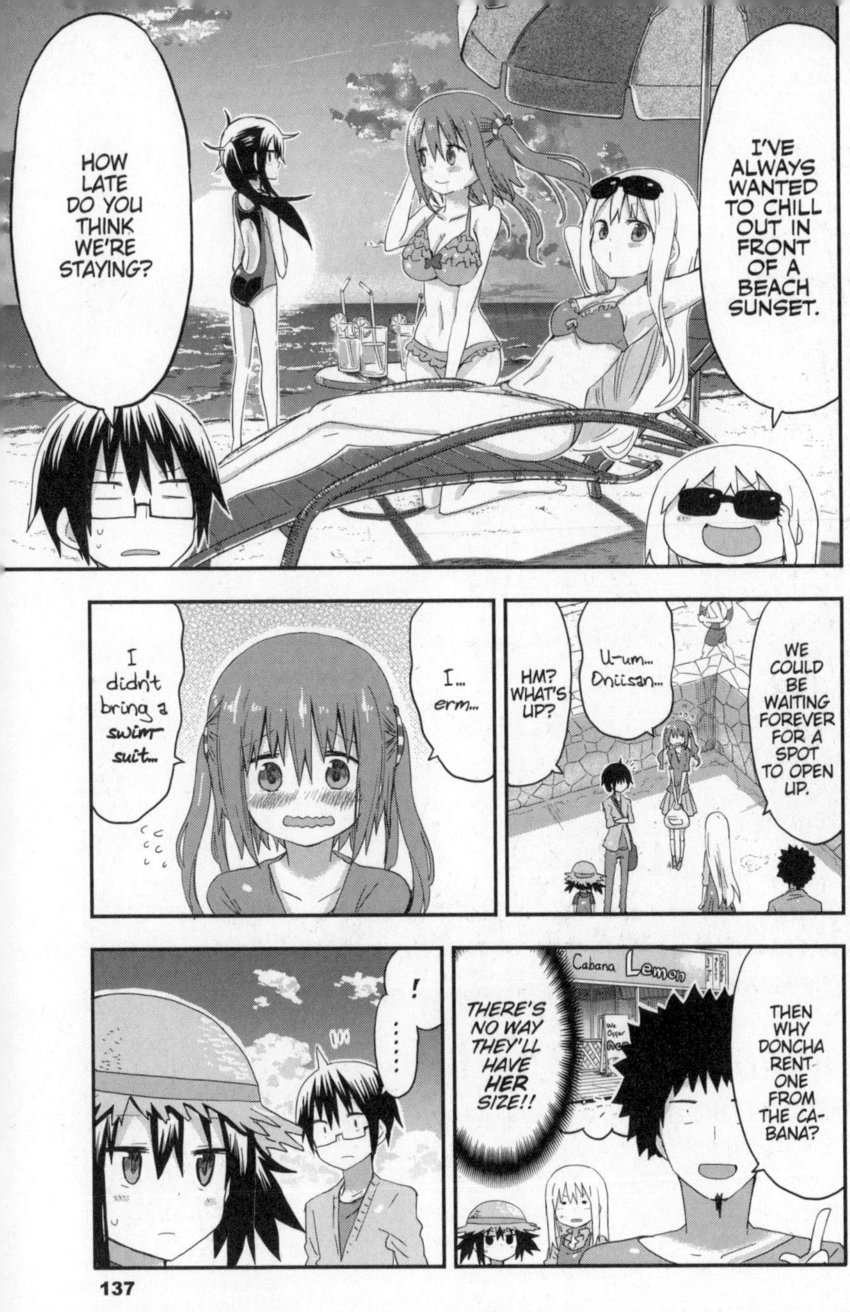
I'VE ALWAYS WANTED TO CHILL OUT IN FRONT OF A BEACH SUNSET.
HOW LATE DO YOU THINK WE'RE STAYING?
WE COULD BE WAITING FOREVER FOR A SPOT TO OPEN UP.
U-um... Oniisan...
HM? WHAT'S UP?
I... erm...
I didn't bring a swim suit...
THEN WHY DONCHA RENT ONE FROM THE CA-BANA?
Cabana Lemon
THERE'S NO WAY THEY'LL HAVE HER SIZE!!
!
......

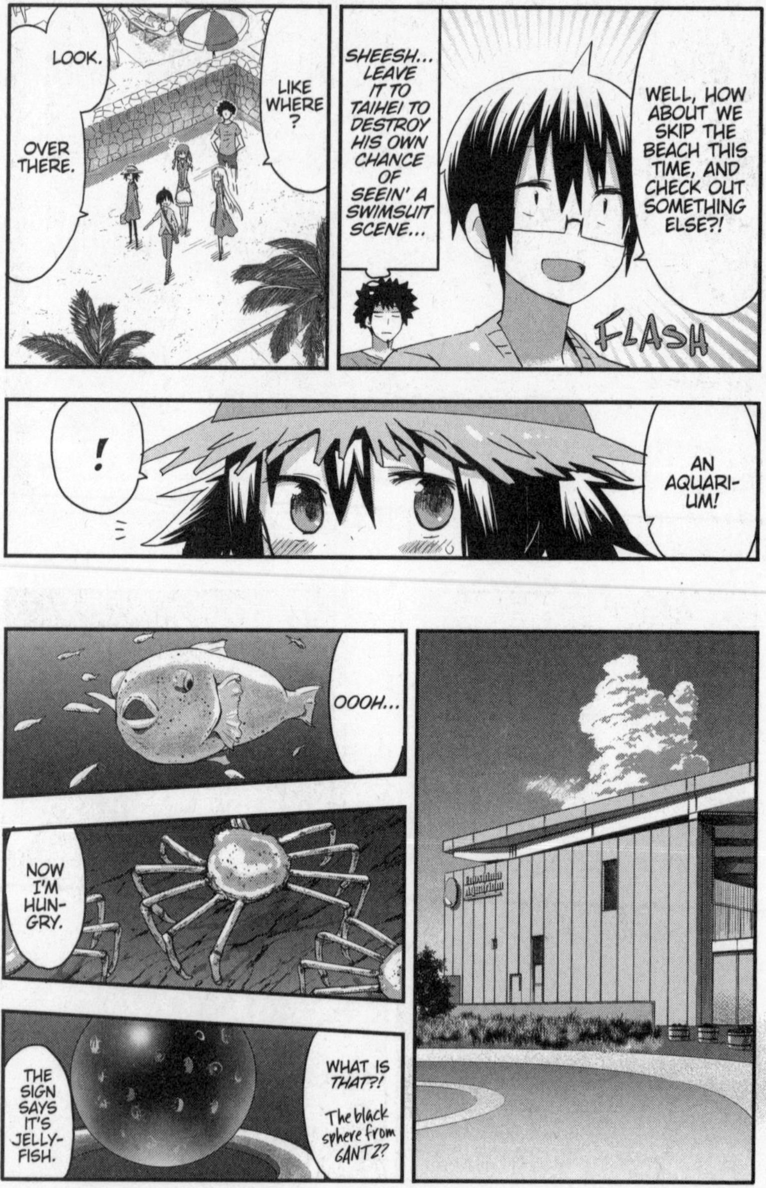
WELL, HOW ABOUT WE SKIP THE BEACH THIS TIME, AND CHECK OUT SOMETHING ELSE?!
FLASH
SHEESH... LEAVE IT TO TAIHEI TO DESTROY HIS OWN CHANCE OF SEEIN' A SWIMSUIT SCENE...
LIKE WHERE?
LOOK.
OVER THERE.
AN AQUARIUM!
!
OOOH...
NOW I'M HUNGRY.
WHAT IS THAT?!
The black sphere from GANTZ?
THE SIGN SAYS IT'S JELLYFISH.

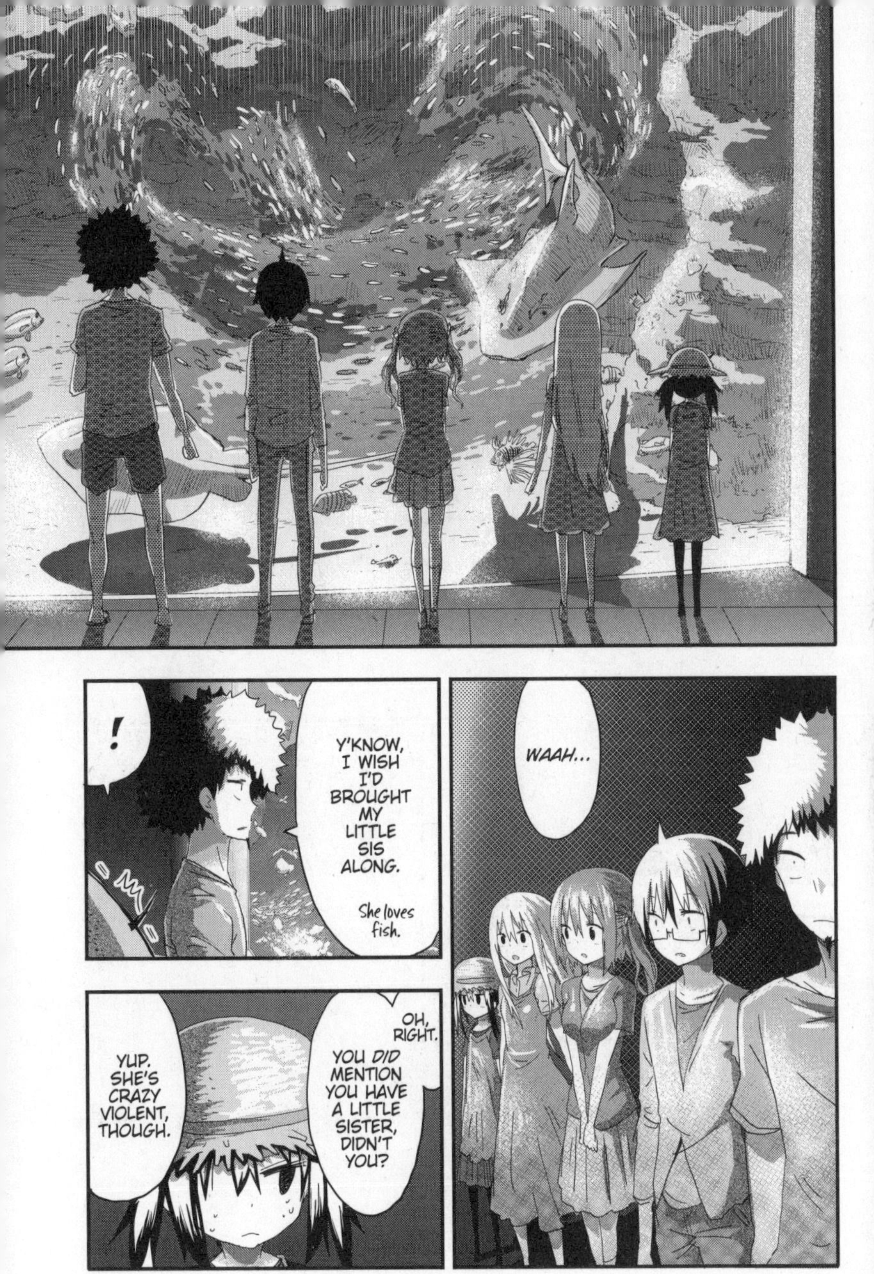
WAAH...
Y'KNOW, I WISH I'D BROUGHT MY LITTLE SIS ALONG.
She loves fish.
!
OH, RIGHT. YOU *DID* MENTION YOU HAVE A LITTLE SISTER, DIDN'T YOU?
YUP. SHE'S CRAZY VIOLENT, THOUGH.

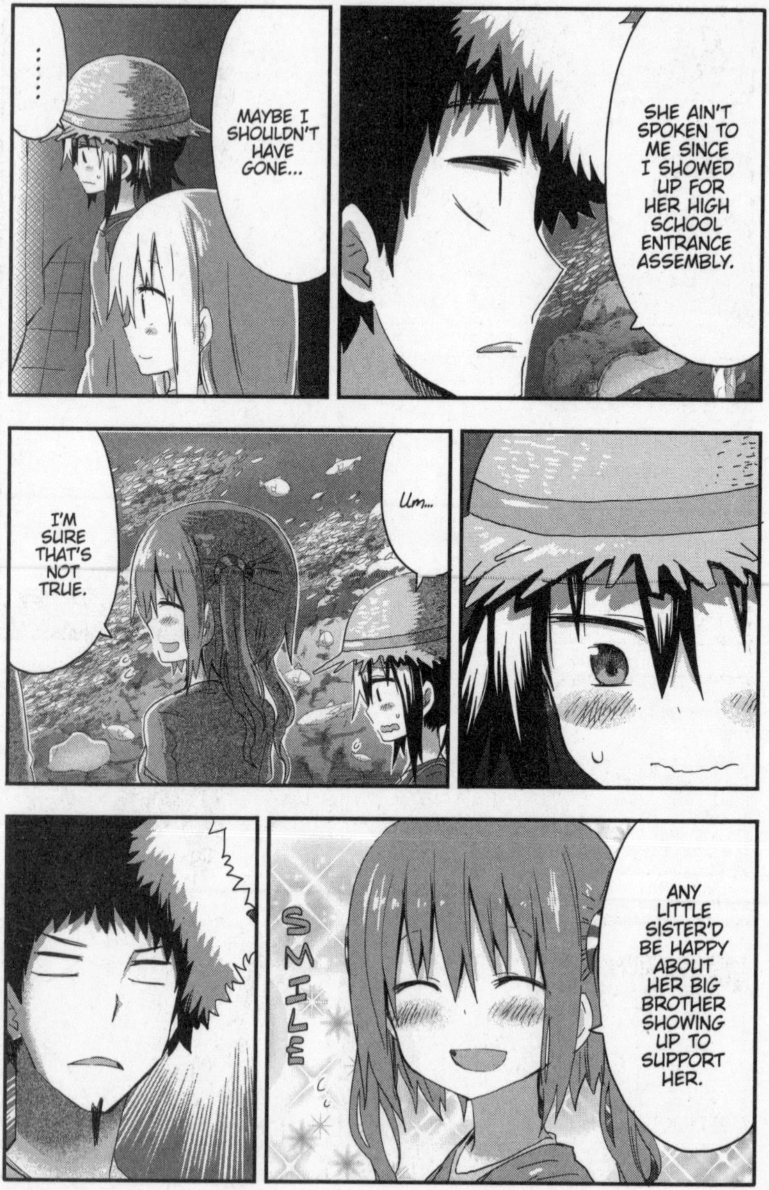
SHE AIN'T SPOKEN TO ME SINCE I SHOWED UP FOR HER HIGH SCHOOL ENTRANCE ASSEMBLY.
MAYBE I SHOULDN'T HAVE GONE...
......
Um...
I'M SURE THAT'S NOT TRUE.
ANY LITTLE SISTER'D BE HAPPY ABOUT HER BIG BROTHER SHOWING UP TO SUPPORT HER.
SMILE

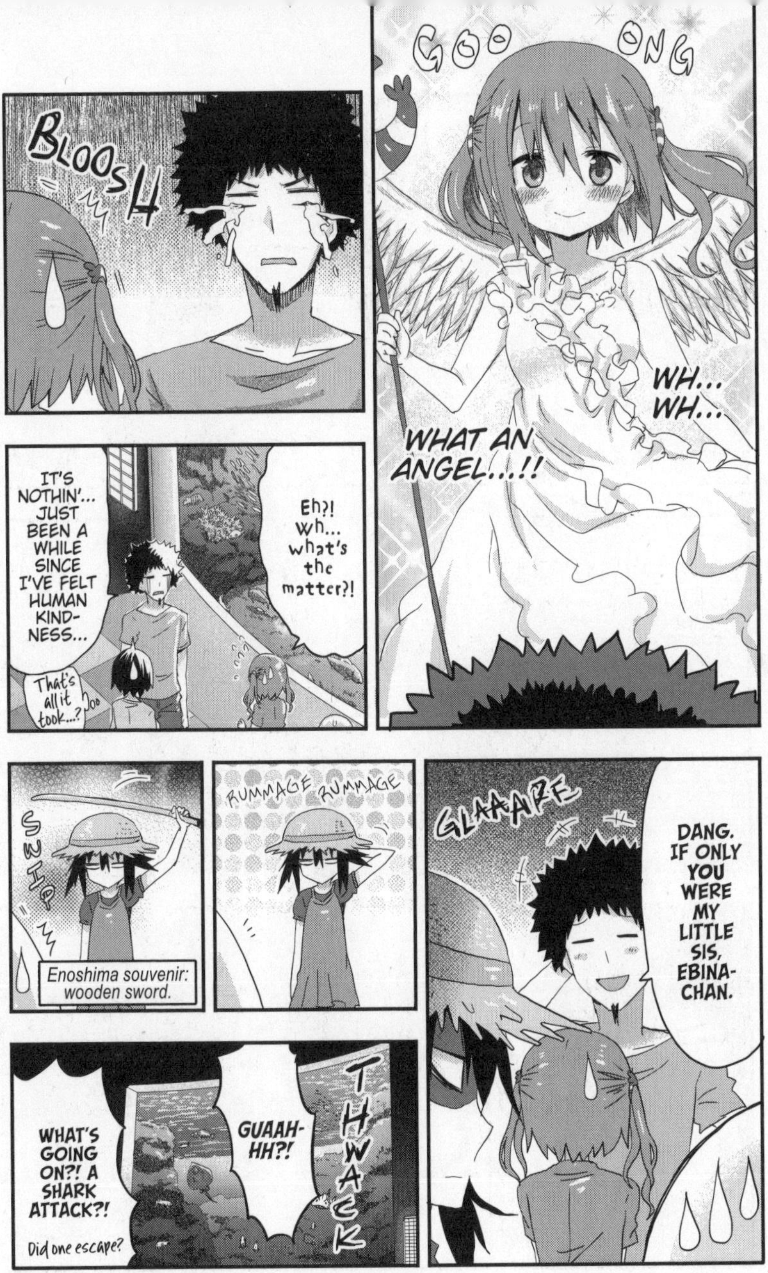
GOO ONG
WH... WH...
WHAT AN ANGEL...!!
BLOOSH
Eh?! wh... what's the matter?!
IT'S NOTHIN'... JUST BEEN A WHILE SINCE I'VE FELT HUMAN KINDNESS...
That's all it took...?
GLAAARE
DANG. IF ONLY YOU WERE MY LITTLE SIS, EBINA-CHAN.
RUMMAGE RUMMAGE
SWIP
Enoshima souvenir: wooden sword.
THWACK
GUAAHH?!
WHAT'S GOING ON?! A SHARK ATTACK?!
Did one escape?

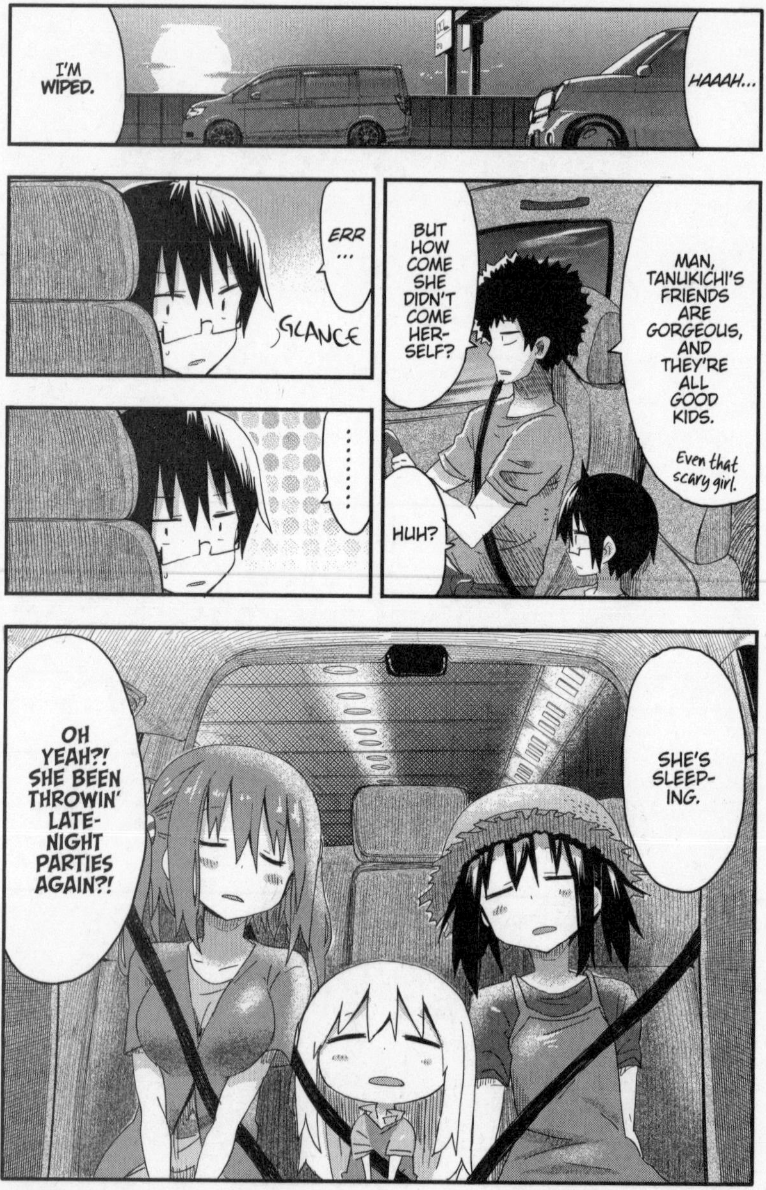
HAAAH...
I'M WIPED.
MAN, TANUKICHI'S FRIENDS ARE GORGEOUS, AND THEY'RE ALL GOOD KIDS.
Even that scary girl.
BUT HOW COME SHE DIDN'T COME HER-SELF?
HUH?
ERR...
GLANCE
......
SHE'S SLEEP-ING.
OH YEAH?! SHE BEEN THROWIN' LATE-NIGHT PARTIES AGAIN?!

Umaru & Unpacking

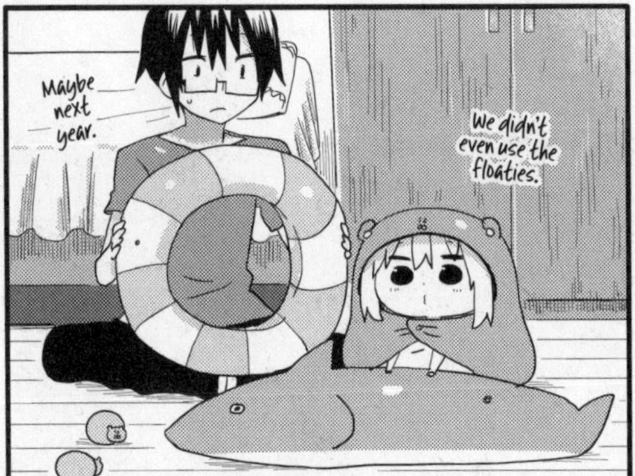
We didn't even use the floaties.
Maybe next year.

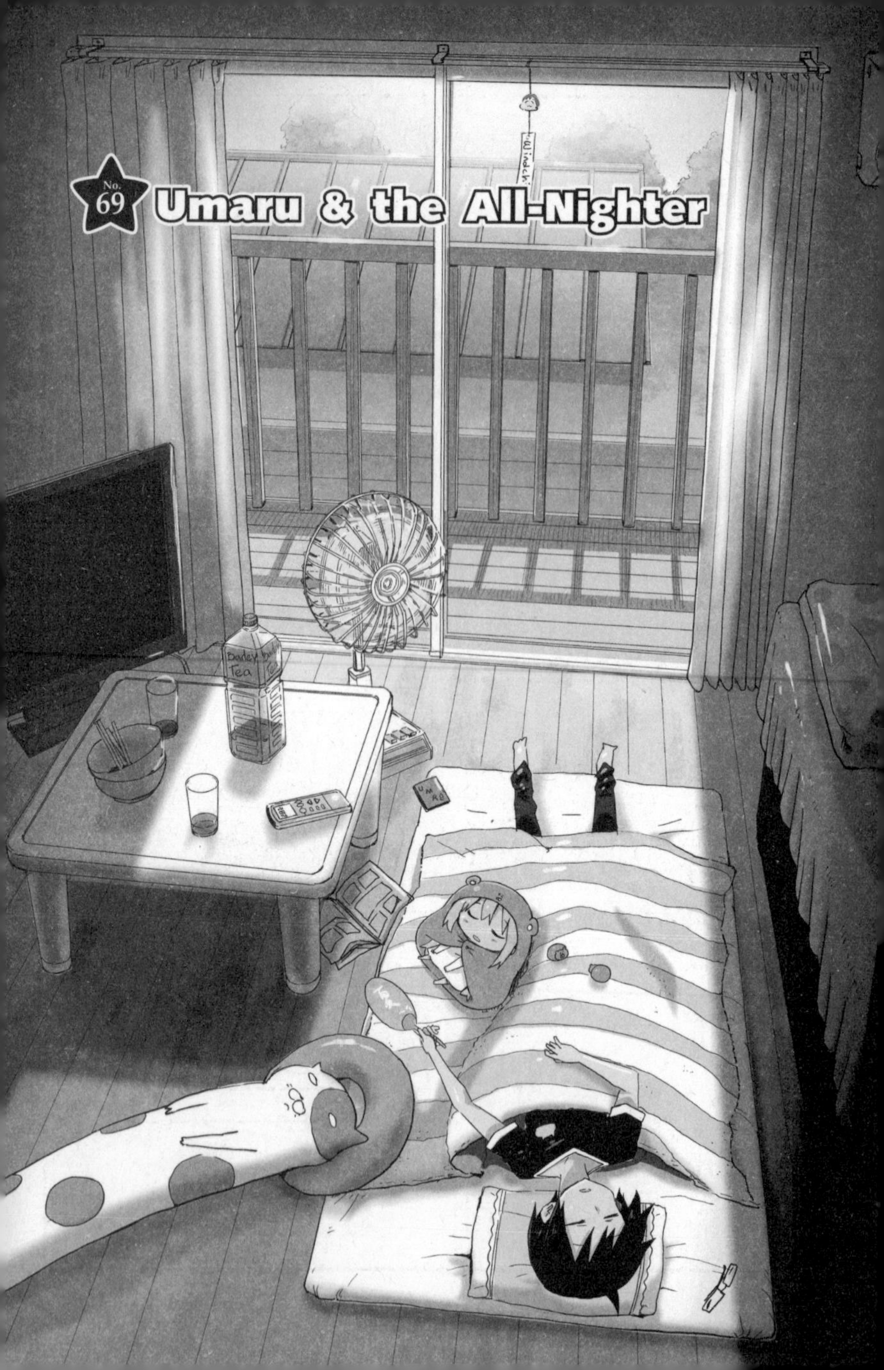
No. 69
Umaru & the All-Nighter
Barley Tea

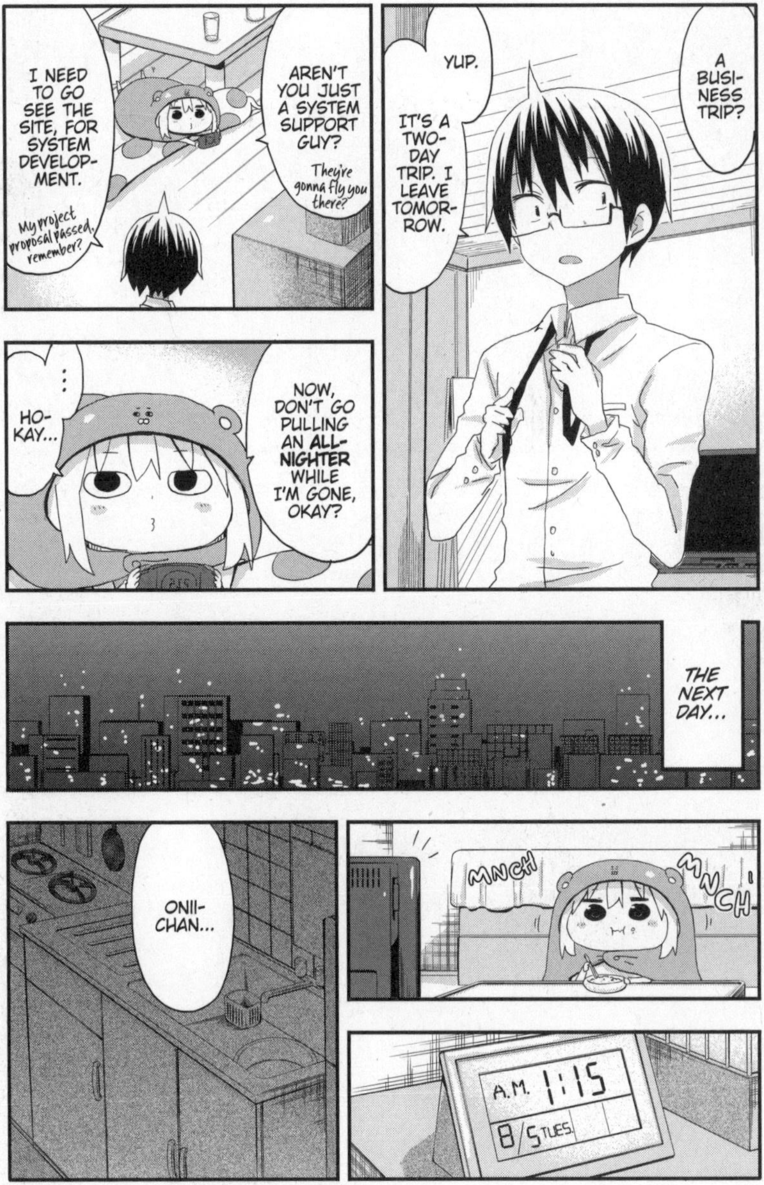
A BUSI-NESS TRIP?
YUP.
IT'S A TWO-DAY TRIP. I LEAVE TOMOR-ROW.
AREN'T YOU JUST A SYSTEM SUPPORT GUY?
They're gonna fly you there?
I NEED TO GO SEE THE SITE, FOR SYSTEM DEVELOP-MENT.
My project proposal passed, remember?
NOW, DON'T GO PULLING AN **ALL-NIGHTER** WHILE I'M GONE, OKAY?
...
HO-KAY...
THE NEXT DAY...
MNCH
MNCH
A.M. 1:15
8/5 TUES.
ONII-CHAN...

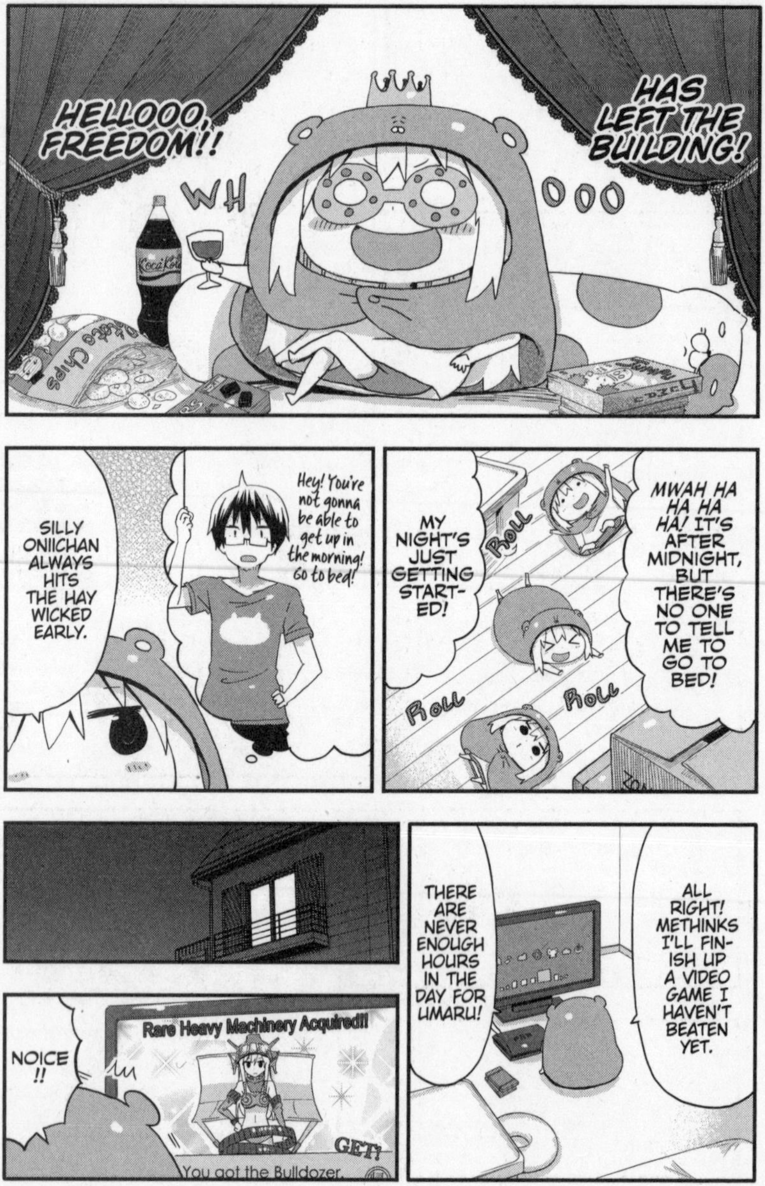
HAS LEFT THE BUILDING!
HELLOOO, FREEDOM!!
WH
OOO
MWAH HA HA HA HA! IT'S AFTER MIDNIGHT, BUT THERE'S NO ONE TO TELL ME TO GO TO BED!
MY NIGHT'S JUST GETTING START-ED!
Roll
Roll
Roll
Hey! You're not gonna be able to get up in the morning! Go to bed!
SILLY ONIICHAN ALWAYS HITS THE HAY WICKED EARLY.
ALL RIGHT! METHINKS I'LL FIN-ISH UP A VIDEO GAME I HAVEN'T BEATEN YET.
THERE ARE NEVER ENOUGH HOURS IN THE DAY FOR UMARU!
Rare Heavy Machinery Acquired!!
NOICE!!
GET!
You got the Bulldozer.

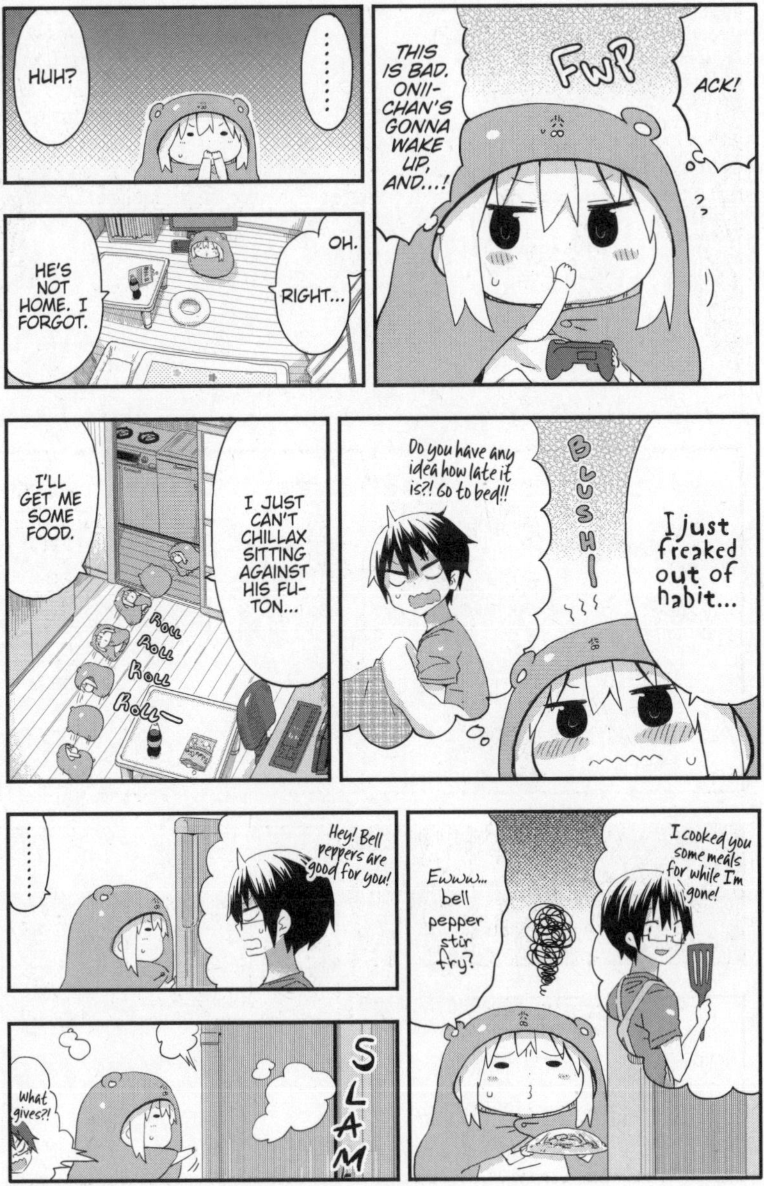
ACK!
FWP
THIS IS BAD. ONII-CHAN'S GONNA WAKE UP, AND...!
....
HUH?
OH.
RIGHT...
HE'S NOT HOME. I FORGOT.
I just freaked out of habit...
BLUSH
Do you have any idea how late it is?! Go to bed!!
I JUST CAN'T CHILLAX SITTING AGAINST HIS FU-TON...
I'LL GET ME SOME FOOD.
Roll
Roll
Roll
Roll—
I cooked you some meals for while I'm gone!
Ewww... bell pepper stir fry?
Hey! Bell peppers are good for you!
....
SLAM
What gives?!

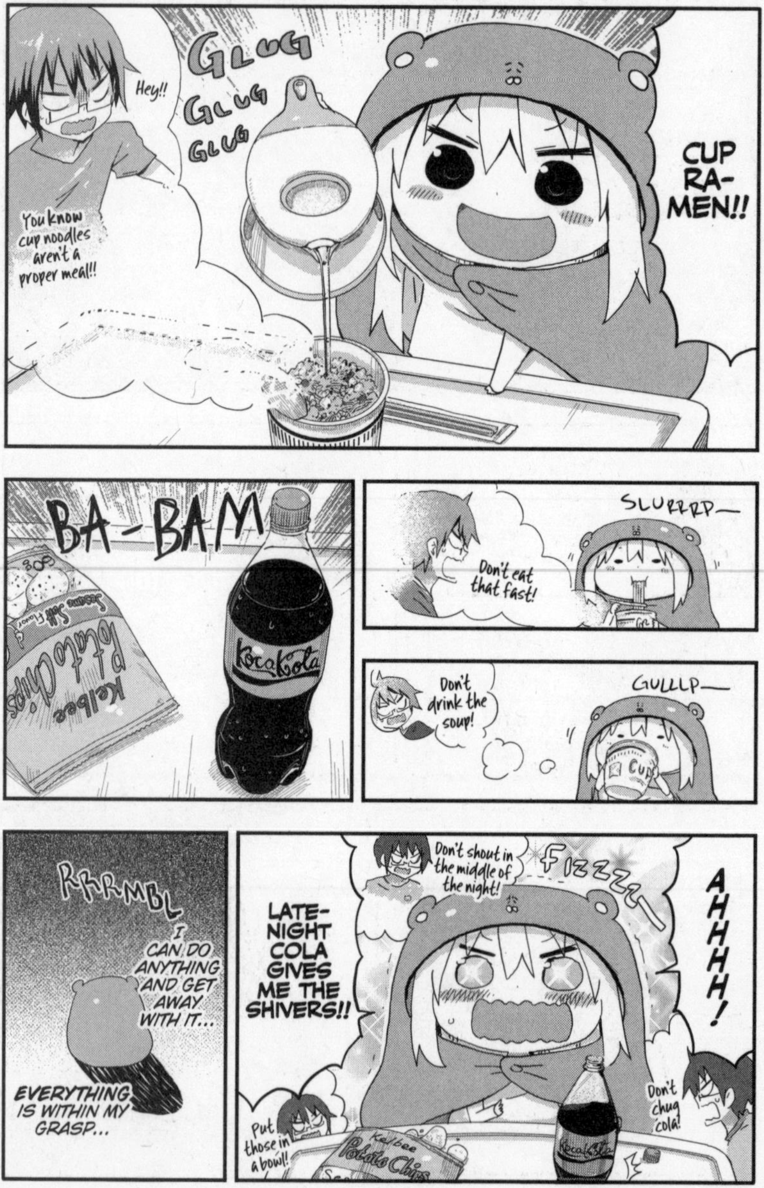
CUP RA-MEN!!
GLUG GLUG GLUG
Hey!!
You know cup noodles aren't a proper meal!!
SLURRRP—
Don't eat that fast!
GULLLP—
Don't drink the soup!
BA-BAM
KocaKola
Kelbee Potato chips
AHHHHH!
FIZZZZ—
Don't shout in the middle of the night!
LATE-NIGHT COLA GIVES ME THE SHIVERS!!
Don't chug cola!
Put those in a bowl!
Kelbee Potato Chips
RRRMBL
I CAN DO ANYTHING AND GET AWAY WITH IT...
EVERYTHING IS WITHIN MY GRASP...

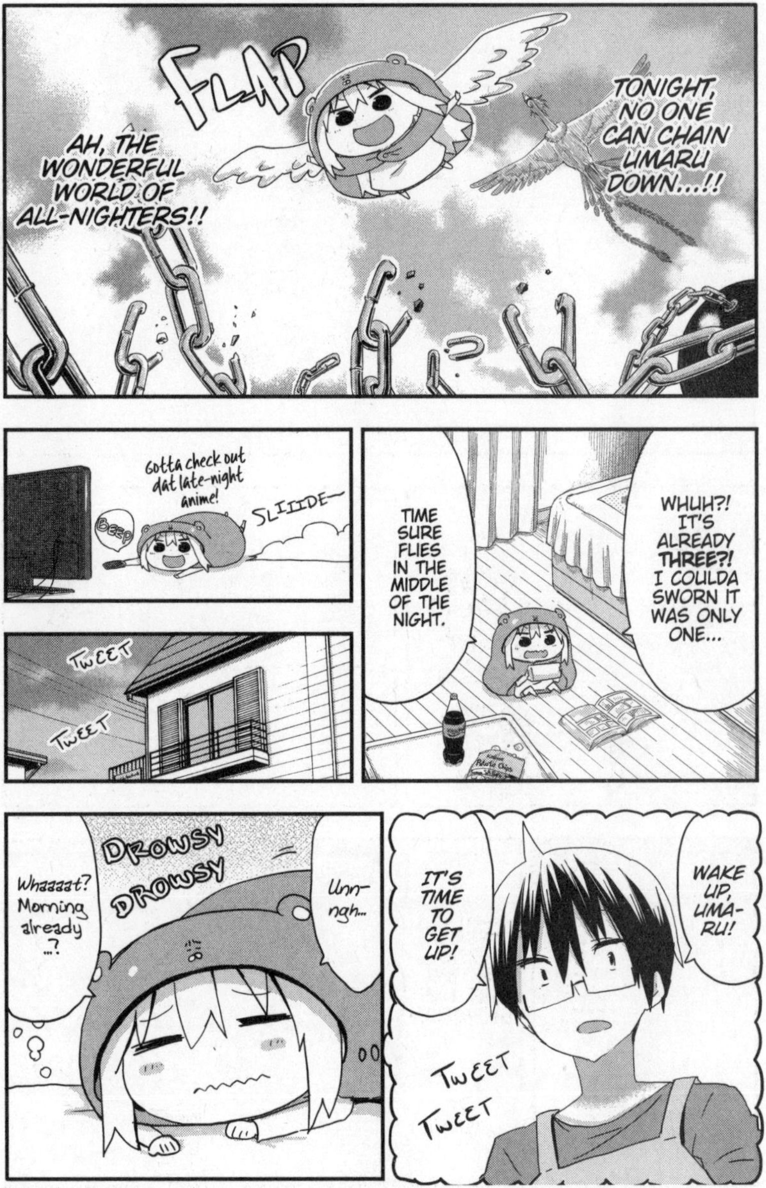
TONIGHT, NO ONE CAN CHAIN UMARU DOWN...!!
FLAP
AH, THE WONDERFUL WORLD OF ALL-NIGHTERS!!
WHUH?! IT'S ALREADY THREE?! I COULDA SWORN IT WAS ONLY ONE...
TIME SURE FLIES IN THE MIDDLE OF THE NIGHT.
Gotta check out dat late-night anime!
SLIIIDE~
BEEP
TWEET
TWEET
WAKE UP, UMARU!
IT'S TIME TO GET UP!
TWEET
TWEET
Unnn-ngh...
DROWSY
DROWSY
Whaaaat? Morning already ...?

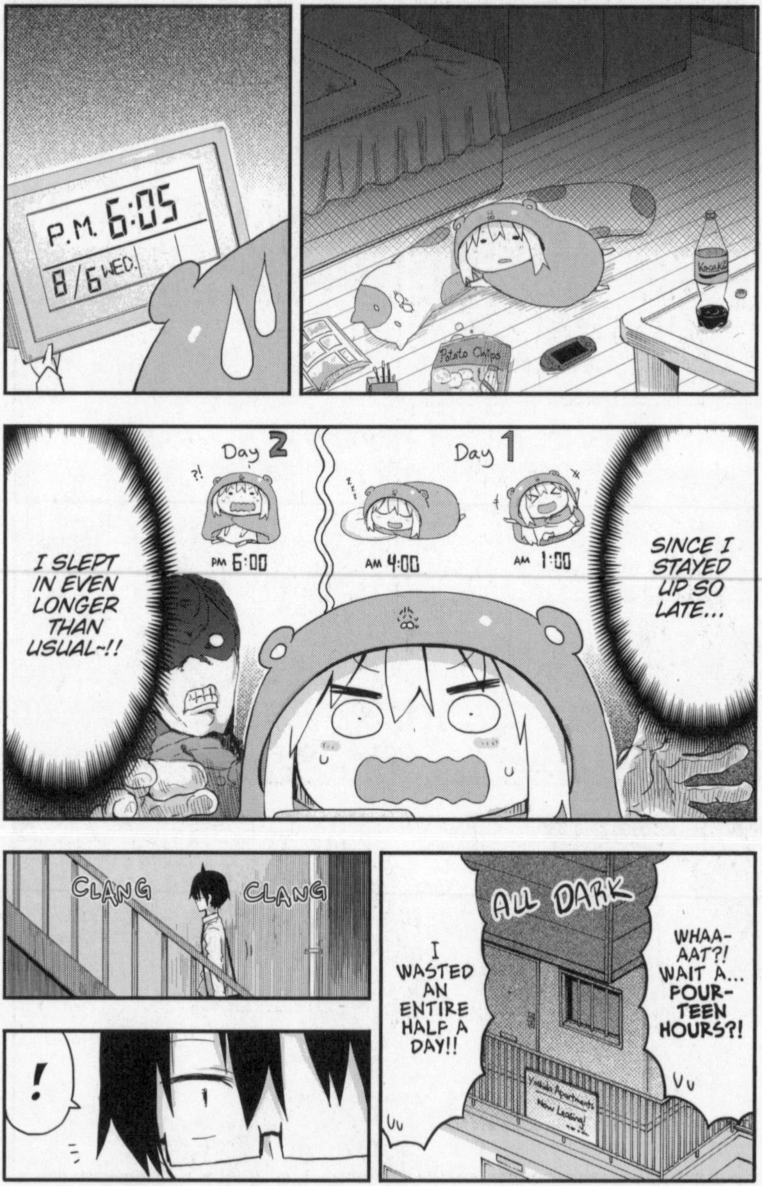
Potato Chips
P.M. 6:05
8/6 WED.
SINCE I STAYED UP SO LATE...
Day 1
AM 1:00
AM 4:00
Day 2
PM 6:00
I SLEPT IN EVEN LONGER THAN USUAL~!!
ALL DARK
WHAA-AAT?! WAIT A... FOUR-TEEN HOURS?!
I WASTED AN ENTIRE HALF A DAY!!
CLANG
CLANG
!

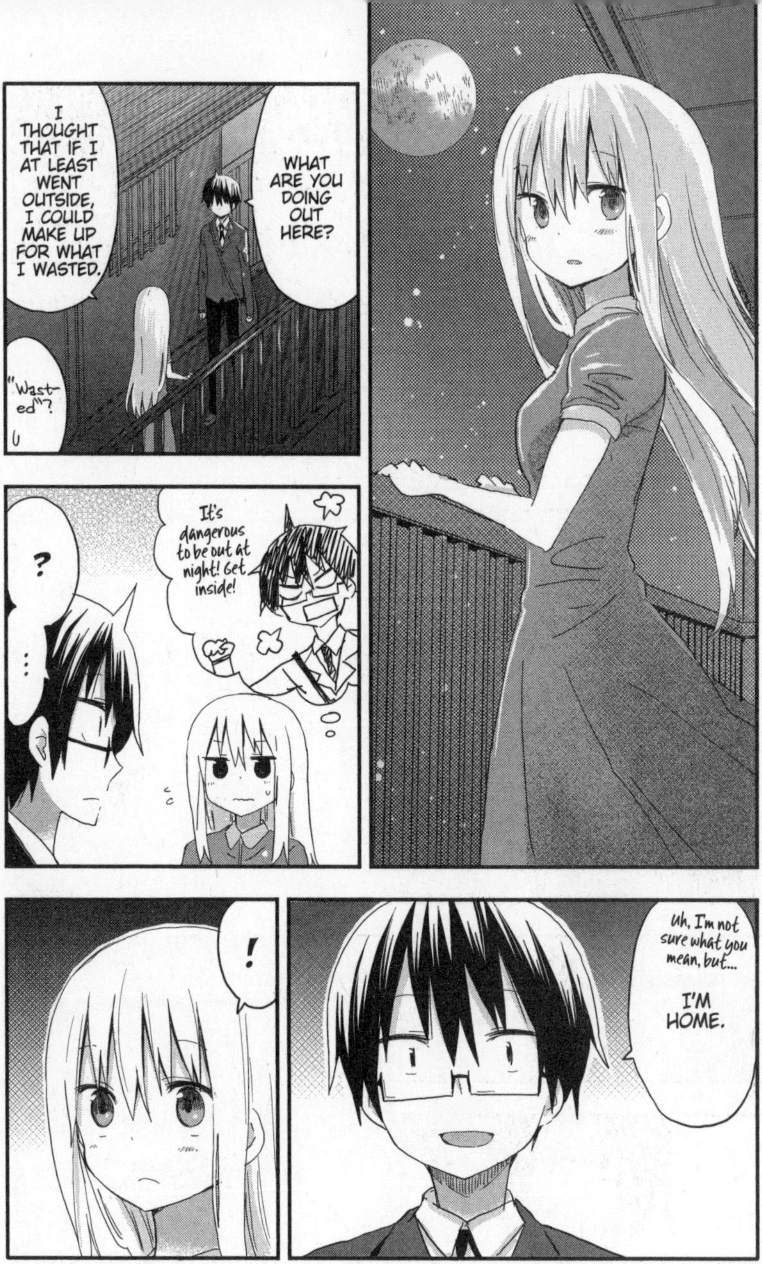
WHAT ARE YOU DOING OUT HERE?
I THOUGHT THAT IF I AT LEAST WENT OUTSIDE, I COULD MAKE UP FOR WHAT I WASTED.
"Wasted"?
It's dangerous to be out at night! Get inside!
?
...
Uh, I'm not sure what you mean, but...
I'M HOME.
!

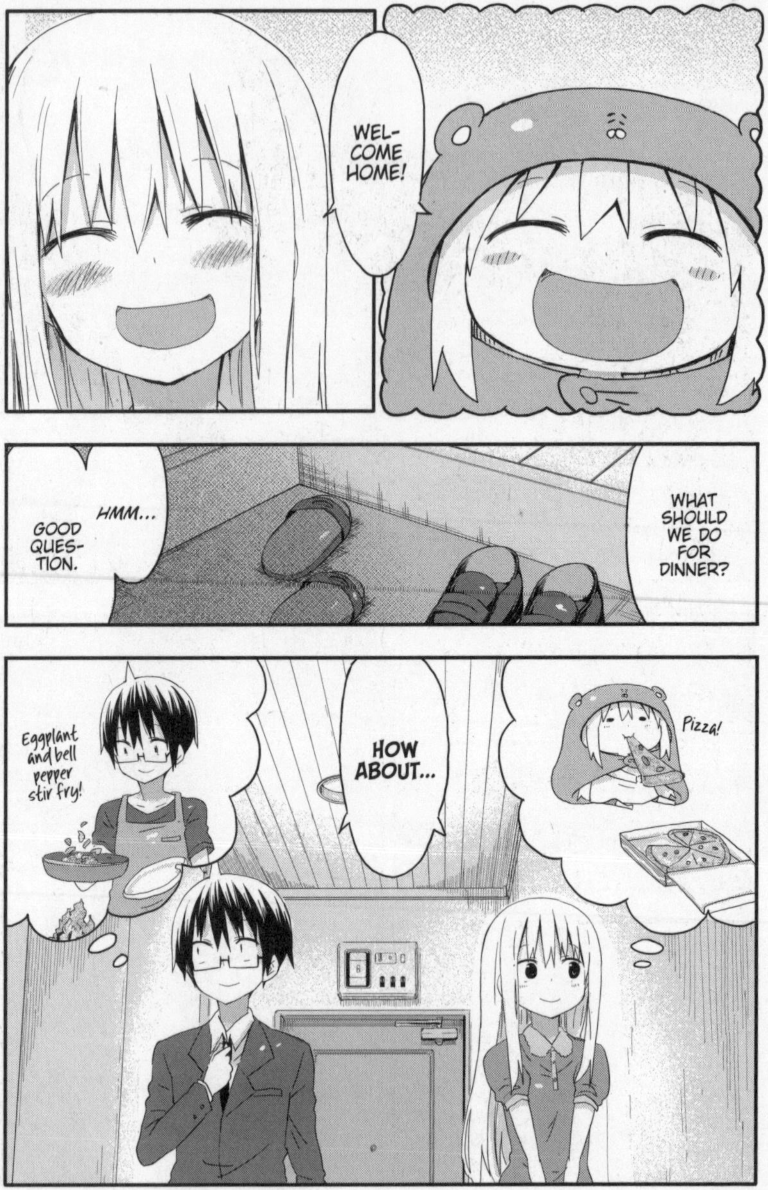
WEL-COME HOME!
WHAT SHOULD WE DO FOR DINNER?
HMM...
GOOD QUES-TION.
Pizza!
HOW ABOUT...
Eggplant and bell pepper stir fry!

No. 70 Umaru & the Electronics Store

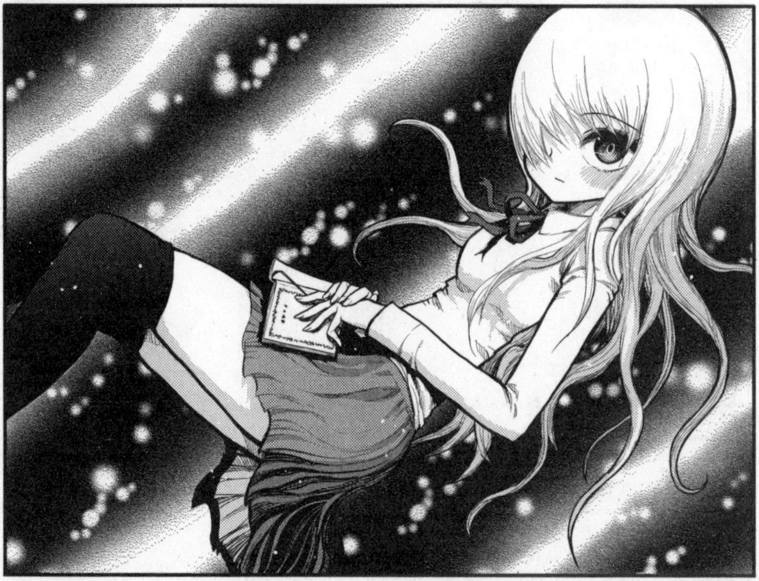

Guest Illustrator: Nakayama Atsushi

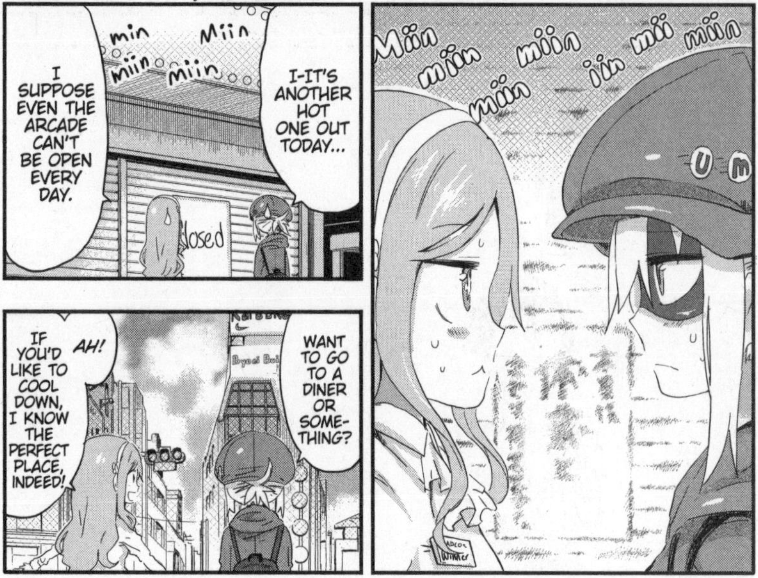

Miin miin miin miin iin mii miin
min Miin miin miin
I-IT'S ANOTHER HOT ONE OUT TODAY...
I SUPPOSE EVEN THE ARCADE CAN'T BE OPEN EVERY DAY.
closed
WANT TO GO TO A DINER OR SOMETHING?
AH!
IF YOU'D LIKE TO COOL DOWN, I KNOW THE PERFECT PLACE, INDEED!

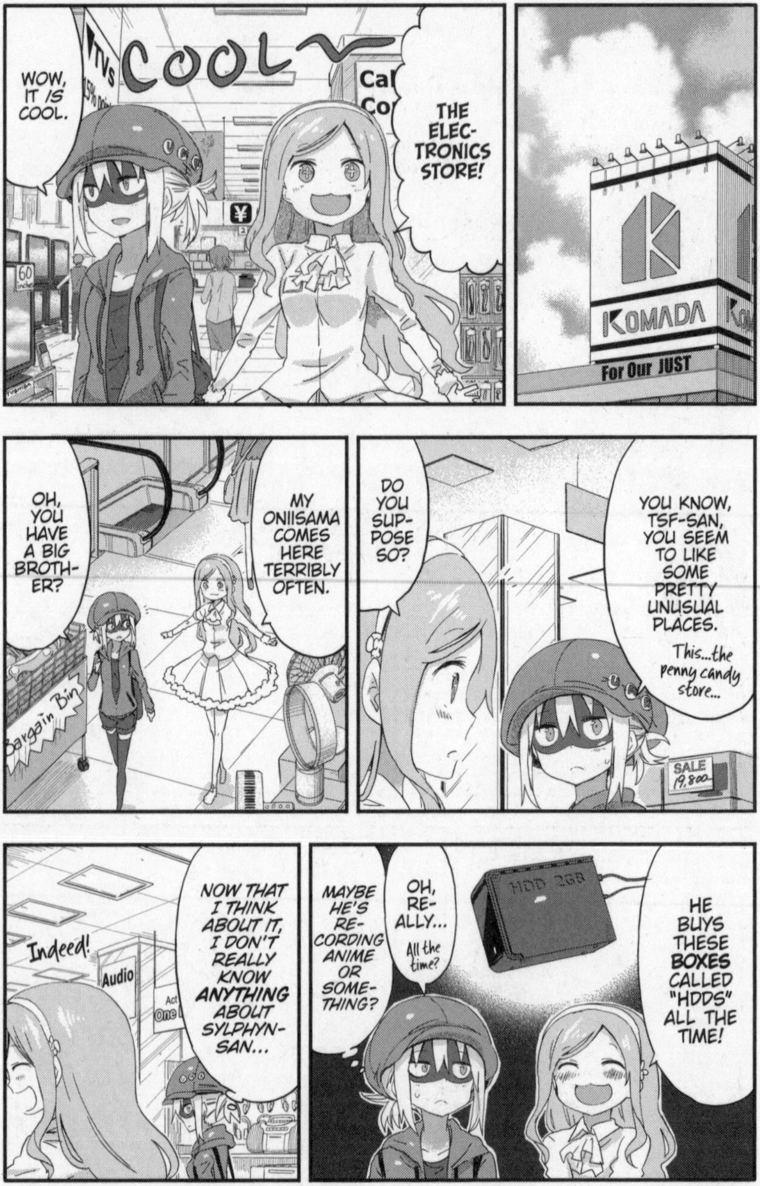
KOMADA
For Our JUST
THE ELECTRONICS STORE!
COOL~
WOW, IT IS COOL.
TVs
60 inches
YOU KNOW, TSF-SAN, YOU SEEM TO LIKE SOME PRETTY UNUSUAL PLACES.
This...the penny candy store...
DO YOU SUPPOSE SO?
SALE 19,800
MY ONIISAMA COMES HERE TERRIBLY OFTEN.
OH, YOU HAVE A BIG BROTHER?
Bargain Bin
HDD 2GB
HE BUYS THESE **BOXES** CALLED "HDDS" ALL THE TIME!
OH, REALLY...
All the time?
MAYBE HE'S RECORDING ANIME OR SOMETHING?
NOW THAT I THINK ABOUT IT, I DON'T REALLY KNOW **ANYTHING** ABOUT SYLPHYN-SAN...
Indeed!
Audio

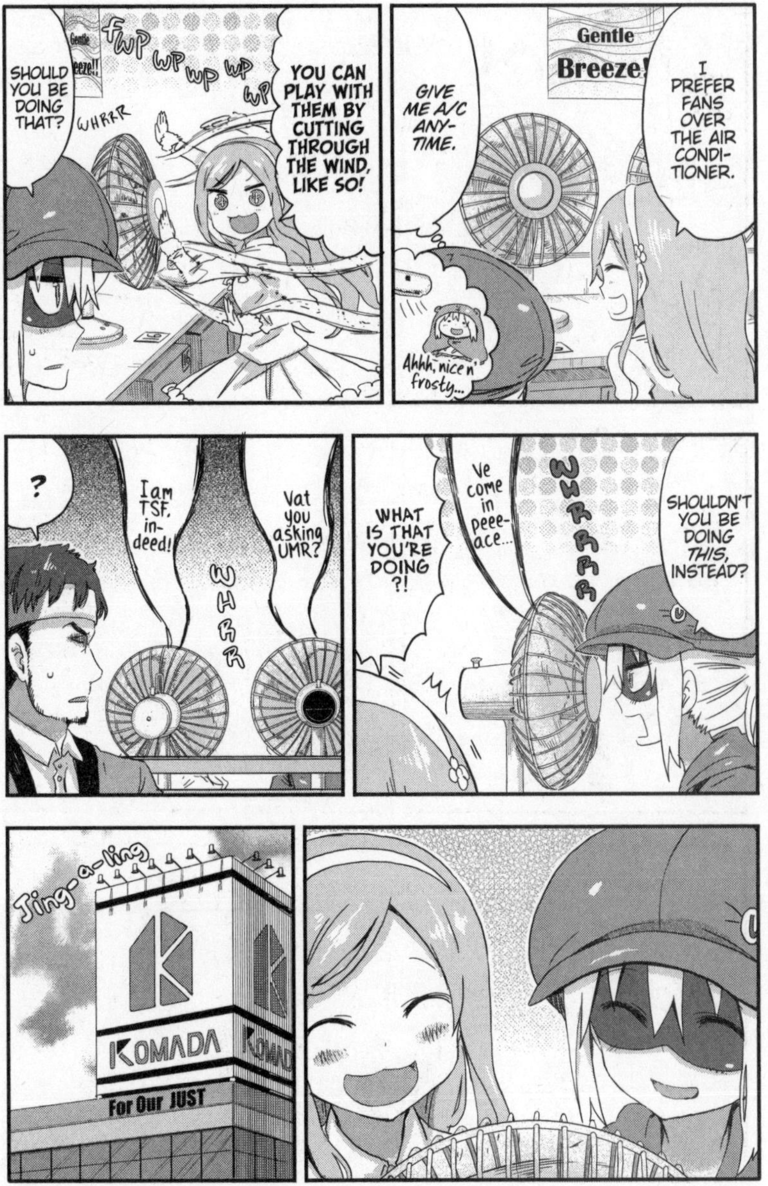
I PREFER FANS OVER THE AIR CONDITIONER.
Gentle Breeze!
GIVE ME A/C ANY-TIME.
Ahhh, nice n' frosty...
YOU CAN PLAY WITH THEM BY CUTTING THROUGH THE WIND, LIKE SO!
FWP WP WP WP WP
Gentle
eeze!!
SHOULD YOU BE DOING THAT?
WHRRR
SHOULDN'T YOU BE DOING THIS, INSTEAD?
WHRRRR
Ve come in peeeace...
WHAT IS THAT YOU'RE DOING ?!
Vat you asking UMR?
WHRR
I am TSF, indeed!
?
Jing-a-ling
KOMADA
For Our JUST

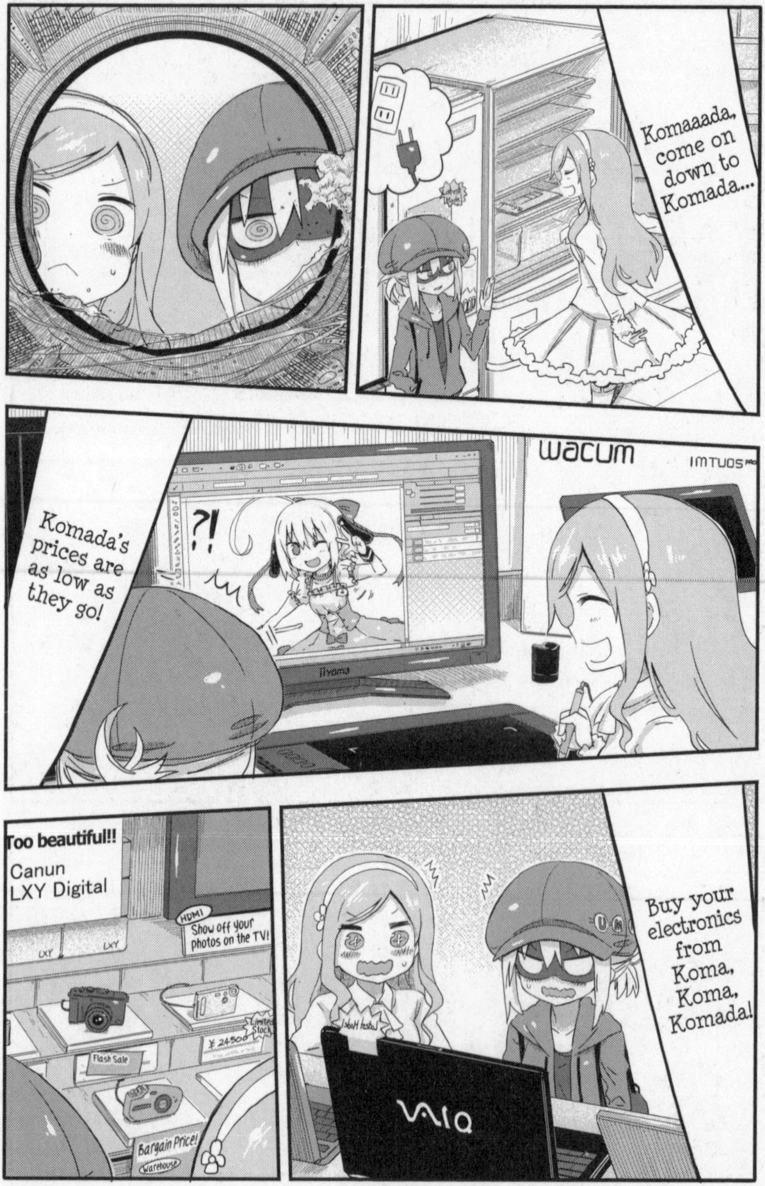
Komaaada, come on down to Komada...
Komada's prices are as low as they go!
?!
wacum
IMTUOS
iiyama
Buy your electronics from Koma, Koma, Komada!
VAIO
Too beautiful!!
Canun LXY Digital
HDMI
Show off your photos on the TV!
LXY
LXY
Limited Stock
¥24500
Flash Sale
Bargain Price!
Warehouse

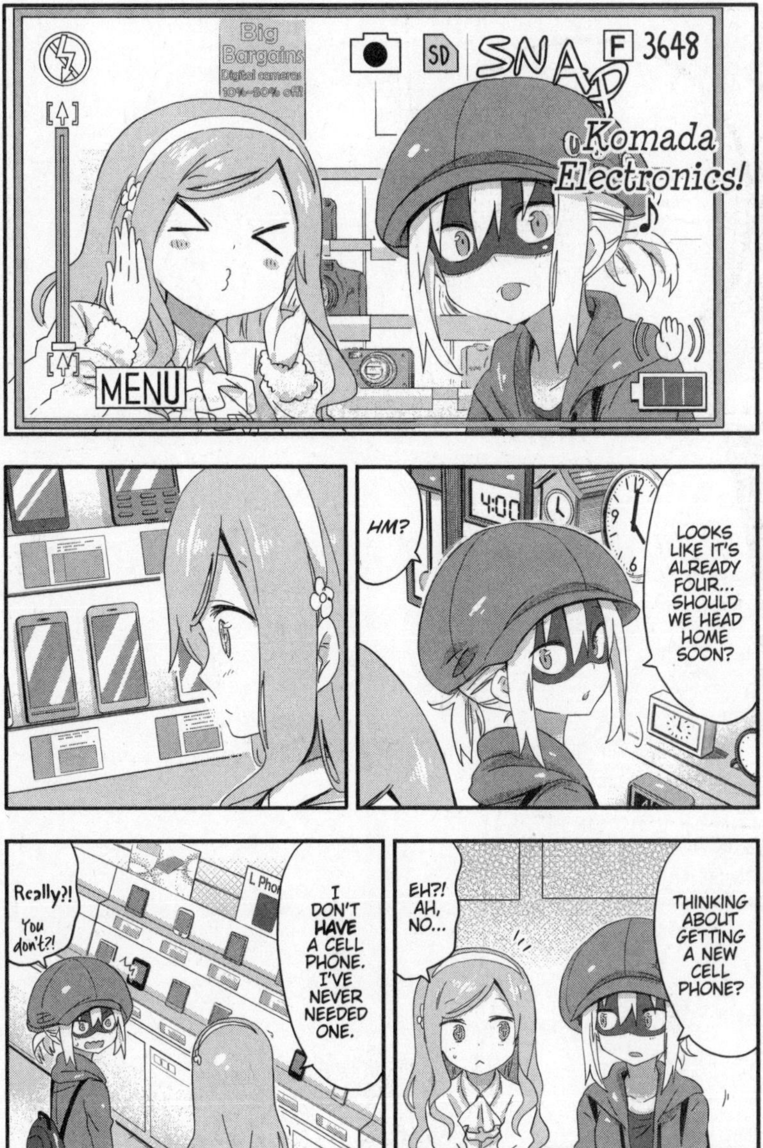
SNAP
F 3648
Komada Electronics! ♪
SD
Big Bargains
Digital cameras 10%-60% off!
MENU
LOOKS LIKE IT'S ALREADY FOUR... SHOULD WE HEAD HOME SOON?
4:00
HM?
THINKING ABOUT GETTING A NEW CELL PHONE?
EH?! AH, NO...
I DON'T **HAVE** A CELL PHONE. I'VE NEVER NEEDED ONE.
Really?!
You don't?!

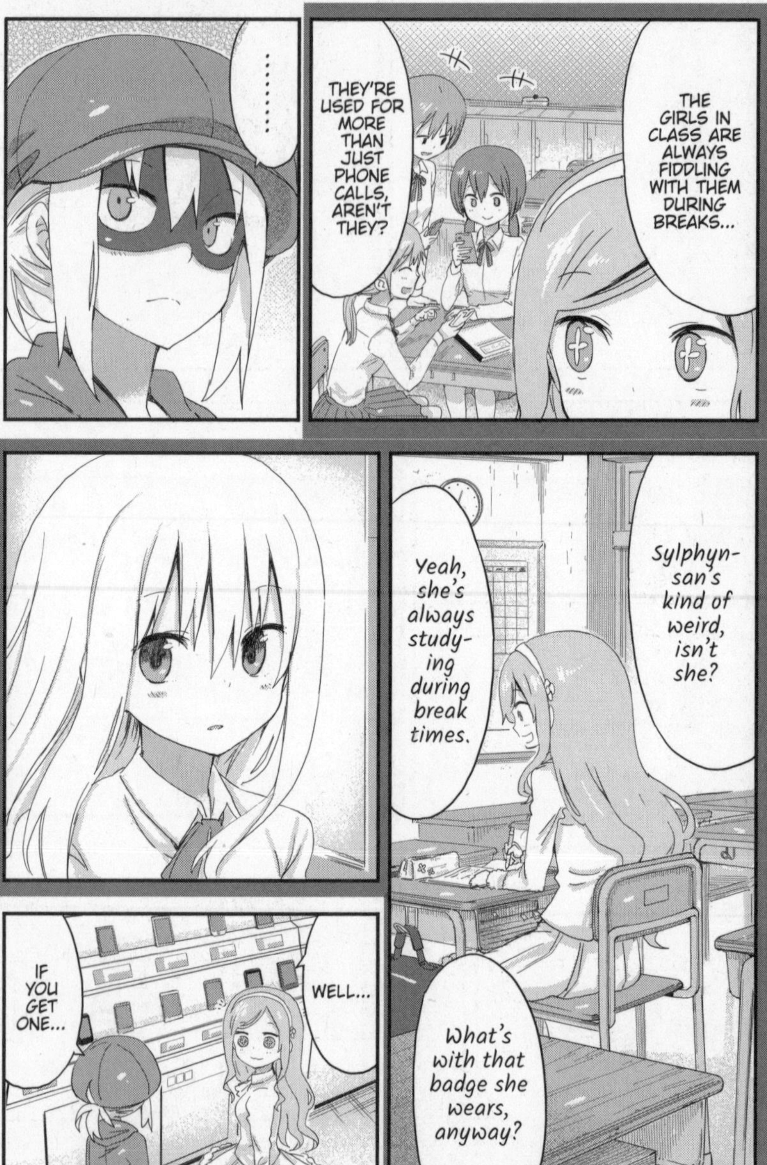
THE GIRLS IN CLASS ARE ALWAYS FIDDLING WITH THEM DURING BREAKS...
THEY'RE USED FOR MORE THAN JUST PHONE CALLS, AREN'T THEY?
......
Sylphyn-san's kind of weird, isn't she?
Yeah, she's always study-ing during break times.
What's with that badge she wears, anyway?
WELL...
IF YOU GET ONE...

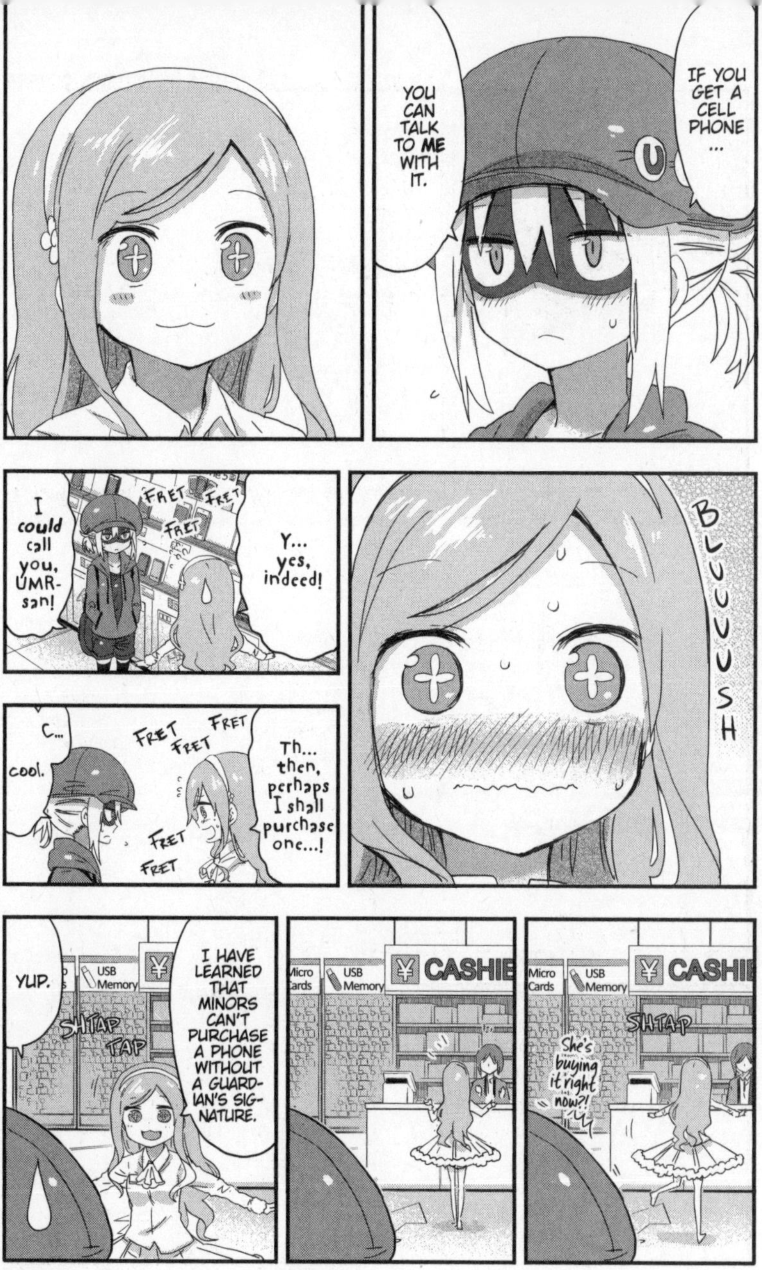
IF YOU GET A CELL PHONE ...
YOU CAN TALK TO ME WITH IT.
BLUUUUUSH
Y... yes, indeed!
FRET FRET FRET
I could call you, UMR-san!
Th... then, perhaps I shall purchase one...!
FRET FRET FRET
FRET FRET
C... cool.
Micro Cards
USB Memory
¥ CASHIE
SHTAP
She's buying it right now?!
Micro Cards
USB Memory
¥ CASHIE
I HAVE LEARNED THAT MINORS CAN'T PURCHASE A PHONE WITHOUT A GUARDIAN'S SIGNATURE.
YUP.
SHTAP TAP
USB Memory

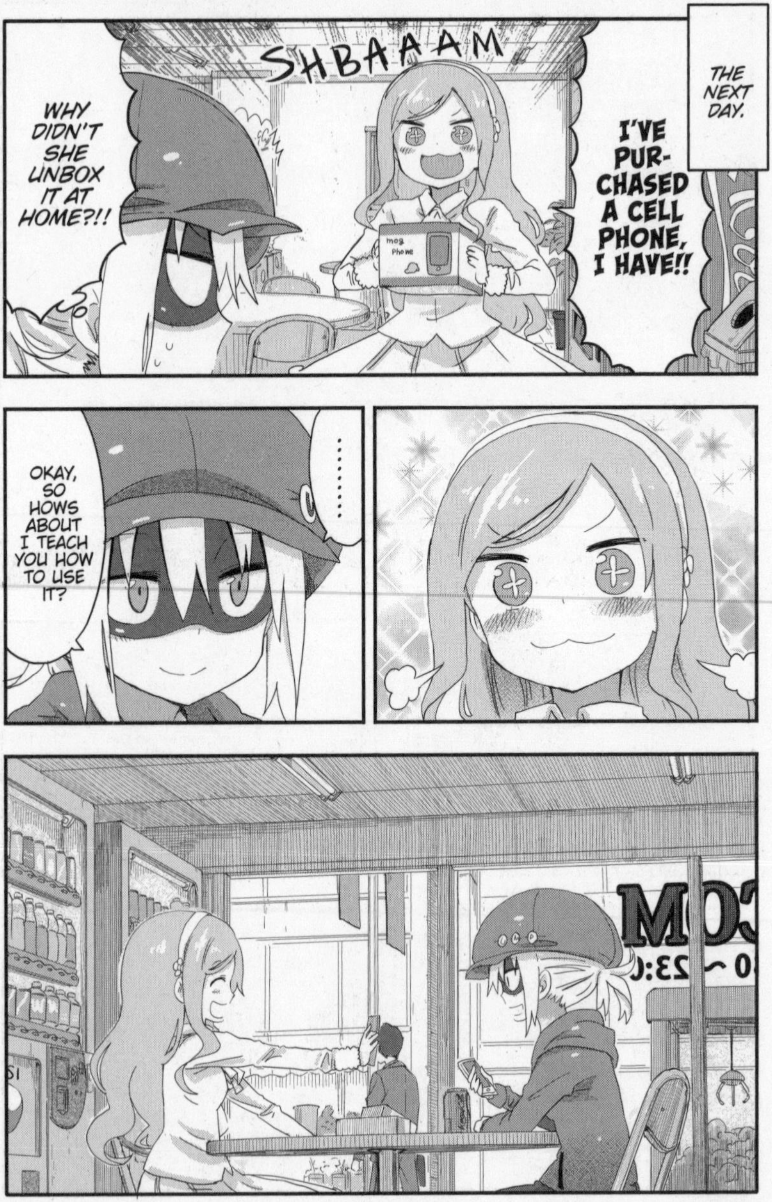
THE NEXT DAY.
SHBAAAM
I'VE PURCHASED A CELL PHONE, I HAVE!!
WHY DIDN'T SHE UNBOX IT AT HOME?!!
......
OKAY, SO HOWS ABOUT I TEACH YOU HOW TO USE IT?

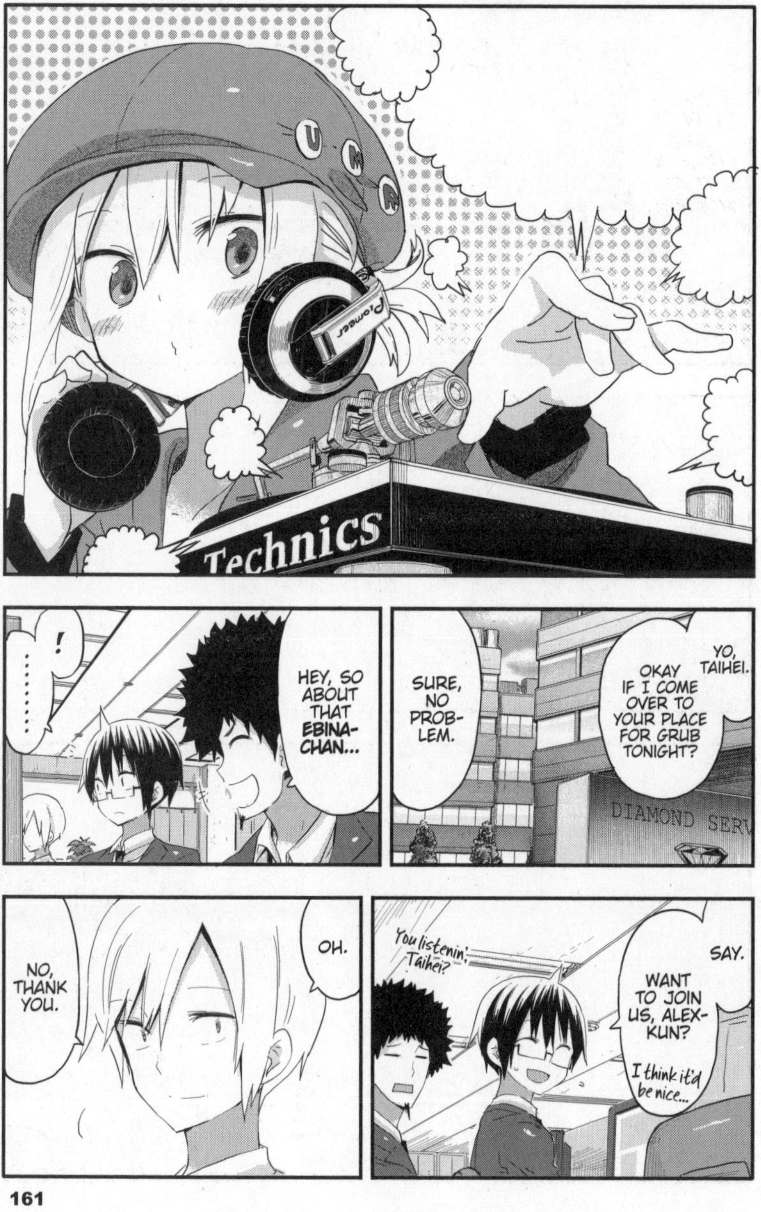
Technics
Pioneer
YO, TAIHEI.
OKAY IF I COME OVER TO YOUR PLACE FOR GRUB TONIGHT?
SURE, NO PROBLEM.
DIAMOND SERV
HEY, SO ABOUT THAT EBINA-CHAN...
!
......
SAY.
WANT TO JOIN US, ALEX-KUN?
I think it'd be nice...
You listenin', Taihei?
OH.
NO, THANK YOU.

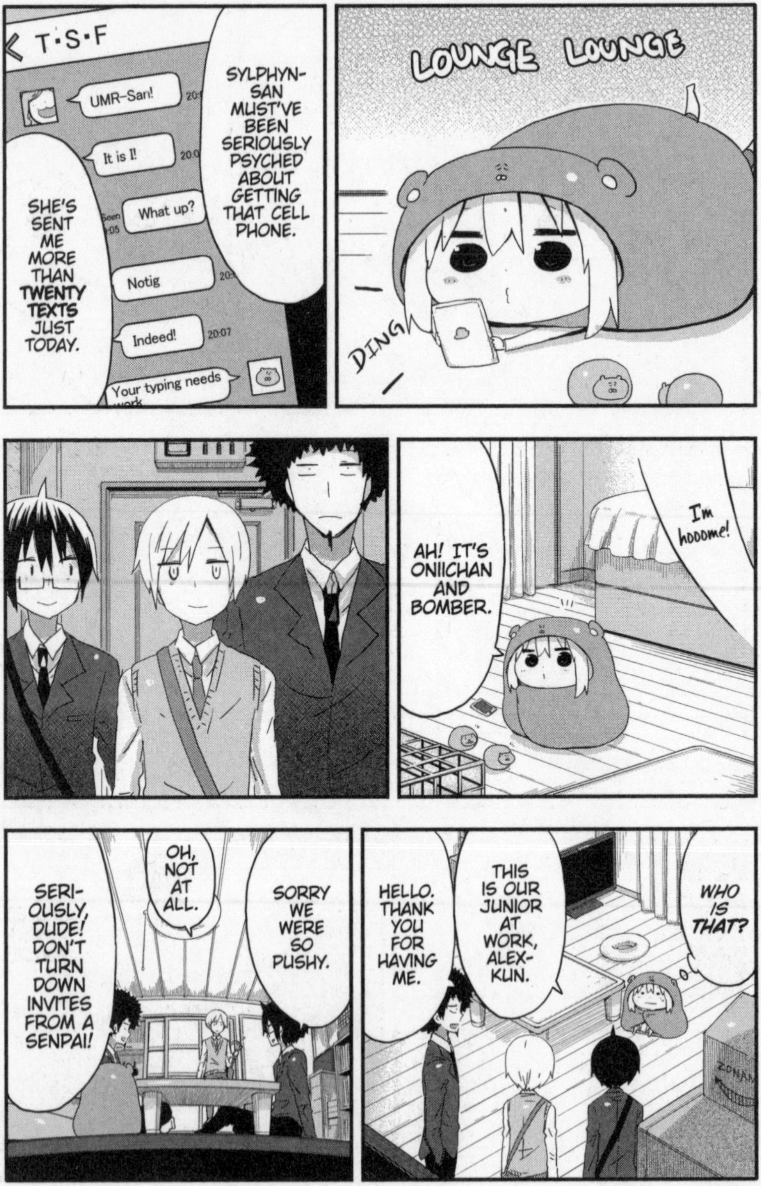
LOUNGE LOUNGE
DING
SYLPHYN-SAN MUST'VE BEEN SERIOUSLY PSYCHED ABOUT GETTING THAT CELL PHONE.
SHE'S SENT ME MORE THAN **TWENTY TEXTS** JUST TODAY.
T·S·F
UMR-San!
It is I!
What up?
Seen
Notig
Indeed!
20:07
Your typing needs
I'm hooome!
AH! IT'S ONIICHAN AND BOMBER.
WHO IS *THAT?*
THIS IS OUR JUNIOR AT WORK, ALEX-KUN.
HELLO. THANK YOU FOR HAVING ME.
SORRY WE WERE SO PUSHY.
OH, NOT AT ALL.
SERI-OUSLY, DUDE! DON'T TURN DOWN INVITES FROM A SENPAI!
ZONAM

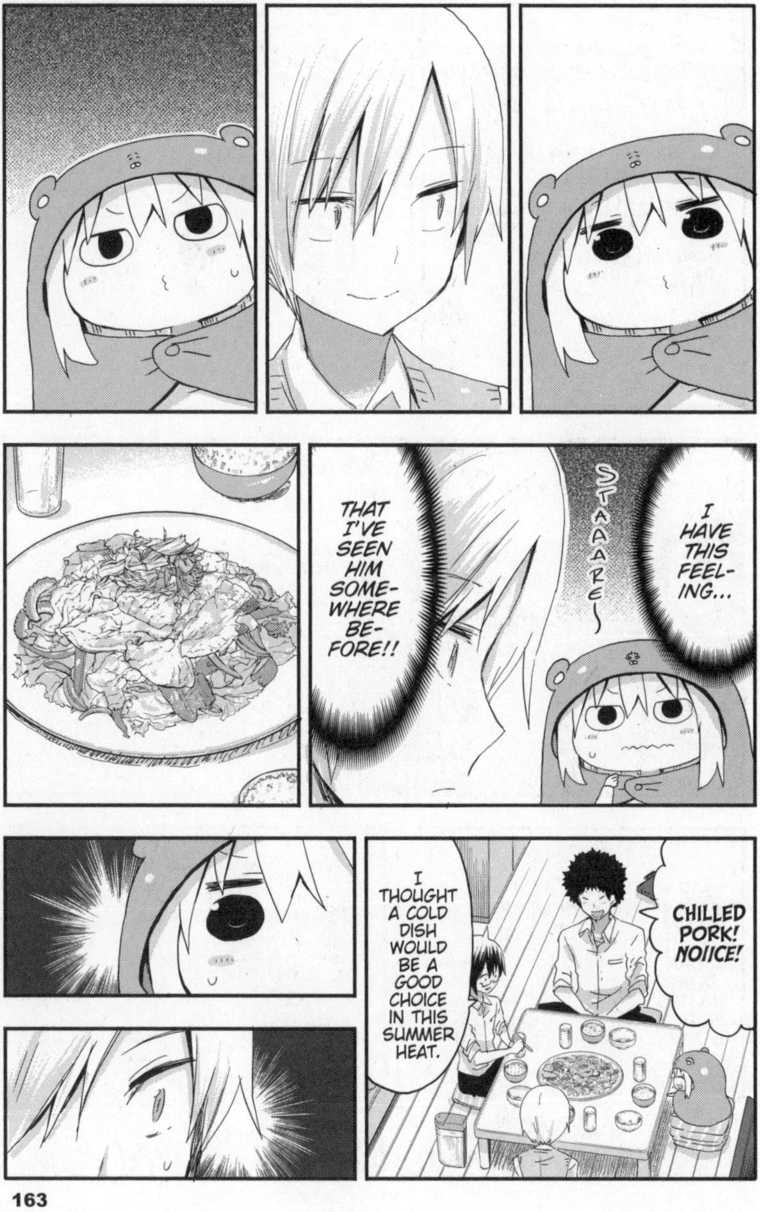
I HAVE THIS FEELING...
STAAARE~
THAT I'VE SEEN HIM SOMEWHERE BEFORE!!
CHILLED PORK! NOIICE!
I THOUGHT A COLD DISH WOULD BE A GOOD CHOICE IN THIS SUMMER HEAT.

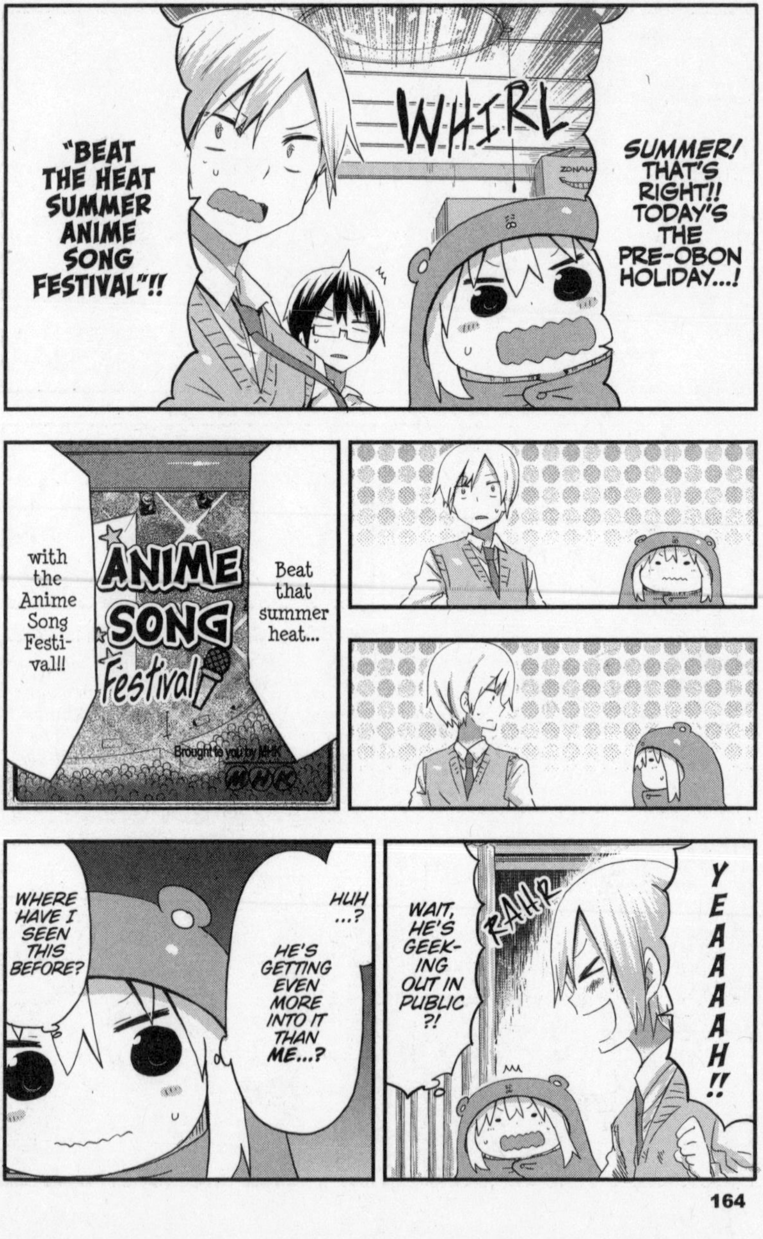
SUMMER! THAT'S RIGHT!! TODAY'S THE PRE-OBON HOLIDAY...!
WHIRL
"BEAT THE HEAT SUMMER ANIME SONG FESTIVAL"!!
Beat that summer heat...
ANIME SONG Festival
Brought to you by MHK
with the Anime Song Festival!!
YEAAAAH!!
RAHR
WAIT, HE'S GEEKING OUT IN PUBLIC?!
HUH...?
HE'S GETTING EVEN MORE INTO IT THAN ME...?
WHERE HAVE I SEEN THIS BEFORE?

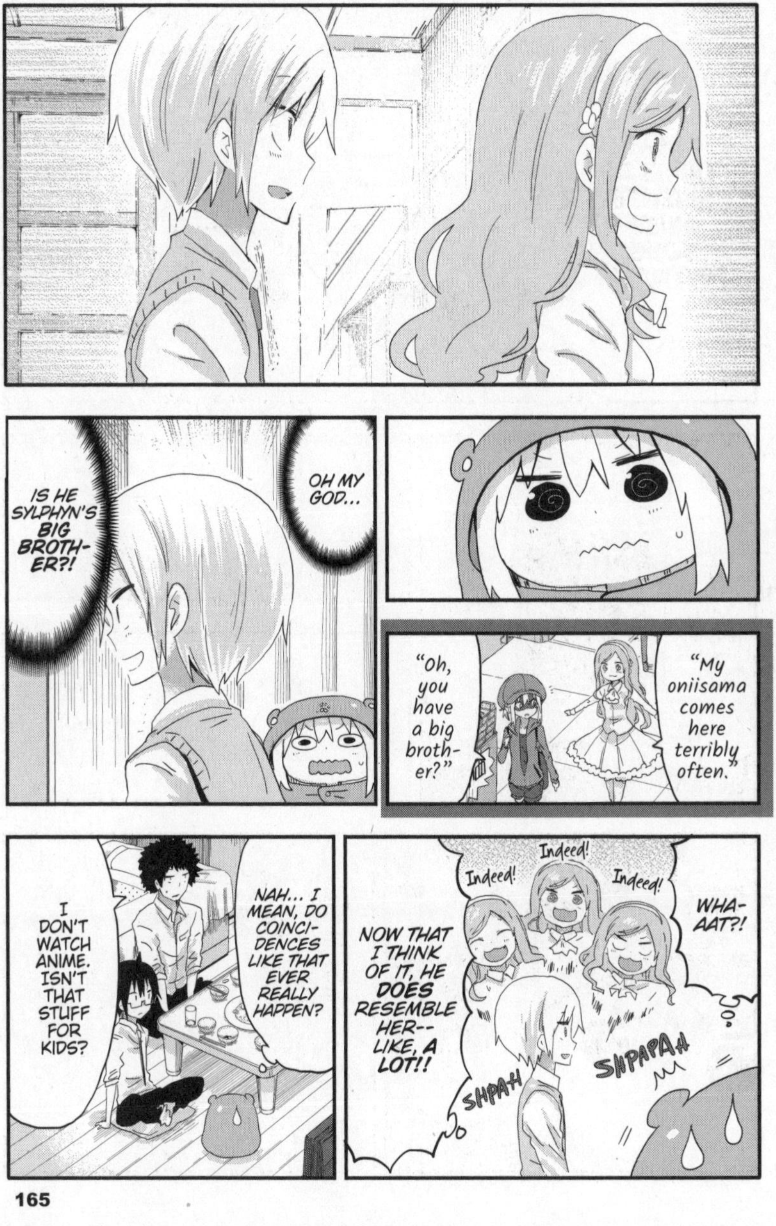

"My oniisama comes here terribly often."
"Oh, you have a big brother?"
OH MY GOD...
IS HE SYLPHYN'S BIG BROTHER?!
WHA-AAT?!
Indeed!
Indeed!
Indeed!
NOW THAT I THINK OF IT, HE DOES RESEMBLE HER-- LIKE, A LOT!!
SHPAPAH
SHPAH
NAH... I MEAN, DO COINCIDENCES LIKE THAT EVER REALLY HAPPEN?
I DON'T WATCH ANIME. ISN'T THAT STUFF FOR KIDS?

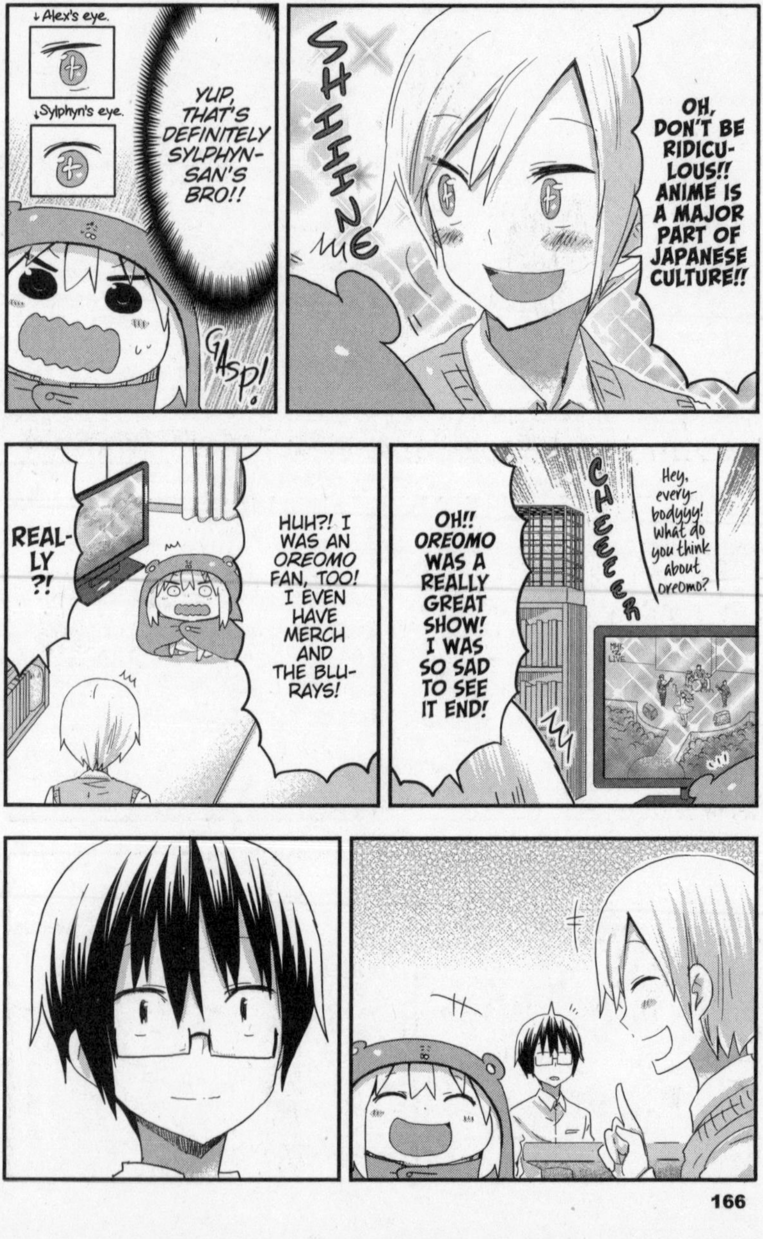
OH, DON'T BE RIDICULOUS!! ANIME IS A MAJOR PART OF JAPANESE CULTURE!!
SHIIIINE
↓Alex's eye.
↓Sylphyn's eye.
YUP, THAT'S DEFINITELY SYLPHYN-SAN'S BRO!!
GASP!
Hey, everybodyyy! what do you think about oreomo?
CHEEEER
OH!! OREOMO WAS A REALLY GREAT SHOW! I WAS SO SAD TO SEE IT END!
HUH?! I WAS AN OREOMO FAN, TOO! I EVEN HAVE MERCH AND THE BLU-RAYS!
REALLY?!

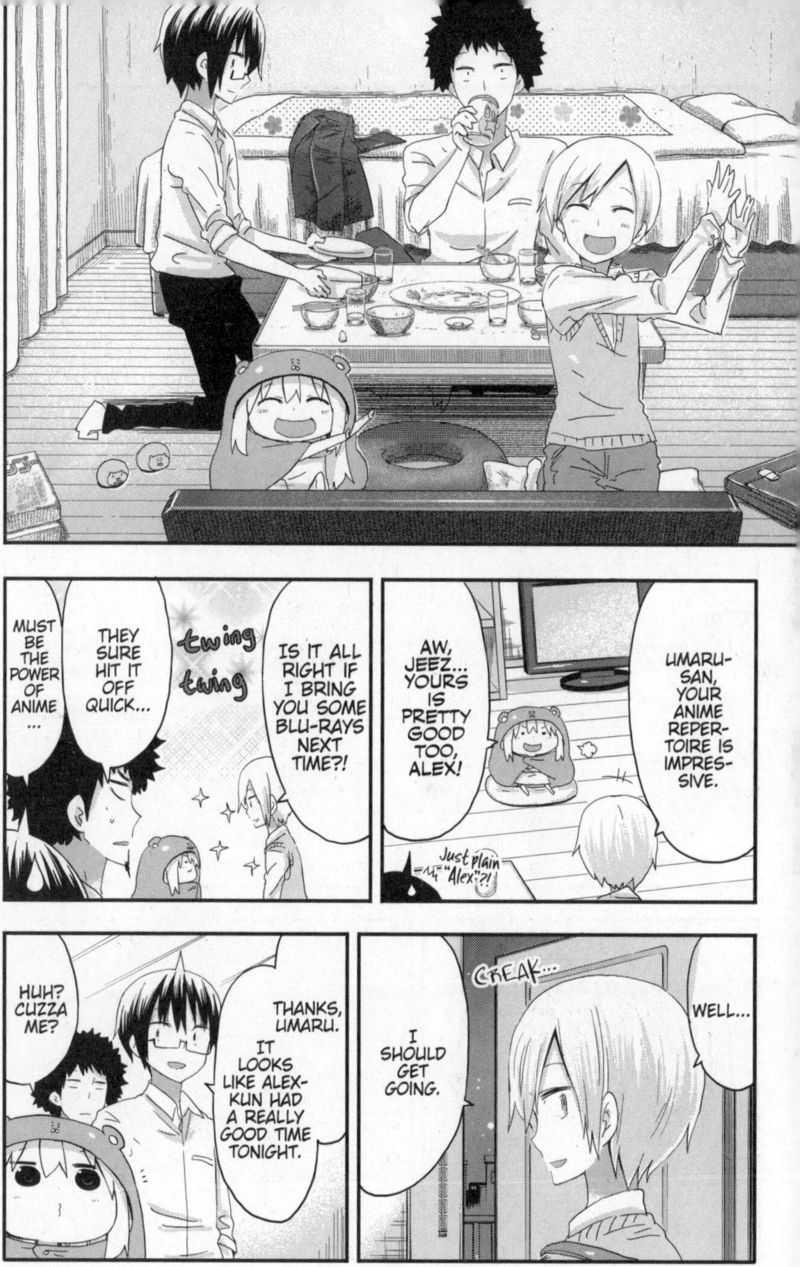
UMARU-SAN, YOUR ANIME REPERTOIRE IS IMPRESSIVE.
AW, JEEZ... YOURS IS PRETTY GOOD TOO, ALEX!
Just plain "Alex"?!
IS IT ALL RIGHT IF I BRING YOU SOME BLU-RAYS NEXT TIME?!
twing twing
THEY SURE HIT IT OFF QUICK...
MUST BE THE POWER OF ANIME...
WELL...
CREAK...
I SHOULD GET GOING.
THANKS, UMARU.
IT LOOKS LIKE ALEX-KUN HAD A REALLY GOOD TIME TONIGHT.
HUH? CUZZA ME?

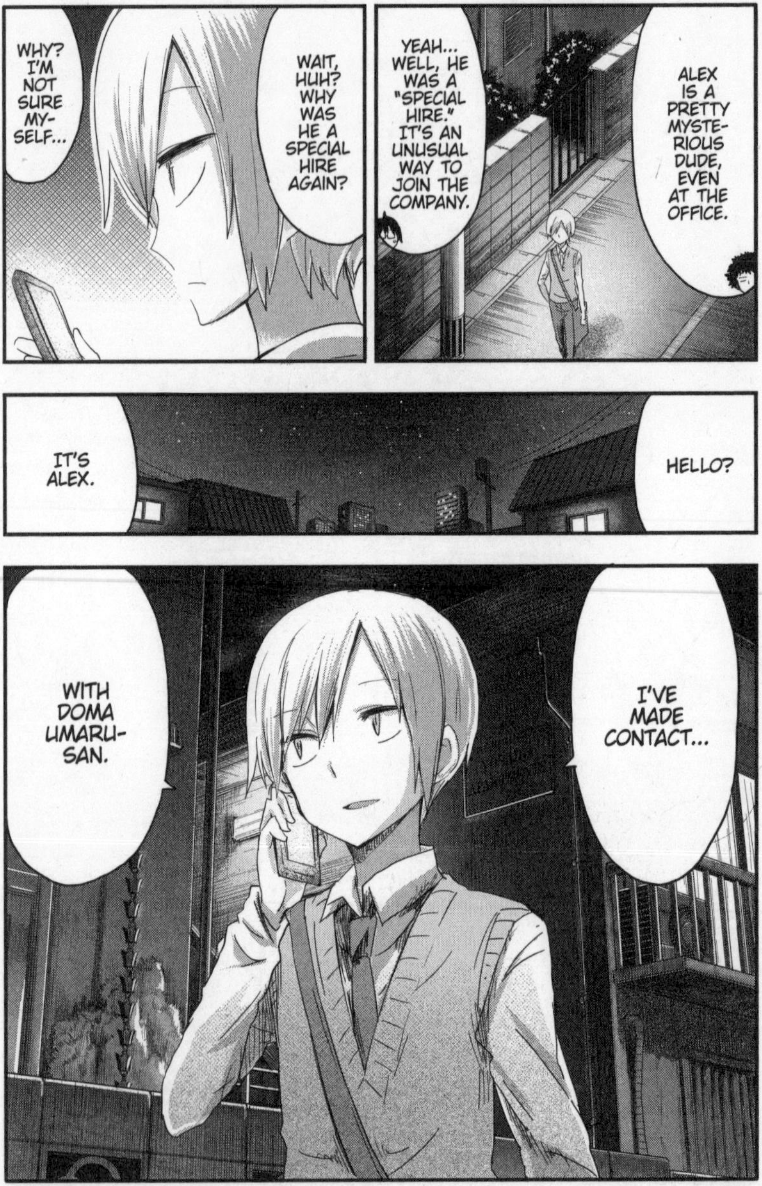
ALEX IS A PRETTY MYSTERIOUS DUDE, EVEN AT THE OFFICE.
YEAH... WELL, HE WAS A "SPECIAL HIRE." IT'S AN UNUSUAL WAY TO JOIN THE COMPANY.
WAIT, HUH? WHY WAS HE A SPECIAL HIRE AGAIN?
WHY? I'M NOT SURE MYSELF...
HELLO?
IT'S ALEX.
I'VE MADE CONTACT...
WITH DOMA UMARU-SAN.

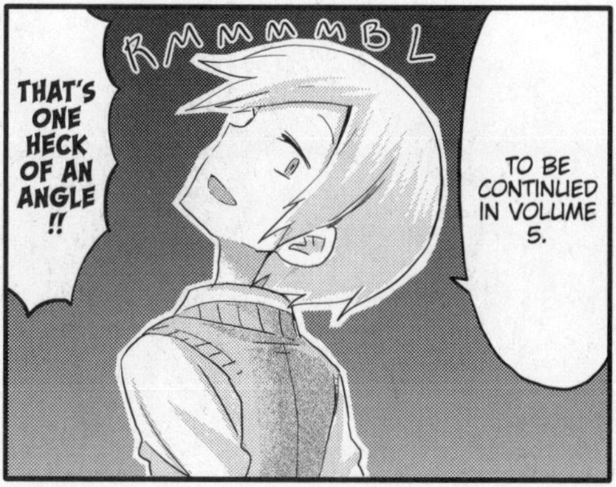
RMMMMBL
THAT'S ONE HECK OF AN ANGLE!!
TO BE CONTINUED IN VOLUME 5.

HIMOUTO! UMARU-CHAN

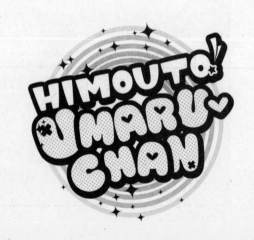

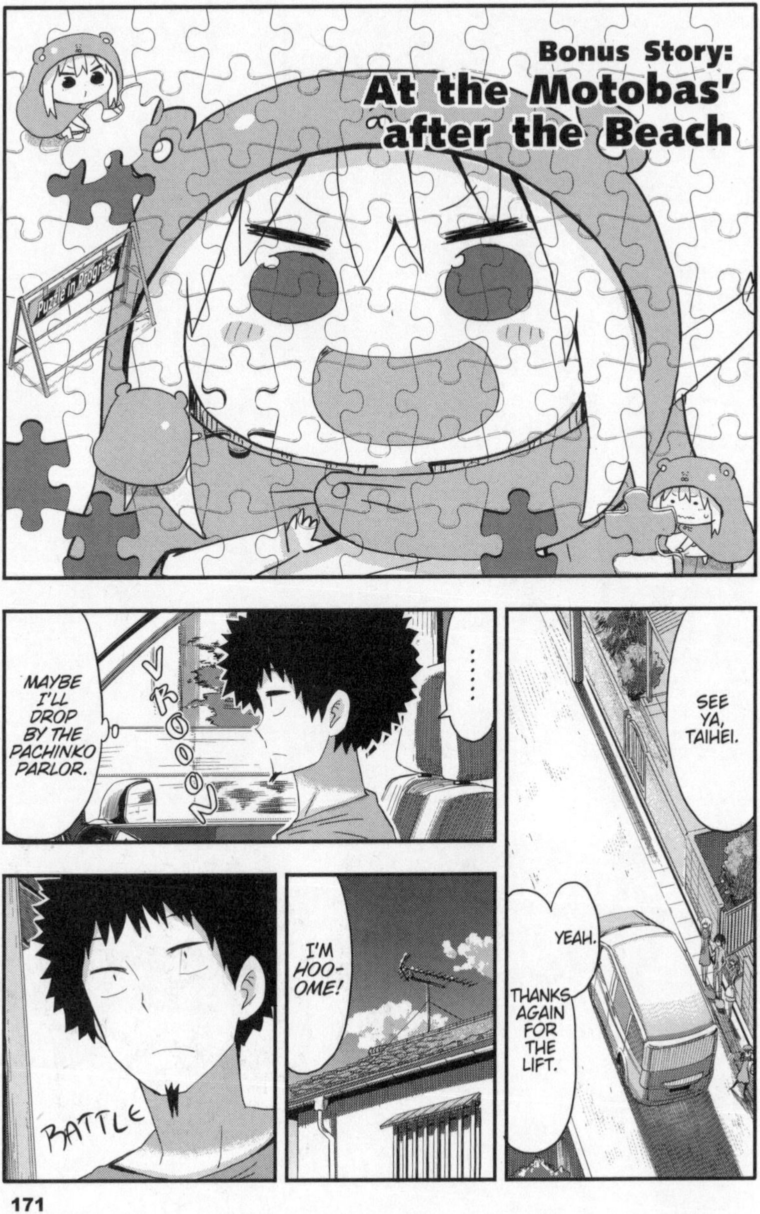
Bonus Story:
At the Motobas' after the Beach
Puzzle in Progress
SEE YA, TAIHEI.
YEAH.
THANKS AGAIN FOR THE LIFT.
......
VROOOOON
MAYBE I'LL DROP BY THE PACHINKO PARLOR.
I'M HOO-OME!
RATTLE

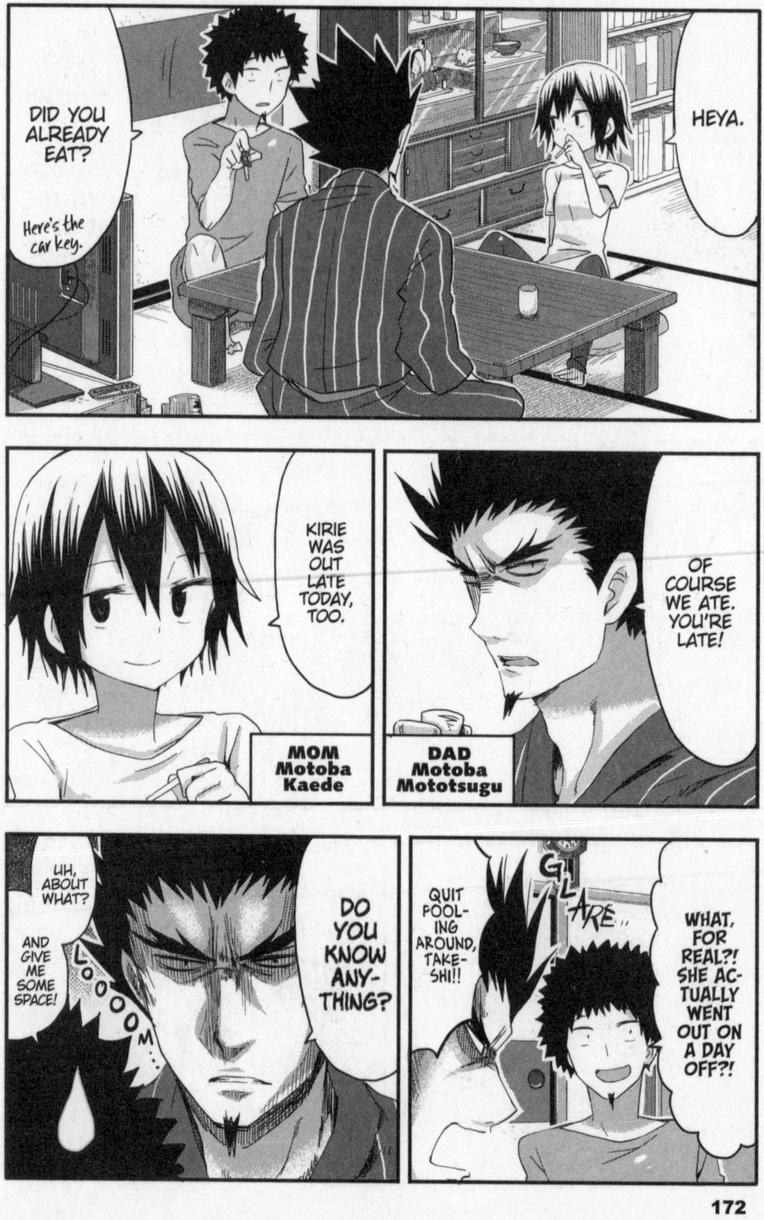
HEYA.
DID YOU ALREADY EAT?
Here's the car key.
OF COURSE WE ATE. YOU'RE LATE!
DAD Motoba Mototsugu
KIRIE WAS OUT LATE TODAY, TOO.
MOM Motoba Kaede
WHAT, FOR REAL?! SHE ACTUALLY WENT OUT ON A DAY OFF?!
GLARE...
QUIT FOOLING AROUND, TAKESHI!!
DO YOU KNOW ANYTHING?
UH, ABOUT WHAT?
AND GIVE ME SOME SPACE!
LOOOOOM...

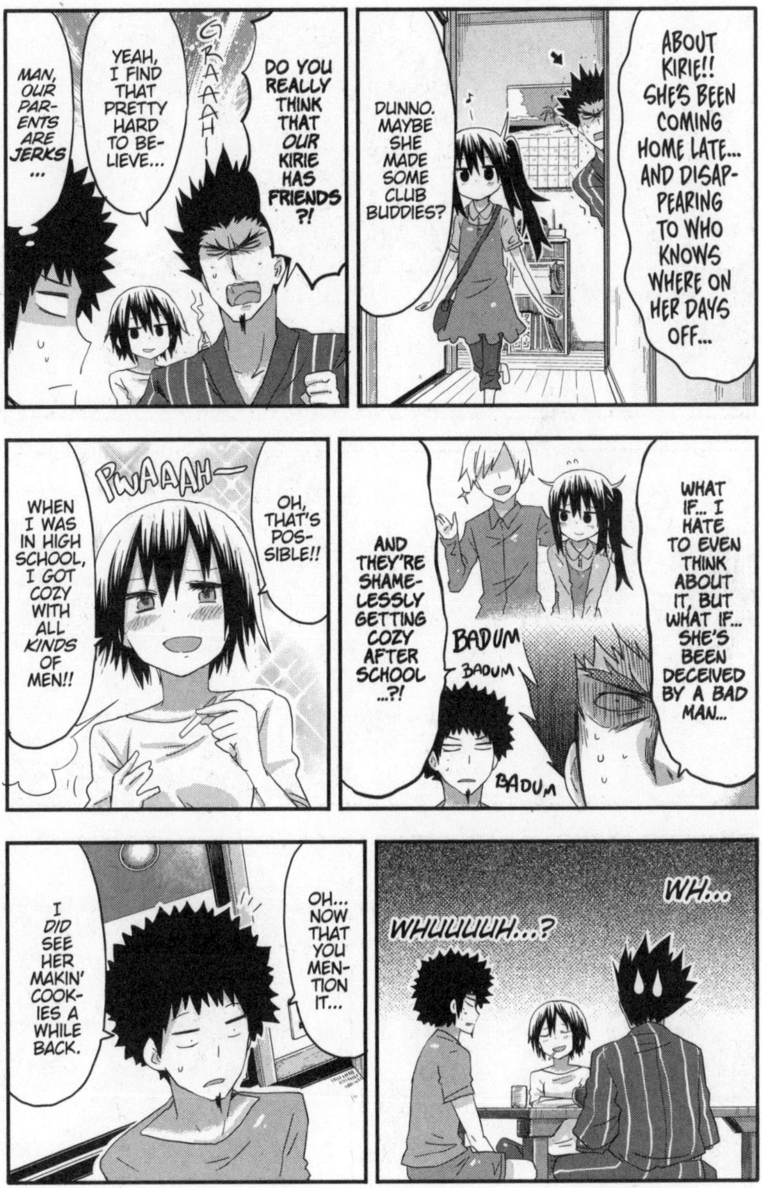
ABOUT KIRIE!! SHE'S BEEN COMING HOME LATE... AND DISAPPEARING TO WHO KNOWS WHERE ON HER DAYS OFF...
DUNNO. MAYBE SHE MADE SOME CLUB BUDDIES?
DO YOU REALLY THINK THAT OUR KIRIE HAS FRIENDS?!
GRAAAH!
YEAH, I FIND THAT PRETTY HARD TO BELIEVE...
MAN, OUR PARENTS ARE JERKS...
WHAT IF... I HATE TO EVEN THINK ABOUT IT, BUT WHAT IF... SHE'S BEEN DECEIVED BY A BAD MAN...
BADUM
BADUM
BADUM
AND THEY'RE SHAMELESSLY GETTING COZY AFTER SCHOOL...?!
PWAAAH—
OH, THAT'S POSSIBLE!!
WHEN I WAS IN HIGH SCHOOL, I GOT COZY WITH ALL KINDS OF MEN!!
WH...
WHUUUUUH...?
OH... NOW THAT YOU MENTION IT...
I DID SEE HER MAKIN' COOKIES A WHILE BACK.

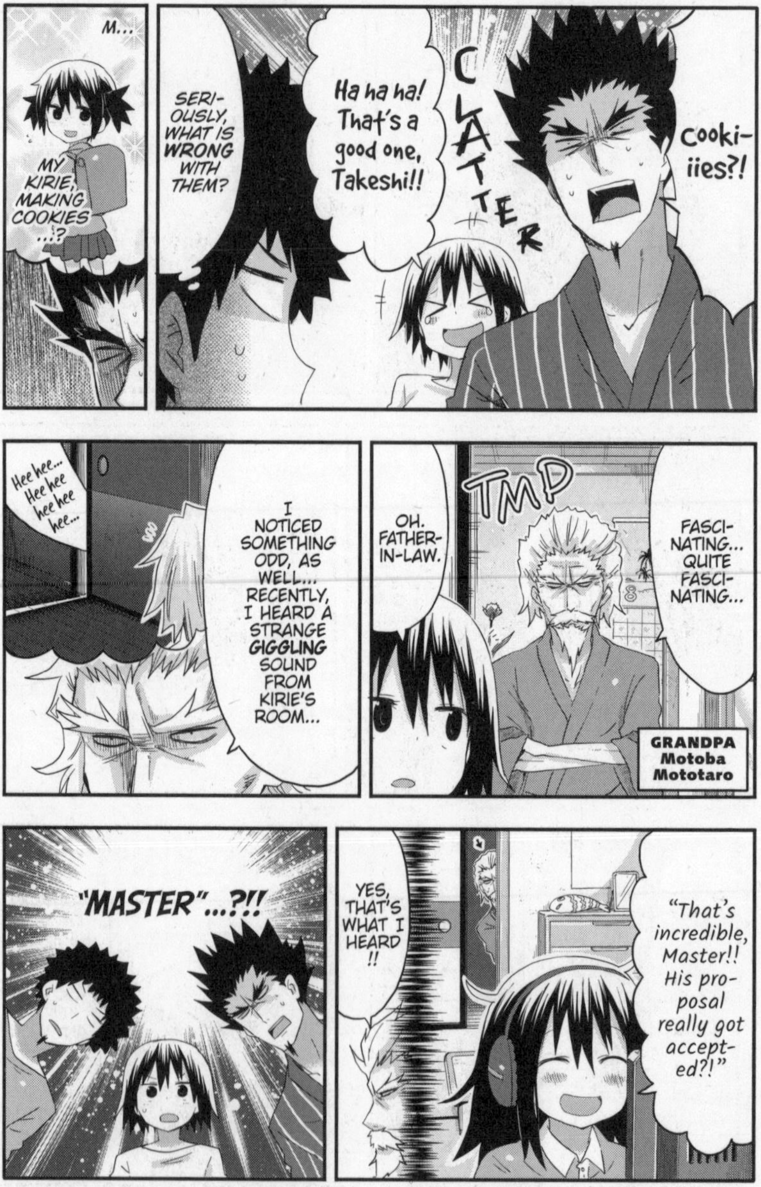
Cooki-iies?!
CLATTER
Ha ha ha! That's a good one, Takeshi!!
SERI-OUSLY, WHAT IS WRONG WITH THEM?
M...
MY KIRIE, MAKING COOKIES ...?
FASCI-NATING... QUITE FASCI-NATING...
TMP
OH. FATHER-IN-LAW.
GRANDPA Motoba Mototaro
I NOTICED SOMETHING ODD, AS WELL... RECENTLY, I HEARD A STRANGE GIGGLING SOUND FROM KIRIE'S ROOM...
Hee hee... Hee hee hee hee hee...
“That's incredible, Master!! His pro-posal really got accept-ed?!”
YES, THAT'S WHAT I HEARD !!
“MASTER”...?!!

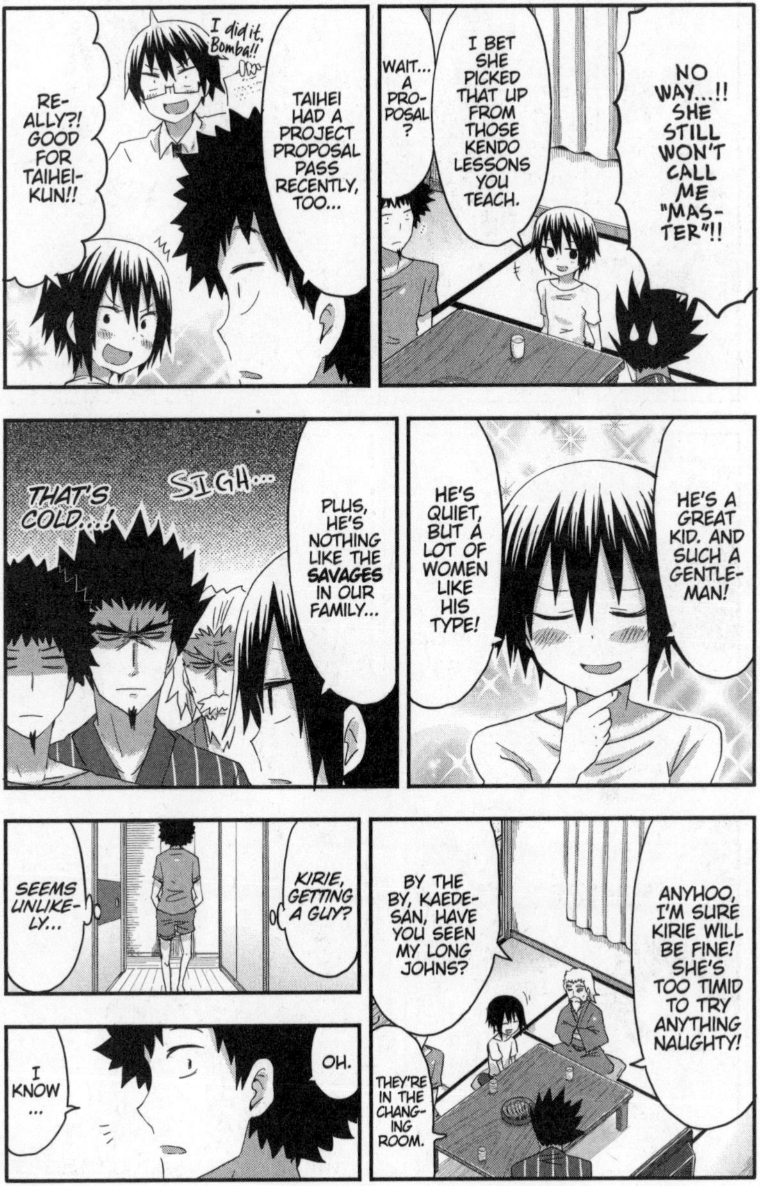
NO WAY...!! SHE STILL WON'T CALL ME "MASTER"!!
I BET SHE PICKED THAT UP FROM THOSE KENDO LESSONS YOU TEACH.
WAIT... A PROPOSAL?
TAIHEI HAD A PROJECT PROPOSAL PASS RECENTLY, TOO...
I did it, Bomba!!
REALLY?! GOOD FOR TAIHEI-KUN!!
HE'S A GREAT KID. AND SUCH A GENTLEMAN!
HE'S QUIET, BUT A LOT OF WOMEN LIKE HIS TYPE!
PLUS, HE'S NOTHING LIKE THE **SAVAGES** IN OUR FAMILY...
SIGH...
THAT'S COLD...!
ANYHOO, I'M SURE KIRIE WILL BE FINE! SHE'S TOO TIMID TO TRY ANYTHING NAUGHTY!
BY THE BY, KAEDE-SAN, HAVE YOU SEEN MY LONG JOHNS?
THEY'RE IN THE CHANGING ROOM.
KIRIE, GETTING A GUY?
SEEMS UNLIKELY...
OH.
I KNOW ...

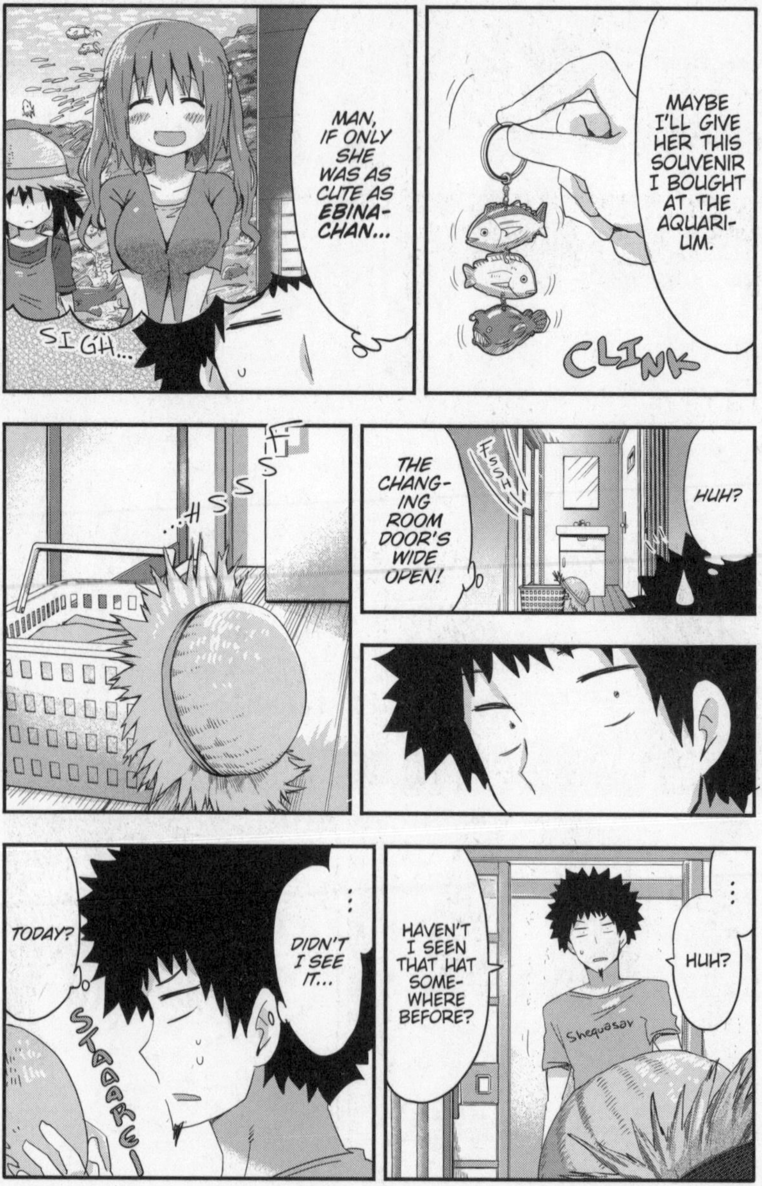
MAYBE I'LL GIVE HER THIS SOUVENIR I BOUGHT AT THE AQUARIUM.
CLINK
MAN, IF ONLY SHE WAS AS CUTE AS EBINA-CHAN...
SIGH...
HUH?
FSSH
THE CHANGING ROOM DOOR'S WIDE OPEN!
FSSSH...
...
HUH?
HAVEN'T I SEEN THAT HAT SOMEWHERE BEFORE?
Shequasar
...
DIDN'T I SEE IT...
TODAY?
STAAARE!

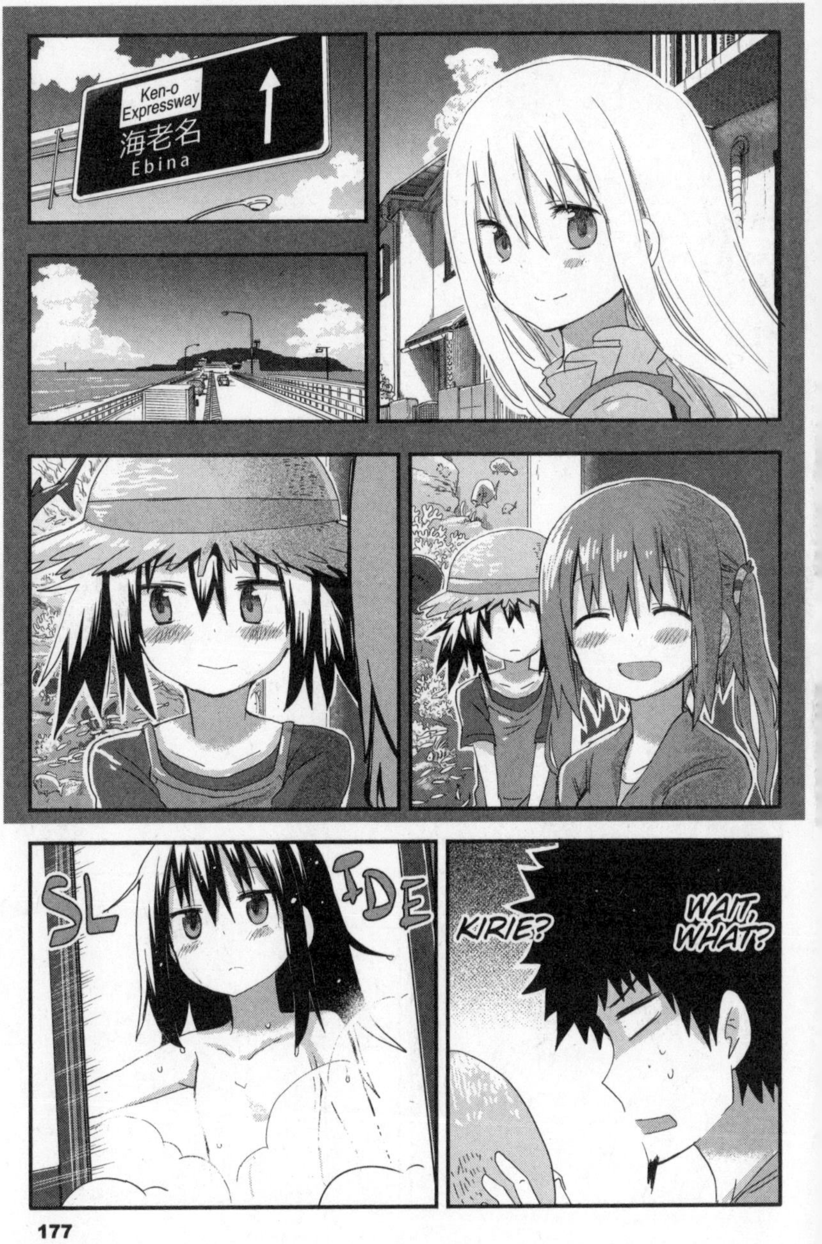
Ken-o Expressway
海老名
Ebina
WAIT, WHAT?
KIRIE?
SLIDE

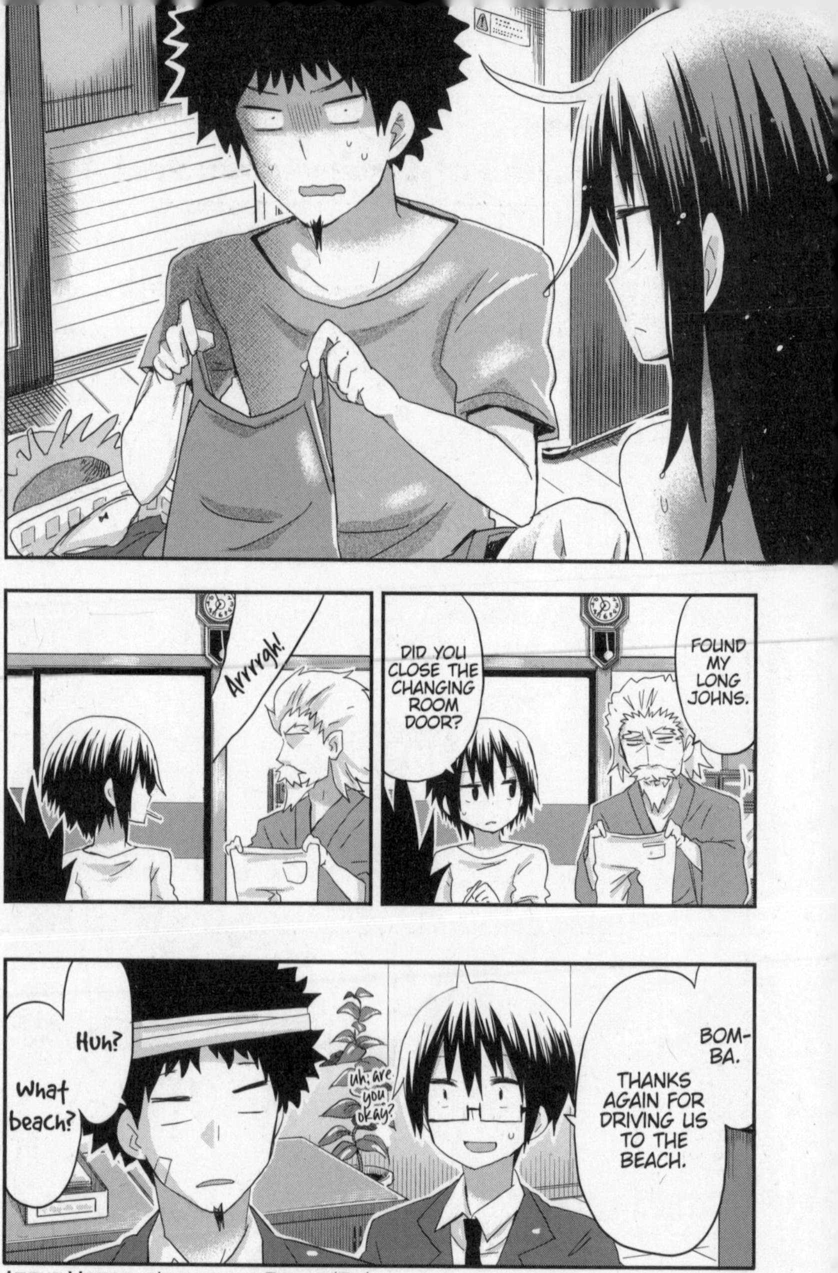
FOUND MY LONG JOHNS.
DID YOU CLOSE THE CHANGING ROOM DOOR?
Arrrrgh!
BOM-BA.
THANKS AGAIN FOR DRIVING US TO THE BEACH.
uh, are you okay?
Huh?
What beach?

At the Motobas' after the Beach (Fin)

Sensei's work was submitted to the Young Jump serialization meeting!! Plus, Sensei's roots revealed!!

AFTERWORD

The Creation of *Umaru-chan:* Part 4

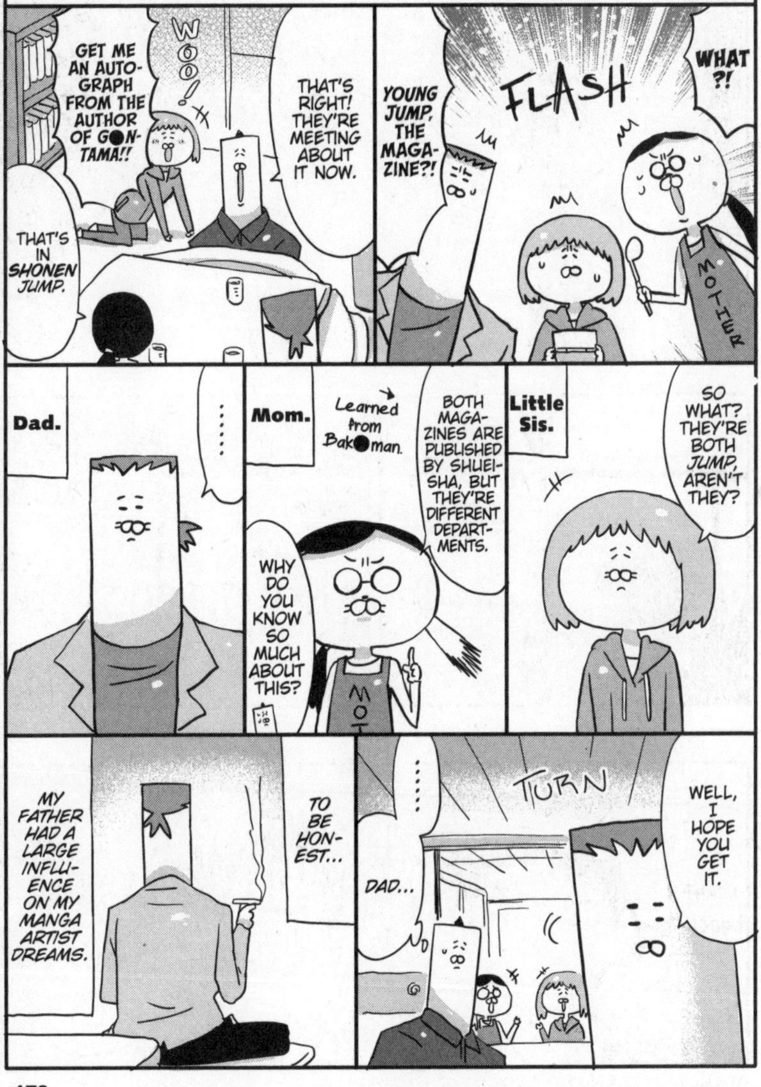
WHAT?!
FLASH
YOUNG JUMP, THE MAGAZINE?!
MOTHER
THAT'S RIGHT! THEY'RE MEETING ABOUT IT NOW.
WOO!
GET ME AN AUTOGRAPH FROM THE AUTHOR OF G●N-TAMA!!
THAT'S IN SHONEN JUMP.
SO WHAT? THEY'RE BOTH JUMP, AREN'T THEY?
Little Sis.
BOTH MAGAZINES ARE PUBLISHED BY SHUEISHA, BUT THEY'RE DIFFERENT DEPARTMENTS.
Learned from Bak●man.
Mom.
WHY DO YOU KNOW SO MUCH ABOUT THIS?
......
Dad.
WELL, I HOPE YOU GET IT.
TURN
......
DAD...
TO BE HONEST...
MY FATHER HAD A LARGE INFLUENCE ON MY MANGA ARTIST DREAMS.

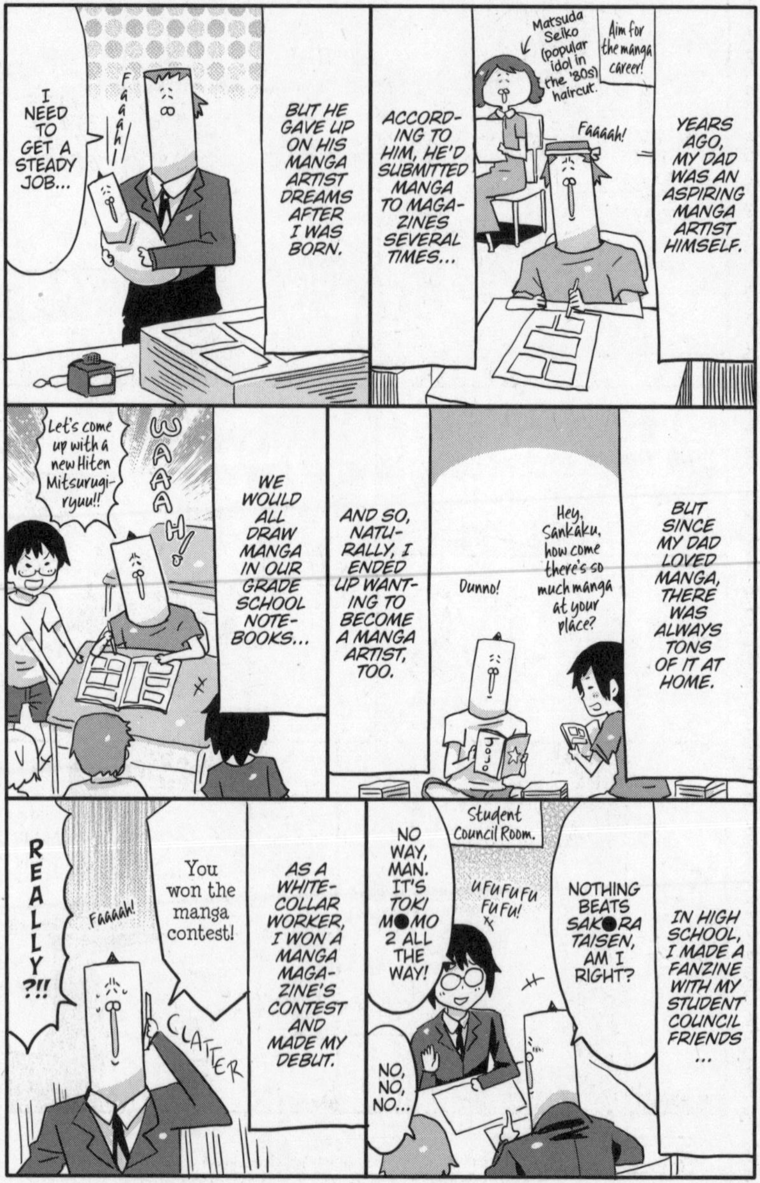
YEARS AGO, MY DAD WAS AN ASPIRING MANGA ARTIST HIMSELF.
Aim for the manga career!
Matsuda Seiko (popular idol in the '80s) haircut.
Faaaah!
ACCORDING TO HIM, HE'D SUBMITTED MANGA TO MAGAZINES SEVERAL TIMES...
BUT HE GAVE UP ON HIS MANGA ARTIST DREAMS AFTER I WAS BORN.
Faaah!
I NEED TO GET A STEADY JOB...
BUT SINCE MY DAD LOVED MANGA, THERE WAS ALWAYS TONS OF IT AT HOME.
Hey, Sankaku, how come there's so much manga at your place?
Dunno!
JOJO
AND SO, NATURALLY, I ENDED UP WANTING TO BECOME A MANGA ARTIST, TOO.
WE WOULD ALL DRAW MANGA IN OUR GRADE SCHOOL NOTEBOOKS...
WAAAAH!
Let's come up with a new Hiten Mitsurugi-ryuu!!
IN HIGH SCHOOL, I MADE A FANZINE WITH MY STUDENT COUNCIL FRIENDS ...
Student Council Room.
NOTHING BEATS SAK●RA TAISEN, AM I RIGHT?
NO WAY, MAN. IT'S TOKI M●MO 2 ALL THE WAY!
UFuFuFuFuFu!
NO, NO, NO...
AS A WHITE-COLLAR WORKER, I WON A MANGA MAGAZINE'S CONTEST AND MADE MY DEBUT.
You won the manga contest!
CLATTER
Faaaah!
REALLY?!!

Come on, this is the afterword! How long are you gonna drag this out?! Next volume, the conclusion of the Umaru creation story!!

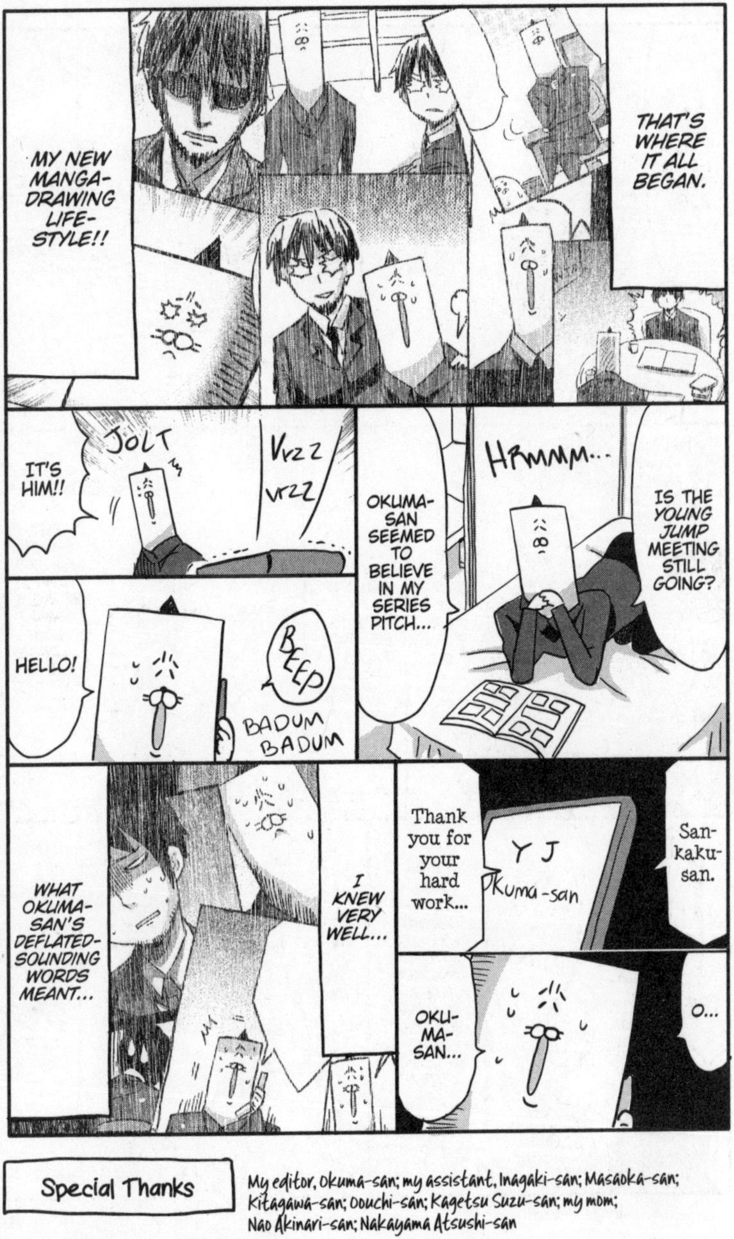
THAT'S WHERE IT ALL BEGAN.
MY NEW MANGA-DRAWING LIFE-STYLE!!
IS THE YOUNG JUMP MEETING STILL GOING?
HRMMM...
OKUMA-SAN SEEMED TO BELIEVE IN MY SERIES PITCH...
VRZZ VRZZ
JOLT
IT'S HIM!!
BEEP
BADUM BADUM
HELLO!
San-kaku-san.
YJ
Kuma-san
Thank you for your hard work...
O...
OKU-MA-SAN...
I KNEW VERY WELL...
WHAT OKUMA-SAN'S DEFLATED-SOUNDING WORDS MEANT...

Special Thanks

My editor, Okuma-san; my assistant, Inagaki-san; Masaoka-san; Kitagawa-san; Oouchi-san; Kagetsu Suzu-san; my mom; Nao Akinari-san; Nakayama Atsushi-san

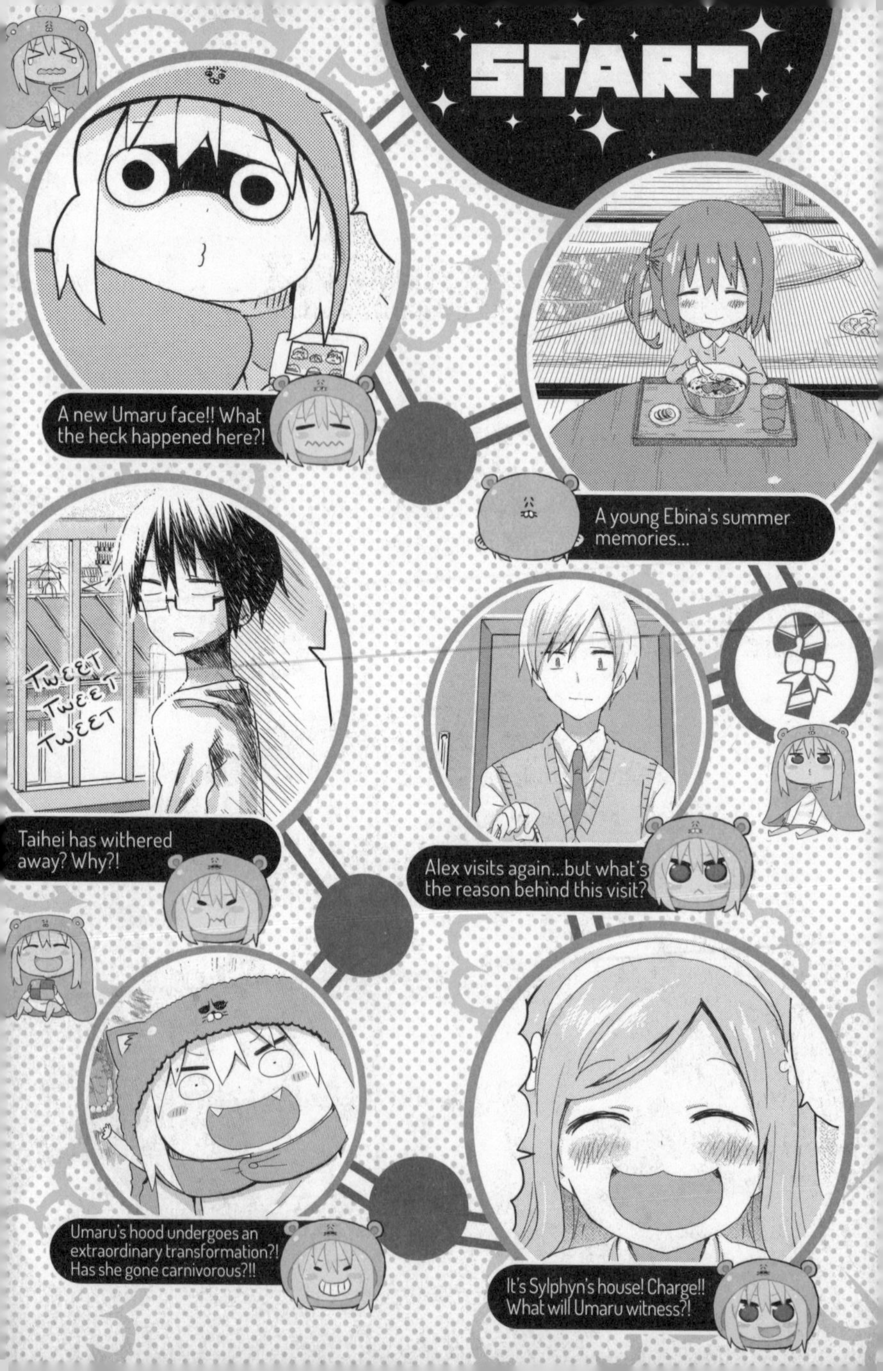
START
A new Umaru face!! What the heck happened here?!
A young Ebina's summer memories...
Alex visits again...but what's the reason behind this visit?
Taihei has withered away? Why?!
TWEET TWEET TWEET
It's Sylphyn's house! Charge!! What will Umaru witness?!
Umaru's hood undergoes an extraordinary transformation?! Has she gone carnivorous?!!

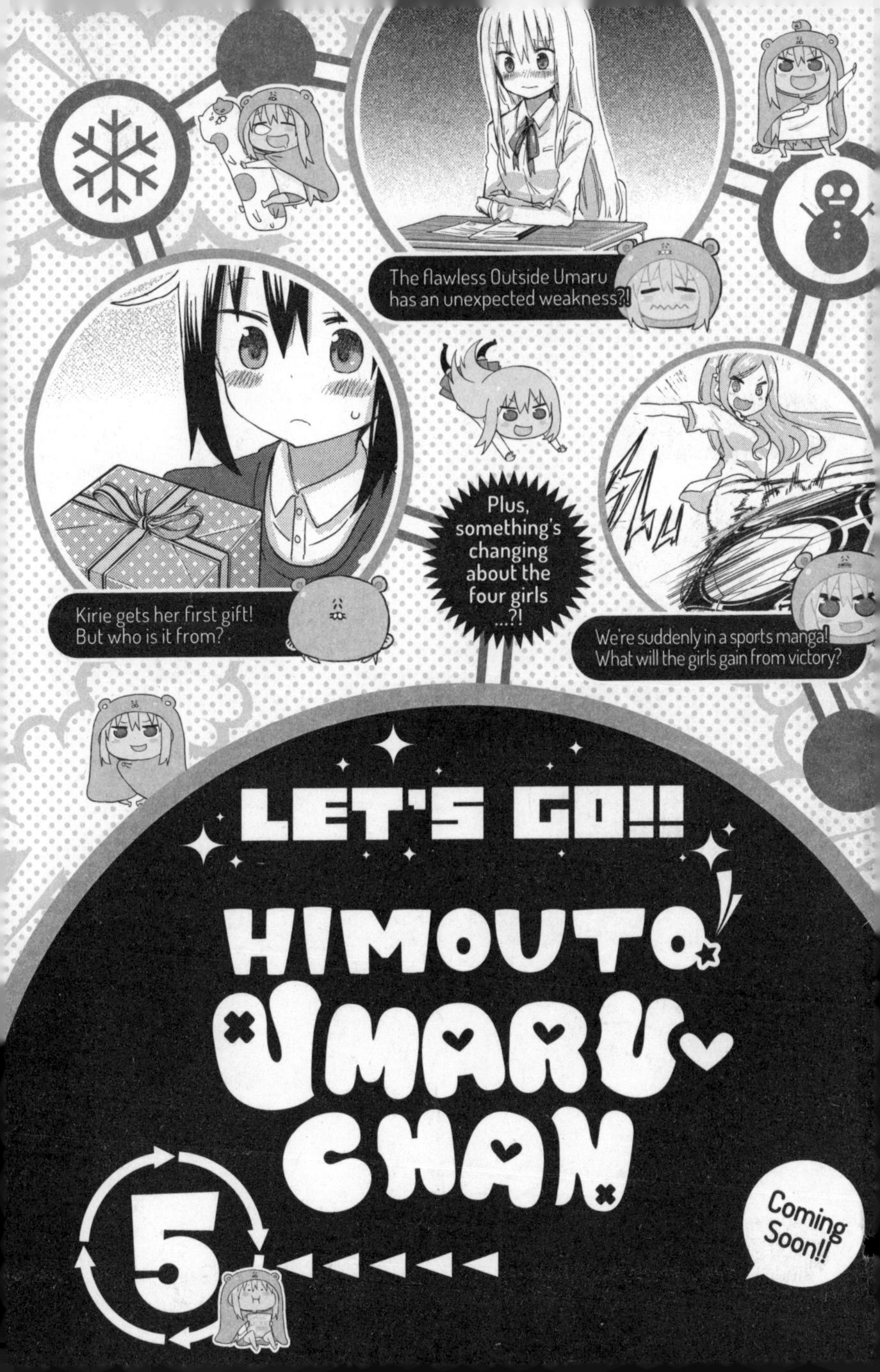
The flawless Outside Umaru has an unexpected weakness?!
Kirie gets her first gift! But who is it from?
Plus, something's changing about the four girls ...?!
We're suddenly in a sports manga! What will the girls gain from victory?
LET'S GO!!
HIMOUTO! UMARU-CHAN
5
Coming Soon!!

SEVEN SEAS ENTERTAINMENT PRESENTS

HIMOUTO! UMARU-CHAN

Volume 4

story and art by SANKAKUHEAD

TRANSLATION
Amanda Haley

ADAPTATION
Shanti Whitesides

LETTERING AND RETOUCH
Carolina Hernández Mendoza

COVER DESIGN
Nicky Lim

PROOFREADER
Janet Houck

EDITOR
Jenn Grunigen

PRODUCTION ASSISTANT
CK Russell

PRODUCTION MANAGER
Lissa Pattillo

EDITOR-IN-CHIEF
Adam Arnold

PUBLISHER
Jason DeAngelis

HIMOUTO ! UMARUCHAN
© 2012 by Sankakuhead
All rights reserved.
First published in Japan in 2012 by SHUEISHA Inc., Tokyo.
English translation rights arranged by SHUEISHA Inc.
through TOHAN CORPORATION, Tokyo.

Seven Seas books may be purchased in bulk for promotional, educational, or
business use. Please contact your local bookseller or the Macmillan Corporate
and Premium Sales Department at 1-800-221-7945, extension 5442, or by
e-mail at MacmillanSpecialMarkets@macmillan.com.

Seven Seas and the Seven Seas logo are trademarks of
Seven Seas Entertainment, LLC. All rights reserved.

ISBN: 978-1-626929-80-7

Printed in Canada

First Printing: January 2019

10 9 8 7 6 5 4 3 2 1

FOLLOW US ONLINE: www.sevenseasentertainment.com

READING DIRECTIONS

This book reads from *right to left*, Japanese style.
If this is your first time reading manga, you start
reading from the top right panel on each page and
take it from there. If you get lost, just follow the
numbered diagram here. It may seem backwards at
first, but you'll get the hang of it! Have fun!!

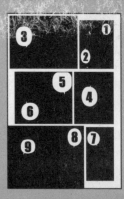